Hiding in Plain Sight

Hiding in Plain Sight

Women Warriors throughout Time and Space

Christian P. Potholm

ROWMAN & LITTLEFIELD
Lanham • Boulder • New York • London

016.355

Published by Rowman & Littlefield
An imprint of The Rowman & Littlefield Publishing Group, Inc.
4501 Forbes Boulevard, Suite 200, Lanham, Maryland 20706
www.rowman.com

86-90 Paul Street, London EC2A 4NE, United Kingdom

British Library Cataloguing in Publication Information Available

Library of Congress Cataloging-in-Publication Data

Names: Potholm, Christian P., 1940– author.
Title: Hiding in plain sight : women warriors throughout time and space / Christian P.
   Potholm.
Other titles: Women warriors throughout time and space
Description: Lanham : Rowman & Littlefield Publishing Group, [2021] | Includes
   bibliographical references and index. | Summary: "Hiding in Plain Sight: Women
   Warriors Throughout Time and Space takes the many, long-standing dimensions
   of military history, including the various modalities of warfare across cultures and
   periods, and integrates them with the more recent and very substantial contributions of
   social history, women's history, black history, feminist theory, LGBTQ community,
   and other perspectives. By providing an extensive annotated bibliography of the new
   findings, the work provides the reader with an exciting compilation of new knowledge
   placed within a longstanding military historical framework, one which provides
   a broader study and understanding of warfare into which to put the very recent,
   disparate findings culled from many disciplines"—Provided by publisher.
Identifiers: LCCN 2021023892 (print) | LCCN 2021023893 (ebook) | ISBN
   9781538162712 (cloth) | ISBN 9781538162729 (epub)
Subjects: LCSH: Women and war—Bibliography. | Women and the military—
   Bibliography. | Military history—Bibliography. | Women soldiers—Bibliography.
Classification: LCC Z7963.S55 P68 2021 UB416 (print) | LCC Z7963.S55 UB416
   (ebook) | DDC 016.3550082—dc23
LC record available at https://lccn.loc.gov/2021023892
LC ebook record available at https://lccn.loc.gov/2021023893

To the Wonder Women of Our Family
Erica, Heather, and Sandy
What would we ever do without you?

Contents

Preface

Writing a book is such an adventure. It always fills me with excitement and stimulation. The research, writing and rewriting are so interesting and thought-provoking. You are transported beyond your comfort zone, forced to confront new information and new ideas and meet such interesting new people across time and space. Writing is also a process that can be therapeutic as well as exhilarating. It can become something of an obsession, albeit a good one. I have always enjoyed doing a book.

Certainly, writing a book for me was a magnificent obsession to have during the COVID-19 pandemic. The action became refuge and a diversion as well as a purposeful occupation. While working on it during the COVID-19 lockdown of 2020, I stopped to realize that I had been writing books for 57 years, ever since I began my master's thesis in 1964. I realized I had been teaching even longer, having given a lecture to a Bowdoin history class in 1961, and subsequently teaching as a teaching assistant at Tufts with later stints at Dartmouth, Vassar, and finally at Bowdoin. Lecturing for 60 years. That's a lot of time at the podium.

During my whole adult life I have been writing a book.

And I have been teaching.

I have truly loved teaching and writing both, especially that powerfully rewarding, never-ending feedback loop with research and writing and delivery and being questioned in class and doing more research and subsequent writing and then more teaching.

Teaching with Zoom, while it turned out to be necessary and useful, was nowhere near as rewarding (or effective) as teaching in person. But continuing to write books and creating lectures in anticipation of a return to the classroom remained intensely rewarding and fulfilling.

Fortunately, when COVID-19 hit, I was already researching and outlining *Hiding in Plain Sight: Women Warriors throughout Time and Space*, which was an expansion of my Bowdoin course "The Daughters of Mars." Having taught courses on the Korean War, government, war and society, and conflict simulation and conflict resolution, I was intrigued by the tantalizingly brief accounts of women in much of traditional military writing and with the now-ongoing reevaluation of the role of women in warfare from Black history, social history, women's studies, and LGBTQ? studies. Explorations with their new perspectives have proceeded rapidly in recent years. Indeed, over time, there was a true flood of new or newly examined material including the myriad of findings (some real, some suspect) provided by the Internet on such sites as Wikipedia and Military Wiki.

This book then arose out of my explorations and extrapolations from my first-year seminar, "The Daughters of Mars" which featured women in warfare throughout history. In this regard, I am very grateful to Bowdoin's Dean of Faculty, Jennifer Scanlon, who came to the faculty seminar where I first presented some of my most exciting initial findings and from beginning to end, encouraged me with this project. And very high marks go to President Clayton Rose, who managed Bowdoin through the COVID-19 crisis with skill and dispatch and compassion.

Writing a book during the pandemic also offered some additional possibilities as time taken from now-forbidden or truncated activities could be used for research and writing. And distractions, except for the big ones of personal health and safety concerns, were actually fewer and fewer. In addition, writing a book offered a much-needed and welcome distraction from those concerns. It was indeed a relief to be transported through time and space with each new discovery of an understudied or even virtually unknown woman warrior.

The closure of Bowdoin College and the concomitant new sanitizing rules greatly diminished access to the library and interlibrary loan, putting additional strains on both its staff and library patrons. It took the hard work of dedicated professionals to keep the fires of research burning brightly, so I begin here with an extra special thank-you to Carman Greenlee, Jamie Jones, Amy Heggie, and the rest of the Bowdoin Library staff, especially Guy Saldanha, Bart D'Alauro, Alida Snow, Laura Bean, and others for their collective efforts to keep the flow of books coming despite all the impediments of COVID-19 and related shutdown problems.

Thanks too to Peter and Margie Webster, who added numerous women warriors to our investigation of that amazing cohort, as well many trenchant comments about the content of various chapters. They added much zest to the proceedings. And, as always, appreciation goes to Lynn Atkinson, whose labors as executive secretary and governmental coordinator go beyond the call of duty and then some.

Kudos also to Gil Barndollar for providing useful materials and challenging insights as an undergraduate, U.S. Marine, and now think tank maven and encouragement for the title of this work also came from longtime good friends Lyle and John Gibbons. Others, like Andy Rudalevege, added seldom-included women warriors from unusual places. Special appreciation is also expressed to the DeAlva Stanwood Alexander Professorship research fund and for the extra assistance of Lynne Atkinson and Ann Oswald.

I appreciate all of your help.

I have always been most fortunate in having excellent research assistants, and I was truly blessed to have two outstanding ones during these tumultuous times. A heartfelt thanks to Carolyn Shipley, whose inspiration and hard work on finding women warriors during the initial dark days of COVID-19 kept us both sane and focused as she transitioned from teaching assistant to research assistant with skill and dispatch.

Upon her graduation and entrance into the outside workforce, Carolyn's place was taken by the amazing Elise Hocking, whose ability to find scholarly articles on women warriors wherever they have been hiding out quickly became legendary. She plans to be a lawyer, in which profession she will, no doubt, leave no fragment of data unfound. Woe to miscreants from far and wide if she is put on their trail. Elise's work ethic and cheerful demeanor will make her much in demand. I am deeply grateful for all her hard work and engaging insights.

Thanks also to Michy Martinez, as well, for initially stimulating my interest in the *soldaderas* of the Mexican Revolution, their important presence underscoring as it does not only women as supporters of armies, but also as military participants and also, how some of the revolutionary armies and situations provided avenues for transgender migration.

As I have been for these past 40 years, I am most grateful for the friendship, comradeship, and support of Jed Lyons. There are many editors and many publishers, but there is only one Jed Lyons, the author's best and most trusted friend. Nor are there any with a better sense of humor. And we have happily had each other's back for lo these nearly 50 years. His long friendship has been a true blessing and is most gratefully appreciated. Jed is a singular presence.

I especially appreciate the fine editorial supervision of his Roman & Littlefield acquisitions and production teams, including April Snider and Catherine Herman.

In addition, this book is dedicated to three wonderful, strong, and loving women who have made our three-generation family happy beyond words.

In addition to my wife Sandra, Erica Burgess Potholm and Heather Potholm Davis, respectively daughter-in-law and daughter, are touchstone role models for our entire family. Warm and caring, infused with a joy for life and a desire to make all more content, grandly nurturing, they have provided wonderful home environments for our three grandchildren, Noah, Aiden, and Will and admirable partners for their husbands, Erik Dodds Potholm and Bruce Davis (both of whom themselves are inspirational as well). Their collective astute inspections of, and interactions with, life and people are a joy to behold. They are generous, gracious, and loving partners and have greatly enriched our family's collective life.

And to my students over the years at Tufts, Dartmouth, Vassar, and Bowdoin—you have kept me young at heart and spirit, and fully and happily engaged in the educational process. It has been truly joyful.

Finally, as with every other book I have ever written, including my 1964 MALD thesis, I hasten to deeply acknowledge the many contributions of Sandy Quinlan Potholm, whose unstinting support and assistance, including a most careful proofreading and editing of the entire manuscript, were outstanding contributions to the entire project. Sandra is the love of my life, my inspiration, my muse, and my best editor ever. With great love and appreciation I ask of her only one more thing, *Lascia Che Duri*.

And if that cannot be, let Heaven be where we live our married life all over again.

Thank you all,
Christian Potholm
DeAlva Stanwood Alexander
Professor of Government
Bowdoin College
2021

Part I

HIDING IN PLAIN SIGHT

Women Warriors throughout Time and Space

THE CONTEXT OF WAR

War is of long standing in human experience and it has been studied for millennia. Yet both our fascination with it, and our knowledge of it, keep expanding, especially as we look backward in time to investigate earlier and earlier examples of inter- and intraspecies violence.

For example, it was long thought that during the Bronze Age in northern Europe, there was no large-scale warfare. Skirmishes between bands and defenses of territory or homesites were assumed, but not large, organized military activities. But recent discoveries now tell a different story. Some 3,200 years ago, for example, two large armies totaling approximately 4,000 warriors fought in what is now northern Germany at the Tollense River. They were not defending their immediate homes, nor was it a chance encounter of rival bands.

In fact, both groups were heavily armed and many miles from any settlements. For several days they fought, maimed, killed, and died. These warriors left behind hundreds and hundreds of remnants and shards of that battle. This extensive site is now considered the first Bronze Age battle discovered in northern Europe. It is remarkable for its character as a full-fledged war on open ground in northern Europe.[1]

Coincidentally, perhaps, the battle at the Tollense River took place in roughly the same time frame as dozens of other major battles and wars occurred all across Europe and the Mediterranean basin, including the sack of Troy, the destruction of various Mycenean cities, the occupation of Cyprus and Crete, the destruction of the Hittite, and in other cities all across the Levant as well as in parts of Egypt.

3

Termed "The Catastrophe"—although it was probably not one for many of the successful "Sea Peoples" who caused it—its widespread nature remains a cautionary tale of how war is old, large-scale, and destructive.[2]

Indeed, by the time of the Tollense River battle and "The Catastrophe" of the Mediterranean, war was already many millennia of years old, as Wayne Lee indicates in his intriguing article, "When Did Warfare Begin?" For him, "War does not dominate the archaeological record but it does suffuse it."[3] He then cites evidence of intra- and interspecies violence found in walled cities 9,000 years ago in Turkey. Lee also sees what he terms "warfare" even much earlier than that, in the butchered and presumably eaten human remains found in the caves of 35,000 years (Les Rois in France) and 50,000 years (El Sidrón in Spain). It is even likely, he claims, that warfare extended far back into the unrecorded history of hunter-gatherer bands, although, because of their very transitory and migrant nature, that is very difficult to prove. Other writers such as Nichols Longrich also hypothesize that Neanderthals and modern Homo sapiens engaged in armed conflict for 100,000 years over Europe, Asia, and the Middle East.[4]

War thus seems to predate "government" or "civilization." We have, of course, no way of telling exactly when wars really began but we have these beguiling hints that it is very, very old.

We know that war also dominates some of our oldest and most influential written accounts, illustrating our species' commitment to purposeful violence. Think, for example, of the earliest writings on the subject. Almost 3,200 years ago, the longest poem (with 2,000 verses) in the world, the Sanskrit *Mahabharata* (attributed to Vyas), celebrates an intense struggle between two Aryan forces in what is now India. The war and description of its concomitant violence exceeds even that found in the very bloody *Iliad* of Homer, which is more familiar to European or American readers.

The *Mahabharata* portrays what is essentially a dynastic struggle between two clans, the Kauravas and the Pandavas, for the throne of Hastinapura, a conflict culminating in a final cataclysmic battle, Kurukshetra, between them. The battle is eventually won by the Pandavas, and in the description of the battle, there is one haunting, overpowering, intense image which for me sums up the impact of war on humankind.

During the final climatic battle of Kurukshetra, the elder warrior Bhisma is shot with so many arrows by his foe Arjuna that when he falls from his chariot, his body cannot touch the ground: "There was not in Bhisma's body space of even two fingers' breath that was not pierced with arrows."[5]

What better metaphor for human suffering caused by war and its claustrophobic embrace?

Likewise, 2,500 years ago, Thucydides, writing in the last decade of the 5th century BCE in his *The History of the Peloponnesian War*, captures in book 3 the wild, untamed nature of conflict and war, even among people of the same language and culture, which can be overwhelmingly violent. He points to the seemingly unending nature of war when, writing about the Corcyran Revolution, declaring, "The suffering which revolution entailed upon the cities were many and terrible, such as have occurred and always will occur as long as the nature of mankind remains the same."[6]

And of course, what of the most celebrated of stories from the Western tradition, Homer's 2,700–year-old *Iliad*, which is a long and very detailed account of war in all its glory and pathos?[7]

Its story of Achilles, the ultimate warrior, has been told and retold countless times, but it still provides perspective and context for our appreciation of war's influence on human history. If even a half-god can be ultimately destroyed by war, what will be the fate of humans throughout time and space ever since?

On the surface, of course, the central story of the *Iliad* is about gods and human interactions set against the backdrop of a 10-year-old war. But as Simone Weil so cogently and profoundly asserts in her long 1939 poem, "The Iliad, or the Poem of Force," it is the war itself that is the real subject of the *Iliad*.

> The true hero, the true subject, the center of the *Iliad* is force. Force as a man's instrument, force as man's master, force before which human flesh shrinks back. The human soul seems ever conditioned by its ties with force, swept away, blinded by the force it believes it can control, bowed under the constraint of the force it submits to.[8]

It is precisely that force and its compelling nature that provides the holistic background for this book, as the nature of warfare presented in all three works gives us the added horror of familiarity because the participants speak the same language, worship the same gods, share the same cultural norms, and yet fight as if their opponents were only true "Others," worthy of slaughter.

The long arc of the Tollense River, the *Mahabharata*, and the *Iliad*, then, all tell of war's supremacy and ultimate power, which remain with us today. War is thus an institution and a beguiling attraction seemingly unstoppable throughout human history and prehistory as well as into its future.

Humans have long tried to grapple with war's impact and nature. Virtually since its inception in the human record, war has been studied, pondered, and written about, yet much of its ultimately metaphysically true nature remains unknown, perhaps unknowable, even as the same questions are asked over and over.

Despite thousands of years of study, then, the ultimate causes and roots and ubiquitous nature of war remain elusive. Some say war is in our genes and therefore nearly immutable. Others say war begins with our cultures and that if we change cultural norms, we can reduce, even eliminate war. Still others believe war is a combination of genes and culture. But, and this is a big "but," no one knows for certain. All we know, and continue to know, is that as a species, Homo sapiens has shown an enduring propensity for war's practice and perfection.

Is war the results of hormones and DNA or more prosaic causes such as lust, greed, desire to dominate, to seek freedom, gain riches, subjugate, enslave, take, or defend?[9]

We do not know. Perhaps we cannot know, even though many of us may have once thought we knew or could know or were certain we did know. Perhaps from time to time, we came close to pinning down the hows and whys as well as the wheres of war, but we still do not really know its ultimate nature.

Luckily then, the metaphysical essence of war is not the subject of this book. For our purposes, war is simply the space-time milieu, the phenomenon, the matrix and context within which humans kill others for a multiplicity of purposes. It remains with us in all its horrible and monstrous power.

Again, as Simone Weil so cogently puts it,

> For those who have supposed that force, thanks to progress now belong to the past, have seen a record of that in Homer's poem; those wise enough to discern the force at the center of all human history, today as in the past, find in the *Iliad* the most beautiful and flawless of mirrors.[10]

WOMEN'S PLACE IN WAR

It is within that matrix of the harsh reality of the contemporary and seemingly ubiquitous nature of war that we examine force, but from a different central focus: where are the women warriors in that long arc from the Tollense Bridge, the *Iliad*, and the *Mahabharata* to the present?

This volume seeks to put women in their rightful place into that most powerful and destructive of matrices, for they have so long been denied their fair positioning in its holistic nature and nearly ubiquitous past. They are, and have been, a fundamental part of the war space and processes, not just as victims, but also as planners, participants, and leaders. Women deserve belated recognition as purposeful actors in the history of warfare.

We are fortunate to be examining this subsection of topic today and not much earlier, because we find that the last few decades have seen scholarship not only focused more on the roles women play in war, but also new perspectives and new sources have emerged that highlight the positions of women in the historical landscape of war, illuminating their extensive participation across time and space.

As we begin our examination of women in the context of war, then, it is fitting therefore that the first recorded author in history was a woman; and she was indeed writing about war. Enheduanna was the Sumerian/Akkadian chief priestess who, during the reign of Sargon the Great (2285–2275 BCE) wrote, "You hack everything down in battle. . . . God of War, with your fierce wings." Enheduanna

> is where we start.
> She, and her pronouncement, begin our search.

7

As we will see later in this volume, there are ancient echoes of women warriors far back in the mists of time: the Egyptian Queen Hatshepsut led armies
in both Canaan and Nubia in the 15th century BCE; Lady Fu Hao in China
in the 13th century BCE also captained a number of military campaigns; the
Rigveda was written in the same time period, and also contains verses of
praise for the women warrior Vishpala; while in the 6th century BCE Queen
Tomyris led her army to a stunning victory over Cyrus the Great.

Accounts, however tantalizingly brief in many cases, suggest that women
have been in the military sphere, albeit often underreported in that canon. One
initial question of import, therefore, is that if women have been such widespread participants in warfare until recently, why have they been so neglected
and understudied in the history of war?

Certainly, some of the biggest Anglo-American names in the study of
warfare during the last generation—Michael Howard, Jeremy Black, Donald
Kagan, John Keegan, Victor Hanson, Williamson Murray, Paul Kennedy,
Allan Millett, and others—have spent very little time investigating women at
war or have ignored them altogether. Some have gone farther, even denying
their widespread participation, such as John Keegan, who confidently asserts
"Warfare is . . . the one human activity from which women, with the most
insignificant exceptions, have always and everywhere stood apart."[11]

Nor are women exegetes on war immune to disregarding or substantially
ignoring the combat history of women. Margaret MacMillan, in her widely
praised contemporary account *War: How Conflict Shaped Us*, after giving
women wide coverage as cheerleaders, excuses for war, victims of rapes
in warfare, their roles as camp followers and in the peace movement, gives
virtually no coverage to women warriors in combat, concluding her few examples with the caveat, "they are exceptions, seen as outside the normal order
of things where war is the male sphere."[12]

Others have been even more overtly dismissive.

For example, Israeli Martin van Creveld, who has dealt extensively with
warfare, finds women's contributions and even their potential as singularly
unimpressive. He also states categorically and incorrectly, "Women have
never taken a major part in combat—in any culture, in any country, in any
period of history."[13]

More recently, there have been substantial attacks on van Creveld's positions vis à vis women in combat. One well worth noting here is Nina Liza
Bode, in her *The Imaging of Violent Gender Performances*, which conclusively underscores his lack of familiarity with non-Western women warriors.[14] Using the case studies of Tanja Nijmeijer, Xarema Muzhakhoyeva,
Wafa Idris, and Pauline Nyiramasuhuko, Bode cogently attacks his assertions

that warfare is not for women because biologically they are incapable of the heinous actions that are central to war.

By providing a refined and holistic image of the female participators of political violence, she shows how they are as capable of men of perpetrating mass slaughter and in the process refutes Creveld's biological determinism. Bode also puts women realistically and squarely in the space/time continuum of purposeful war acts, including as perpetrators of genocide. The case studies she uses are worthwhile in and of themselves, for they show the wide range of motives and actions involved in these five women's stories.

Part of the problem of the suppression of the deeds of women warriors is also cultural, for many societies did/do not think that women should be involved in war and therefore treated those who did as aberrations, oddities, anomalies or totally atomized and brainwashed by the experience, hence there is no real reason to explore it.

For example, the feminist theorist Cynthia Enloe writes,

> None of these causes and consequences of militarization are more significant than the entrenchments of ideas about "manly men" and "real women." I am convinced that women have special roles to play in exposing and challenging militarization, not because women are somehow innately, biologically wired for peacefulness, but because women are so often outside the inner circles where militarizing decisions are being made yet are likely to be called upon to support, and even work on behalf of, militarizing agendas.[15]

Although worldwide the military field remains a primarily masculine space, the existence and accomplishments of the women warriors included in this bibliography challenge the notion that war and militarization only re-entrench gendered conceptions of "manly men" and "real women."

While the military space is certainly not female-dominated, the success of women warriors across space and time rejects the false dichotomy between femininity and military strength and positive participation. Joan of Arc and her military exploits stimulated proto-nationalism, which in turn freed northern and western France from English domination, and Queen Isabella of Spain personally oversaw the military campaigns to drive the Moors from Spain, so far permanently altering the political and religious contours of that country.

Another element in that denial may come from another source. And that is that for much of human history, most military historians were and even now are men, and many of the most celebrated simply did not want to include women, finding them so small in numbers and so scattered as to be useless in looking at the broader questions of waging war—or simply because they do not believe that women belonged in the sphere of war-making except as victims. Finally, many of them often lack extensive knowledge of women warriors (and warriors in general) in a non-Eurocentric context except as those societies defeated by "The Western Way of War."

Perhaps Adrian Goldsworthy puts it best, especially for the earlier eras:

> Women tend to be a shadowy presence in much of ancient history, and although it is obvious that they were often highly influential, their own voices are not preserved and they are seen solely through the prism of others.[16]

Part of the problem is also the scope of the data involved. With tens of thousands of battles, describing them and interpreting them required a broad brush in terms of sweep and detail. The bias for historians of military strategy and decisions was that even when women made those decisions, it was assumed that there were men behind the scenes actually making those choices for war and peace, for strategy and tactical actions. Hence it was safe to ignore them.

But they were there and in significant enough numbers to enable us to ask the following question: how many more women would have entered the armed forces and combat without the host of prohibitions in so many societies and polities preventing them from doing so?

At the present time, however, a number of mainstream male historians—such as Max Boot, John Lynn, Geoffrey Parker, and Robert Kaplan to name a few of the more prominent—are now paying more attention to the role of women, even when they have had to search for them resolutely in previously examined times and spaces.[17] In the process, they are contributing to fresh examinations of the true roles played by women in warfare.

For today, if one truly wants to know about the various substantial roles women have played throughout history, it is now quite easy to find evidence of their activities and import across a wide array of time periods and societies. They are not, for the most part, hidden; they have simply been ignored. They are now, and have always been, in plain sight.

That is the theme of this book.

In terms of warfare, even with all the biases and submerging of the roles of women, they are still there for all to see.

They have always been there.

Women warriors have simply been hiding in plain sight.

Until fairly recently they have simply not been brought together in any holistic way. Patterns for their involvement have not been studied, and the differing contexts for their participation and success in warfare that exist have been scattered and seemingly random, or presented as sui generis, not placed in the context of the mode of warfare of their time and place.

But now, this highlighting has become something of a self-fulfilling prophecy because almost wherever we have looked, we find women playing important roles in war. As we hope to show in this annotated bibliography, there are thousands and thousands of women who have participated in warfare across the globe and across eons.

There have been some discernable reasons for the flood of articles and books dealing with women warriors over the last few decades: (1) more mainstream male military historians are writing about women in combat; (2) there have also been more women becoming military historians or having an interest in military dimensions involving women; (3) the historical revisionisms of Black history, social history, and women's studies, including several strands of feminist thinking (one that more women engaged in military pursuits would change the nature of the military making it more pacific and another that sees women gaining equality within the military as having positive social value); (4) more recently, there has been considerable interest on the part of the LGBTQ? community in examining LGBTQ? participants throughout history including in the military sphere; and frankly (5) the Internet and sites such as Wikipedia and Military Wiki have greatly enhanced our opportunity for finding stimulating mention of often obscure women warriors. Some Internet "discoveries" turn out to be fantasy, some turn out to be debatable, but many, even most, are real and simply needed to be brought to our attention as contemporary sources are now much easy to access.

But all are stimulating a search for more information about more women in more cultures in military situations. For us, especially, in the present circumstances, it seems preferable to cast a too-wide net than one traditionally too narrow. Hopefully this volume errs on the side of inclusion rather than exclusion.

All five of these strands thus combine to contribute to greatly enriching our knowledge of women warriors and their actions throughout history and the present. We celebrate these activities and the momentum they have produced. Collectively they have greatly added to our store of knowledge about women playing active roles in warfare and stimulated interest in the study of war from different perspectives.

The women's movement in general and gender studies in particular have become a most important part of this process of rediscovery, both in terms of simple description of where and when and how they participated, but also in terms of their multiplicity of intentions.

Women should be able to participate as equals, say many. They have in the past, often under duress and almost always with substantial resistance and difficulties, been present, whether societies have welcomed them or not.

Also, many in women's and gender studies have reexamined history and found widespread cultural and societal censorship, and when that is stripped away, even more women and even greater roles for them have been uncovered.

Happily as a result, the last decades have seen a virtual tidal wave of articles and books and websites devoted to the new knowledge and much of this investigation has found it in the scholarly literature. In the process there have been many books and articles written looking at those various women through new lenses and with new perspectives.

There have been articles and books about the history of women at war. There have been articles and books of great women of history who have made strategic and policy decisions leading to war and it conduct. There has been an outpouring of historical works looking at individual women in action throughout time and space, but often under two rubrics, popular and scholarly.

Here we seek to bring together much of this new scholarship with the older, more popular versions of that interest, in order to present a truly holistic and far-ranging bibliography that melds the popular with the scholarly so that the interested reader can find both in one hopefully convenient resource.

We know of no other major work that seeks to combine the new knowledge about women and their various roles in warfare with the long-studied dimensions of warcraft and differing styles of war throughout human history, so we seek to buttress our collective knowledge of these illuminated women warriors with background and context for their achievements and the limits thereon.

PROVIDING BACKGROUND AND CONTEXT

In order to give the reader quick access to the military dimensions of the period in which the woman warrior appears, we have provided "Notes" in the annotated bibliography section that give some relevant background for the modalities of warfare in effect when particular women warriors operated.

We have included books, articles, essays, and other materials. Several such important companion sources are *MHQ: The Quarterly Journal of Military History* and Osprey Publishing's various series on warriors over the ages which have proven very useful to undergraduates and graduates alike in providing introductory and well-illustrated context for the women highlighted.

The articles and books cited in subsequent chapters are easy to read, yet they are based on superb scholarship and lavishly illustrated. This enables their texts to compete with PowerPoint presentations and the Internet. Many students in my classes have found these articles to be stimulating and enlightening, leading to further research rather easily and productively. By providing context for the women of a particular location or time frame, the interested reader can thus learn of the history of the modes of warfare along with the important dimensions of female participation. Some eras, some societies and some modalities of warfare give women better opportunities to participate than others.

While this annotated bibliography seeks to bring together for undergraduate use the scholarly and some popular works depicting the women we have identified as warriors, it is our hope that it also will prove useful to anyone seeking to examine the thousands of female warriors whose participation has added to that process.

Finally there is the question concerning the criteria for including women in the category of "women warriors." Many other works include only women who have served directly in combat. Others broaden to the scope to any ruler or regent who saw war while they were in charge of its conduct. Still others would have us include women who have dramatically changed or even prophesized change in their broader societies.

Determining what constitutes a woman warrior is a perpetual—and rewarding—undertaking by the classes taking my course "Women at War." Leaving the definition relatively broad but applying it most judiciously has proven to be the best way to understanding the involvement of women across the globe and throughout time and space.

We have thus cast our net most widely, including women generals and military strategists and leaders as well as women in combat, but the inclusion mesh is moderate, hopefully not too large and not too small. We hope readers will end up forming their own conclusions and weaving their own, surely improved, net.

Scholarship remains, and always will be, a collective enterprise.

THE WIDE RANGE OF WOMEN WARRIORS

There is now such a virtual cornucopia of women warriors arrayed across time, space, and cultures that trying to organize them in any coherent way presents considerable problems for those cataloging them.

What are some ways to sort and cluster women warriors? Obviously, they are numerous and varied, but what follows is a very small sampling that students over the years have found useful. These few typologies are meant to be suggestive, not exhaustive. Many cited in one typology could fit in one or more other categories and are kept sparse in the service of brevity. And also, to be honest, so as not to tax the attention span of those younger scholars addicted to the allures of constant screen time and Twitter feeds. In any case, the following categories are meant to be illustrative, not definitive, and the reader is encouraged to come up with additional ways of cataloging these many, many intriguing women.

By Location

One obvious way is to do it geographically, simply where were they located when practicing warcraft, not necessarily where they were born.

Here are some pertinent examples that fit with this approach:

Africa

Berenice II (273–221 BCE) was a Ptolemaic queen married to Ptolemy III Euergetes of Egypt during the Hellenistic period. She is credited with riding with her father Maga, king of Cyrene, into battle before her marriage and when his forces were on the verge of defeat in one, Berenice rallied the remaining troops, leading them to victory on horseback. "Tradition also emphasizes her bravery and even—like her chariot-riding cousin Berenice Syra—a certain blood lust."[18]

Amina of Hausaland (1533–1610) was an African Muslim leader who defied a wide variety of conventions—male dominance, existing Islamic hierarchies, and African traditions—all of which militated against her success, yet she would go on to conquer much of north central Africa. She ruled northern Nigeria, with a capital at Zaria, south of what is now Kano. Born into the ruling house of Zazzau, she took the throne in about 1576. She reportedly refused all suitors and led her armies, fighting for 34 years and presiding over a great expansion of trade. Under her rule, the Hausa language became the language of trade.

In the Kano chronicle it says, "In her time, Amina, a woman as capable as any man." The African playwright Wale Ogunyemi in his play *Queen Amina of Zazzau* goes even further, celebrating her warcraft as well, calling Amina "a strategist for all times."[19]

Masarico (1470–1545) was a Mende woman who hived off from north central Africa and led her followers (subsequently known as the Manes) into what is now Liberia and Sierra Leone. Portuguese sources describe her military innovations, including complex three-pronged attacking units and other strategic imperatives, as well as their own fierce fighting with the Manes at their fortress at Mina.[20]

Or in more modern times, take the example of Rose Kabuye (1961–), a Rwandan freedom fighter for the Rwandan Patriotic Front (RPF) during the 1990–1993 Rwandan War when the Tutsis invaded and again took over that country. She became a lieutenant colonel and highest-ranking female military officer in the Rwandan army. Later she became mayor of Kigali and eventually, chief of protocol under President Paul Kagame.

Finally, we could not really be putting a book together on women warriors throughout time and space in Africa and *not* include the "Amazons," the women warriors of Dahomey in the 19th century.

During the reign of King Ghezo, who ruled over Dahomey from 1818 to 1858), women warriors were officially integrated into the army when faced with various other tribes pressing in upon him and European powers, especially France, trying to colonize and Ghezo faced a "manpower" shortage. His answer was an all-female force, the warrior women of Dahomey. As Stanley B. Alpern writes in his *Amazons of Black Sparta: The Women Warriors of Dahomey*, this all-female unit fought at Abeokuta against the Egba in 1851 and 1854, and later against the French in 1890 and 1892. While some (such as Martin van Creveld) have questioned their battle worthiness, it is worth quoting one of the French Legionaries who fought them:

> These warrioresses fight with extreme valor,
> always ahead of the other troops. . . .
> They are outstandingly brave . . .
> well trained for combat
> and very disciplined.[21]

And Major Grandin, who published a two-volume work in 1895, concluded:

> The valor of the amazons is real. Trained from childhood in the most arduous exercises, constantly incited to war, they bring to battle a veritable fury and a sanguinary ardor . . . inspiring by their courage and their indomitable energy the other troops who follow them.[22]

Asia

For her part, Rani Lakshmibai (1834–1858) led her Jhansi State troops against the British during the Sepoy Rebellion of 1857–1858 (or as many Indians call it, "The Great Rebellion"). She exhorted her troops to die in battle if necessary and is today regarded as one of the pioneers for Indian independence. Michael Edwardes provides an interesting account of the role played by the Rani of Jhansi in the uprising and quotes the general who defeated her in battle, Sir Hugh Rose, who called her "the bravest and best of the military leaders of the rebellion" after she was killed in action during the Battle of Gwalior.[23]

Another Rani, Abbakka Chowta, the Rani of Ullal, "The Fearless Queen," who reigned from 1525 to 1570, fought off the Portuguese for four decades, defending her port city of Ullal. Regarded as the "first woman freedom fighter of India," she was later captured after attacking the Portuguese fort at Mangalore. There she led a revolt in prison and died in the subsequent fighting.

Or take Chand Bibi (1550–1599), a Muslim woman warrior who acted as Regent of Jaipur and Ahmednagar and led her soldiers against the Mughal forces of Emperor Akbar in 1595. She also personally put down various rebellions, reportedly taking her own life by filling a well with acid and then jumping into it as the Mughals closed in (although other accounts have her killed by her own troops for negotiating with the same Mughals).[24]

From China we find Quin Liang-Yu (1574–1648) in the Ming Dynasty period. Her well-documented life as a Ming female general in Sichuan Province indicates that she fought against the Manchus invading in the north and also put down a series of peasant revolts in the south. Leading an elite unit in a variety of combat situations, she is the only woman known to have been a regional military commander under the Mings. Taught by her father and initially accompanying her husband into battle, she took over his command in 1613 when he was killed. For her battlefield exploits, she was highly decorated and was appointed the Crown Prince's Guardian by the Chongzhen Emperor.

Japan too is well represented in the field of women warriorhood. Although we feature the most famous one here, Tomoe Gozen, there were many others. Tomoe Gozen is of legendary proportions. She purportedly commanded 300 samurai in a battle against the Taira clan and later, fighting at the battle of Awazu in 1184, where she fought valiantly until told by Lord Kiso to flee, whereupon she immediately charged the leader of the opponents, Onda no Hachiro Moroshige of Musashi, and his thirty men, killing him and cutting off his head. Only then did she deign to leave the battlefield and according to Stephen Turnbull, who provides much background on female samurai, Tomoe's near contemporary, Hangaku Gozen, fought at the siege of Torisaka Castle in 1201 and Tsuruhime took part in the naval battles of 1541 as well.[25]

It should be noted there are obviously many more Indian and Chinese and other Asian women who have not only been in battle but led in battle: Abbakka Chowta, who in the late 16th century fought off the Portuguese from Goa for 40 years, and Mah Chuchak Begum, who led an army to defeat Munim Khan at Jalalabad in the mid-16th century; the Thai queen Suriyothai, whose battle elephants helped defeat the invaders from Burma in 1548 when she fought with King Maha Chakkraphat during the 1547–1549 war between Siam and Burma,[26] and the Sikh warrior Mai Bhago, who led soldiers against the Mughals in 1705.

Australia and New Zealand

Here we can cite Heni Te Kiri Karamu (1840–1933), a Maori woman warrior from northern New Zealand. Normally in Maori society women warriors were not encouraged to take part in battle except in exceptional circumstances. Heni's clan, the Koherki, joined the Nga Te Pangi group that was being hard pressed by the British. Their defensive *pa* (fortified trench and dugout) was under attack and Heni went in action during the battle. Ironically, she is best remembered in Britain for giving water to wounded British soldiers before the Koherki retreated rather than for having fought against them.

There is also the Australian Women's Auxiliary Australian Air Force (WAAF) (1941–1947)—Australian women who from 1941 to 1947 were a branch of the Australian armed forces and numbered 27,000. Machinists, signals traffic, intelligence, bomb armers, munitions experts, and many other positions were filled by them. They came under attack by the Japanese at various points and eventually paved the way for women to become regular members of the Australian Air Force after World War II.

Note: This is a good juncture to pay homage to the many women in many countries who participated in World War II in other "auxiliary" organizations. Some examples of these include: The Australian Women's Royal Australian Army Corps (WRAAC) and Women's Royal Australian Naval Service (WRANS), the American Women's Airforce Service Pilots (WASP), the U.S. Coast Guard Reserve (SPAR), the U.S. Marine Corps Women's Reserve, the Women's Auxiliary Ferrying Squad (WAFS), Women Accepted for Voluntary Emergency Service (WAVES), Women's Auxiliary Army Corps (WAAC) later the Women's Army Corps (WAC), the British Women's Auxiliary Air Force-UK (WAAF), the British Air Transport Auxiliary (ATA), the Women's Auxiliary Army Corps-UK (WAAC) and the First Aid Nursing Yeomanry Corps (FANY).

These women were vital to the war effort, many had very dangerous jobs (such as ferrying aircraft across countries and continents), and some, like the Australians cited above, came under fire. This was especially true for such units such as the various antiaircraft battalions.

Caribbean

A number of Indigenous women stand out here, women such as Queen Nanna of the Maroons (c. 1686–c. 1755) who was the acknowledged leader of escaped slaves in the eastern part of Jamaica. Originally from what is now Ghana, she led this cluster of "Windward Maroons." Over the course of a decade, she thwarted and eventually defeated the British in the First Maroon War (1728–1734) using guerrilla tactics. The British eventually sued for peace and signed a treaty in 1740 giving her Maroons a land grant on which was built "New Nanny Town," today known as Moore Town. She was a superb tactician and strategist, and her military prowess surprised the British.[27]

Or take note of Carlota Lucumi (?–1844). She was an Afro-Cuban woman who led the slave revolt of 1843 at the Triumvirato plantation in Matanzas Cuba. Yoruba African born, she was known as "La Negra Carlota." She died in battle at the end of the revolt in 1844, one of a series of slave uprisings in Cuba that year. Fidel Castro, in sending Cuban forces to Angola in 1975, called the effort "Operation Carlota" in her honor.

Think also of La Mulatresse Solitude (c. 1772–1802). Her mother was raped on a slave ship coming from Africa and she was born on Guadeloupe. When the French Revolution freed the slaves in 1794, she joined a Maroon community in Guadeloupe. Although Napoleon reinstated slavery in 1802, a number of Guadeloupeans resisted under Joseph Ignace and Louis Delgrès. La Mulatresse Solitude joined the band of Delgrès. When the French troops

(4,000) arrived under General Richepance, they attacked some 1,000 former soldiers and rebels at Galion in May 1802 and defeated them. La Mulatresse Solitude was captured, but she was not executed until after the birth of her child in November. She was hanged the next day.

Although mentioned below under slave revolts, Sanite Belair (1781–1802), the Haitian revolutionary, deserves mention here. A lieutenant in the army of Toussaint Louverture, she fought in numerous battles and when captured by the French and executed, she died calling out "Long live Freedom. Down with slavery!"

Europe

Some examples include Kenau Hasselaar (1526–1588) who, during Spanish pacification of the Low Countries under King Philip II of Spain, when the Spanish invaded the town of Haarlem, led a stiff fight against the invaders for seven months. In the process, Kenau Hasselaar organized and led a group of 300 women in defense of the city. When Haarlem finally surrendered, the garrison was put to death, but she survived. A great hero of Holland, she has had many ships named after her.

Then there is Cynane (357–323 BCE). Half sister of Alexander the Great (and daughter of Philip II and the Illyrian Audata), Cynane was a warrior princess in her own right. Illyrian women often were engaged as fighters and Cynane had considerable military training. She fought in a number of early battles with Alexander and, according to Polyaenus,

> Cynane, the daughter of Philip, was famous for her military knowledge: she conducted armies, and in the field charged at the head of them. In an engagement with the Illyrians, she with her own hand slew Caeria their queen; and with the great slaughter defeated the Illyrian army.[28]

Eventually Cynane was killed by Alcetus after the death of Alexander as she was speaking to the Macedonian troops.

Or take Grace O'Malley/Gráinne Mhaol (1530–1603), the Lord of the Ó Máille dynasty in the west of Ireland. Upon her father's death, she took over active leadership of the lordship on land and sea. She led raids and attacks and involved herself in Irish/English politics. Called "the nurse of all rebellions in the province for this forty years," she interacted with Queen Elizabeth I, claiming equal status as Queen of Ireland. She also insisted on a personal meeting with her—and got one. A pirate's pirate, Grace is now a feminist legend to boot.

Another interesting case is Laudomia Forteguerri (1515–1555), one of three women leaders in resisting the siege of Sienna by organizing a militia of 100 women in January 1553. The women built fortifications to resist the 1554–1555 siege of the city. Although she was married and had three children, Forteguerri is also thought to be one of Italy's earliest lesbian writers. The city would eventually fall to the Imperial Spanish forces under Duke Cosimo de Medici after the bloody Battle of Marciano.

In Spain during the Napoleonic Wars, we find Agustina de Aragon (1786–1857). During the siege of Zaragoza in 1808, she stepped up when the French were about to break through the city's defenses. She loaded a cannon and fired at point-blank range. Her courage electrified the defenders, and they fought the French off for the next two weeks. Augustina escaped the siege and became a low-level rebel leader for the guerrilleros. She was eventually painted by many, including Francisco Goya. See his "What Courage!" in the series "The Disasters of War."

Latin America

Four Inca women, Micaela Bastidas (1744–1781), Bartolina Sis (1750–1782), Gregoria Apaza (1751–1782), and Tomasa Tito Condemayta (1729–1781) should be mentioned here as all participated in Tupac Amaru II's revolt against Spanish rule in what is now Bolivia. Tomasa Tito Condemayta was a military strategist of note and led her women's army to defeat the Spanish at Sangarara. There is considerable literature on their roles, much of it quite recent.[29]

Dandara of Palmares (?–1694) was an Afro-Brazilian warrior of Palmares, a settlement of free Afro-Brazilian people established in the 17th century in what is now the state of Alagoas. Dandara fought in many battles as part of that free settlement despite efforts of slave owners to capture or kill her. When the head chief of the region, Ganga Zumba, signed a peace treaty with the government of the state of Pernambuco, she and her husband led another revolt because the treaty did not outlaw slavery. Eventually she was captured and committed suicide to avoid enslavement.

Then there was Rafaela Herrera (1742–1805). She was a Nicaraguan who fought the British at the battle for Rio San Juan de Nicaragua (1762). Educated by her father, who was a captain of artillery, she was put in charge of defense of the Fortress of the Immaculate Conception on the San Juan River when British and Mistiko filibusters attacked. When he died, she directed cannon fire that killed the British commander and led the defenders to a victory in a battle lasting six days.

Finally in this section, we note Juana Azurduy de Padilla (1780–1862). A mestizo (Spanish and Indigenous person), she was born in what is now Bolivia. When her father was killed by the Spanish, she married and, alongside her husband, subsequently gave birth right after the battle of Pintatora in

1815. Subsequently Padilla fought a guerrilla war against the Spanish including 16 major actions from 1809 to 1816. She was wounded in 1816 and her husband was killed trying to rescue her. Padilla then fled into what is now Argentina and established an insurrection commanding an army of 6,000. In one battle she reportedly killed 15 men while leading the all-female battalion of her personal bodyguard. Today, both Bolivia and Argentina recognize her as a national heroine.

Middle East

One prominent example is Hind Bint 'Utbah (late 6th century–early 7th century). Wife of an important pre-Islamic Meccan leader, she fought against the Muslims at Badr 622 (the Meccans lost) and Uhud 624 (the Meccans won). But then she converted to Islam and fought with them at the Syrian Battle of Yarmuk and is credited by Arab sources as playing an important role during the second day (the Battle of Yarmuk lasted six in total) by rallying the fleeing Muslims. This huge Muslim victory over Byzantium at Yarmuk (626) changed the course of history by projecting Muslim military and political power into the Levant from which it has never withdrawn.

After the Battle of Uhud (624), Hind declared "We have paid you back for Badr and a war that follows a war is always violent. . . . I have slaked my vengeance and fulfilled my vow."[30]

Many accounts of the life and time of the Prophet Muhammad omit or downplay the military accomplishments of women in the early years of struggle, yet there were some prominent examples such as Umm 'Umara (a.k.a. Umm 'Uhud). An Arab Muslim woman who fought beside Muhammad in several key battles (including Uhud and Yamma) during his rise to power. After the battle of Uhud (624 CE) in which she was wounded several times including severely in the neck, Muhammed declared "Whenever I looked to the right or left I saw her fighting in front of me." Umm later fought at Yamma (632), was wounded several more times, and lost her hand. For her valor and courage as well as her fighting ability, Umm was granted the high honor as being recognized as one of the "Companions of the Prophet."[31]

There is an interesting contemporary parallel to Umm Umara in the female Kurdish Peshmerga fighters of the present day and the female pilots of the United Arab Emirates, both groups of which are held to be heretical by some in the Muslim world.

Another of the early female Muslim war leaders was Khawla bint Al-Azaar, a commander in the Rashidun army. She was in numerous battles in the Levant, including Syria, Jordan, and Palestine, including the decisive Battle of Yarmouk in 636 against the Byzantine empire (known to the Muslims as "Romans"). She is recognized today in Muslim countries such as Jordan, Iraq and the United Arab Emirates.

Think of how many women who fought in so many wars and who never had their accomplishments celebrated by subsequent historians because they were airbrushed out of those respective narratives or have had their roles downplayed or submerged.

North America

There are numerous examples of women fighters in this category. Here is but a sampling.

The first is an exception to the thesis of this book, because the story of this Native American woman warrior was not hiding in plain sight but actually hidden from view for over a century. Buffalo Calf Road Woman (c. 1850–1879) was a Northern Cheyenne woman who saved her wounded warrior brother, Chief Comes in Sight, at the Battle of the Rosebud in 1876. She later fought alongside her husband, Black Coyote, at the Battle of the Little Bighorn. Eyewitness accounts have her going into battle with a pistol and much ammunition. Credited after 100 years in 2005 (the survivors of the battle took an oath of silence at the time to avoid retribution from the U.S.) for having knocked General George Custer off his horse during that battle by an eyewitness, Kate Bighead, who puts her at the center of the battle:

> Most of the women looking at the battle stayed out of reach of the bullets, as I did. But there was one who went in close at times. Her name was Calf Woman . . . who had a six-shooter, with bullets and powder, and she fired many shots at the soldiers. She was the only woman there who had a gun.[32]

In 1878 she and her family broke out of the reservation with the Northern Cheyenne (from Oklahoma back to Montana). On the way her husband shot a number of Native Americans and U.S. soldiers. Eventually captured along with Black Coyote, she died of diphtheria while he was awaiting trial. Black Coyote then committed suicide in his cell. How many schoolchildren over the years have been deprived of knowing about her exploits?

Or take Harriet Tubman (1822–1913). Well known as an abolitionist and political activist, she was born a slave and escaped to take part in the Underground Railway and helped John Brown recruit men for his attack on Harpers Ferry. During the Civil War she worked for the Union Army, first as a cook and nurse, then an armed scout. But in this latter activity, she was a true pioneer, becoming the first woman to lead a military expedition, one which freed 700 slaves at Combahee Ferry. A major motion picture in 2019 reprised her various accomplishments.

Then there is Francoise Marie De La Tour (1602–1645). French born, in 1625 she went to Nova Scotia, married Charles de La Tour, and helped build Fort La Tour. In a conflict with Jesuit Seigneur d'Aulnay Charnise, she assumed the role of military commander when her husband was absent. In one engagement, she used their three ships to fight Charnise off, although later he returned and captured the fort, putting her soldiers to death and her in prison at Port Royale where she died.

Ignacia Reachy (1816–1866) was from Guadalajara, Mexico, and organized a battalion of women to defend her home during the Second French Intervention in Mexico (1861–1866). However, Reachy soon left Guadalajara to join the Army of the East, what is now the modern-day Mexican Army, and distinguished herself in Mexico's fight against Napoleon's France. Assigned to the Second Division under General Jose Maria Arteaga as a second lieutenant, she was captured for a year in 1862 while trying to protect General Arteaga. However, she escaped after a year and reported back to him, ready for more combat. She was then made the Commander of the Lancers of Jalisco, but in 1866 she was killed in action.

Oceana

Several useful examples from Oceana would include Manono II (c. 1780–1819), a Hawaiian warrior woman who died fighting with her husband in a struggle for the traditional religion at the Battle of Kuamo'o in 1819. They were defending the traditional *Kapu* system, which kept women and men from eating together and prohibited women from eating certain foods.

We should note that while fighting to uphold the gender norms of the *Kapu* system, Manono II did defy the gendered expectations of women to be submissive and pacific. This tension and her actions remind us that we should not assume that the actions women warriors take always fit into the modern, Western understanding of women's liberation.

Another example would be Queen Teriitaria II (1790–1858), Queen of Tahiti. She fought the French in the Franco Tahitian War of 1844–1847, repelling them in the Battle of Maeva in 1846 although she was later deposed by them.[33]

Other Polynesian women warriors of note fought on Tonga, Samoa, Tahiti, the Society Islands, the Cook Islands, and the Marquesas and include the daughter of Chie Ahomee of Tonga and Putahaie, wife of Keatonui of Taiohae Bay, and Nukuhiva in the Marquesas.

By Typology

Another way, more interesting albeit more difficult perhaps, is to look at women warriors in terms of the military typologies or patterns into which many of them seem to fall.

Horse Archers

For many, the Sarmatian/Scythian warrior women horse archers began the "women warriors" saga. These women, like their male counterparts on the steppes, fought primarily from horseback and with composite bows and arrows. Certainly in the Western tradition, the Greeks were the first to describe women warriors known as "Amazons." Interestingly enough, the Greeks were both fascinated and repelled by them. When the numerous Greek polis were established on the Black Sea, they encountered stories of and myths about women who rode horses and shot bows in battle. And although we don't have any reliable records of the Greek phalanx encountering the female horse archers, it seems likely that such interactions occurred on the periphery of the steppe lands north of the Black Sea.

To the Greeks the very idea of women acting as independent beings and going to battle, let along killing men in action, was doubly anathema, although ironically enough, we do have instances of Greek warriors dressing as women for purposes of assassination.[34]

In the first instance, martial women went totally against their well-ordered universe of male hierarchical dominance, with women excluded from voting or participating in warfare. Amazons were a threat to the very underpinning of the patriarchy and thus to be both ridiculed and hated, because their existence upset the "normal" balance of the known universe.

The Greek disdain for women steppe warriors also comes from the nature of the Greek way of war versus the steppe warfare with its mounted horse archers. The steppe horsemen armed with composite bows would dominate many centuries of battle situations in Central Asia and its periphery in an arc of several thousand miles over a thousand years of history.[35]

The Greeks could never seriously challenge the horse archers effectively. The Greeks and their heavily armored infantry phalanx formations were able to operate effectively only in small valleys and for very short periods of time. They could not, and generally did not, do well on the open plains where any horse archers could kill from afar, and never come within striking distance of the Greek spears.

How frustrating then was the very *idea* that these horse archers killed from afar, and women doing some of that killing undoubtedly made it doubly hateful, even shameful, for the Greeks.

But these Amazons were not legends alone, nor did their military process require Greek certification one way or the other. Women horse archers were widespread and extensive across a broad arc among many societies. For over 1,000 years, across a 2,000-mile Eurasian arc, horse archers dominated the Eurasian landmass, leaving behind irrefutable evidence of their presence. With their mobility and standoff fighting ability to inflict casualities, as well as their durability and longevity when in action against heavily armed infantry, the horse archers, male and female, were the premium military formation across the vast steppes from Hungary to China.

In the Don Basin and Central Asia, for example, among the Sarmatians and Scythians and other steppe peoples, 20% of women's graves have bows and other weapons buried with them. More recent archaeological and DNA evidence places these women warriors back as far as 2,500 years ago, thus providing stark new evidence that Herodotus was not wrong is depicting the "Amazons" of the day.[36] They were, in fact, Scythian women engaged in ongoing warfare.

Castle Keepers/Defenders of Home and Hearth

Just as horse archer warfare on the Asian steppes was conducive to women's participation, certain other types of warfare seem to have been more open to female participation than other forms. For example, such as in the Middle Ages, castles and the nature of defensive medieval warfare from the fortifications enabled women to step into leadership roles more easily than at other times and in other situations.

Megan McLaughlin, in her seminal work "The Woman Warrior: Gender, Warfare and Society in Medieval Europe," also draws our attention in this category to several important distinctions between women warriors as foot soldiers and women warriors as generals and points out that much of medieval warfare in Europe involving the defense of castles and therefore should be thought of as "domestic warfare."[37] They also can be thought of as women "military commanders" depending on their time, place in the decision-making apparatus, and activities.

For example, one can look at the large group of women who were in castles or fortresses and, in the absence of a male war leader, took charge during the Middle Ages. One of the most famous of these was Jeanne La Flamme, Jeanne of Montfort (1295–1374), Joanna of Flanders, or "Jeanne La Flamme." She was the consort Duchess of Brittany and showed her skill as a military leader defending her captured husband's (Jeane de Montfort, Duke of Brittany) dukedom against the challenge by the House of Blois during the Breton War of Secession. Jeanne La Flamme actually led her husband's knights in battle when he was in prison and became famous throughout France for burning the tents and supplies of her French opponents.

Or take the even more famous Caterina Sforza (1462–1509). Milan born, she was Countess of Forli and Lady of Imola by her husband Girolamo Riario. After his death, she ruled Imola and Forli before being finally defeated by the Pope Rodrigo Borgia Pope Alexander VI, who sent his illegitimate son

Cesare Borgia to capture her while she and her soldiers waited in a fortress in Ravaldino. Caterina is cited several times by Machiavelli in *The Prince* and *Discourses on Livy* for her harsh treatment of her subjects, but it may be she was only criticized because she was a woman, for contemporary men did all these things as a matter of course.

Elizabeth Lev in her *The Tigress of Forli: Renaissance Italy's Most Courageous and Notorious Countess, Caterina Riario Sforza de 'Medici* gives a fascinating account of her heroic stand in 1499 against Cesare Borgia, his mercenaries, and assisting French forces. For hours Catarina fought in battle with her troops, finally betrayed by someone on her own side "for she had no intention of leaving the battlefield alive."[38]

Indeed, John Lynn, calling this category of women warriors in castles "Besieged," finds that in the early modern period, women defending home and hearth are considered quite acceptable and widespread even when breaking gender norms for their sex, declaring as he does, "Women who fought bravely and publicly as women in siege warfare were anything but rare."[39]

Some other examples include Agnes of Dunbar (1300–1369) in Scotland, Lady Mary Banks (d. 1661) during the English Civil War, and Jeanne d'Albert (1528–1572) during the Wars of Religion. Aluzehen (during the Chinese Jin dynasty [1115–1234]) also led troops against Puxian Wannu during a siege as well.

There was also Stamira of Ancona (1172) who defended the city of Ancona when she fought against the archbishop of Mainz during the Byzantine-Venetian conflict (1170–1177) as did Alruda Frangipani, who liberated the town of Ancona from imperial siege during the same war and Marzia Degli Ubaldini (1330–c. 1374) who defended the castle of Cesena (near Forli) against papal attacks in 1335 and 1357. Emma de Gauder (1059–1096), Countess of Norfolk, also defended her husband's castle against the king as did Nicolaa de la Hay (1160–1230) of Lincoln who commanded during two sieges, one in 1191 and the other in 1216–1217 and Charlotte Stanley, Countess of Derby (1599–1664) who defended Lathom House during the English Civil War. In Poland, Anna Dorota Chrzanowska refused to let her husband surrender the castle of Trembowla during the Polish-Ottoman War of 1672–1676 while Ilona Zrinyi fought off the Habsburgs during the siege of Palanok castle (1685–1688).

In Japan, this phenomenon was also much in evidence during the 16th and 17th centuries. To take but a few examples: Lady Ichikawa defended Konomine Castle in 1569; Akai Teruko served as commander in the Battle of Kanayama Castle in 1574, holding out for 18 months; Kato Tsume fought that same year in the siege of Suemori Castle; Myorin-ni defended Tsurusaki Castle in 1585–1586 and Yuki no Kata defended Anotsu Castle in 1600.

There are many more from a number of countries.
This is thus quite an interesting and far-reaching category.

Admirals and Fleet Commanders

Also, at sea where ships are like little floating castles, there have been women admirals, in charge of their own ships and their fleets, and they successfully appear and reappear across time and space. Women admirals such as Artemisia of Halicarnassus, who was at the battles of Artemisia and Salamis, and her Aceh, Greek, Irish, and Chinese compatriots all show women warriors able to compete with their male counterparts in this type of warfare.

Here we encounter a whole array of successful women admirals such as the legendary Admiral Keumalahayati or Malahayati (c. 1501–16th century). Born into the Aceh Sultanate at the height of its power, Keumalahayati convinced the reigning sultan to form, and put her in charge of, an armada of Acehnese women whose husbands had died in war. This armada was called the Inong Bale, and Keumalahayati led it through successful warfare with the Dutch and diplomacy with the British. She eventually died in battle, at the hands of the Portuguese. The female GAM unit, the Inong Bale Forces of the Free Aceh Movement (1976–2005) was named for her.

Or take one of the most successful pirates in history, Ching Shih, a.k.a. Cheng I Sao (1775–1844). At one time, she commanded and at least loosely controlled as many as 300 ships and 20,000 pirates. At various points, she fought the British, the Portuguese, and the Quin dynasty. In the process, her Red Flag Fleet was never defeated in battle. Unlike most pirates, she knew when to retire and successfully made peace with the Quins and died ashore at age 69 after successfully running a variety of enterprises.

Another Chinese bandit queen and "outlaw of the marshes" is Huang Bamei (1906–1982) who fought in the Second Sino-Japanese War (1937–1945), the Chinese Civil War (1945–1949) and the Cross Strait conflict (1949–1955). Her life quickly became the stuff of legends in both China and Taiwan.[40] She played a number of roles and had a variety of careers, first as a bandit, then as a smuggler who traded with the Japanese, then as an anti-Japanese fighter recruited by the Nationalists. After World War II, she fought the Communists, both during the Chinese Civil War before the Nationalists fled to Taiwan and afterward as a guerrilla leader on the mainland.

Known as "Double Gun" for her ability to shoot with both hands, she joined the Nationalist Army in 1940 as a protégé of Mao Sen, a top commander of the Nationalists. The CIA tried to recruit her for cross-straits operations after 1949, but she preferred to work directly with the Nationalists against Mao's forces.

Authors

Like their male counterparts, numerous women wrote accounts of their military lives and published them, some to considerable acclaim. Some interesting ones include the following:

Loreta Velasquez (1842–1897) who, after her husband was killed in the American Civil War, signed up as Harry T. Buford, and fought at 1st Bull Run, Ball's Bluff, Ft. Donelson, and Shiloh before being wounded and discovered to be a woman. She was then discharged, whereupon she served the Confederacy as a spy. She claims to have gotten close to both U. S. Grant and Abraham Lincoln. Velasquez wrote a book entitled *The Woman in Battle: A Narrative of the Exploits, Adventures, and Travels of Madame Loreta Janeta Velazquez, Otherwise Known as Lieutenant Harry T. Buford, Confederate States Army.*[41]

Nadezhda Durova (1783–1866) was a Russian woman who, disguised as a man, fought for the Czar during the Napoleonic wars. Becoming a cavalry officer and distinguishing herself in battle, she was awarded the Cross of St. George (the first woman ever) and promoted to lieutenant in a hussar (light cavalry) regiment by Czar Alexander I, who found out he had an "Amazon" in his army. By her own account, *The Cavalry Maiden: Journals of Russian Officer in the Napoleonic Wars*, this Russian woman from the Urals, disguised as a boy, joined the Imperial Army, and found herself in the Polish Regiment as a lancer, seeing combat in 1807 and again in 1812–1814 against Napoleon. "At last my dreams have come true! I am a warrior! I am in the Polish Horse, I bear arms and moreover, Fortune has placed me in one of the bravest regiments of our army!"[42] She fought at the Battle of Smolensk and was wounded in the Battle of Borodino in 1812. Durova only left the army in 1816 to take care of her ailing father.

Flora Sandes (1876–1956) was an English woman who went to Serbia to serve as a St. John Ambulance driver, but later enrolled in the Serbian Army and was promoted to the rank of captain. Sandes fought in numerous engagements and earned seven medals. Wounded in battle, she received the highest decoration of the Serbian Military, the Order of the Karadorde's Star. In her book, *An English Woman-Sergeant in the Serbian Army*, she outlines her military career in Serbia, Albania, and Corfu. She apparently loved "becoming an ordinary soldier."[43] Her account is charmingly self-effacing, and humorous and shows a fine eye for detail.

Finally, it is important to include in this section Christine de Pizan who although she was not in combat, nevertheless wrote two very important texts in the Middle Ages dealing with war and the women warriors of the past such as Artemisia: *The Book of the City of Ladies* and *The Book of Feats of Arms and of Chivalry* (see analysis of both in part 2), she was one of the first authors to rediscover and study the earlier Roman texts of military writers such as Vegetius and bring them back into the mainstream.

Guerrilla Warfare/Revolutionary Participants

Here we have one of the largest and most inclusive categories, women who have participated as warriors in guerrilla warfare/revolutionary uprisings.

In modern times, these have included hundreds of thousands of participants in the Cuban, Algerian, Vietnamese, Angolan, Mozambique, South Africa, Eritrean, Guinee Bissau, Salvadorian, Peruvian, Argentinian Nicaraguan, Free Aceh, Huk Philipina, Malaysian, Cambodian, Timoran, and other revolutions. See for example, the women in this volume: the French women of the Paris Commune such as Louise Michel, Spanish Civil War Republican women such as Lina Odean, the Philipina HMB Huks, women of the Peruvian Shining Path, women of the Colombian FARC, Eritrean women of the EPLF, women of Mozambique FRELIMO, women of the Angolan UNITA, MPLA, women of Namibia SWAPO, women of Guinea Bissau PAIGC, women of South West Africa SWAPO, women of the South African ANC, the Rwandan RPF, Zimbabwe ZANU, Vietnamese, Malayan and Chinese women warriors, Cubans, Algerian FLN, Hungarian Freedom fighters, North Vietnamese and Viet Cong, Cambodian Kamer Rouge and Pated Lao women warriors, Nicaraguan Sandinista FSLN, El Salvador FMLA, Free Aceh GAM, Sri Lankan Tamil Tigers, Black Widows of Chechnya, Timoran Falintil-FDTL, the ISIS Al Khansaa Brigade, and Kurdish Peshmerga women warriors.[44]

But before the contemporary era, there were women who fought in earlier revolutions, including the American, the French, the Latin American revolts against the Spanish (Bolivia, Venezuela, Colombia, Peru, etc.)—and against them in the causes of Royalist France and Spain—women such as Renée Bordereau, "The Angevin;" Celeste Bulkekey, Catalina de Erauso, "The Lieutenant Nun," and Rose-Alexandrine Darreou. We also have the example of Maria Lebstuck, the Croatian woman in the revolution of 1848 against the Austrian Empire

One could also include here another potential subcategory, partisans. Women participated in considerable numbers in a variety of partisan operations during World War II, including those in Russian, Yugoslavian, French, Italian, Dutch, Vietnamese, Danish, Belgian, Norwegian, Czech, Greek, Rumanian, Polish, Jewish, Chinese, Indonesian, Burmese, Malayan, Thai, Filipino, and other resistance movements.

Recent scholarship has also finally illuminated the war-making contributions of many Ethiopian women fighters. Wayzaro Shewaraged Gadle, Wayzaro Olamawarq Terunah, Wayzaro Shewanash Abreha, and Wayzaro

Lakelas all fought against the Italian invasion of 1935–1936 and later with the shifta Patriot movement who resisted from 1937 to 1941, when Ethiopia was finally liberated.[45]

Additionally, contemporary studies now accent the key role played by women in the Taiping Rebellion (which lasted from 1850 to 1864) against the Qing Dynasty and resulted in the deaths of 20 million people, making it the most destructive civil war in recorded history. For example, an expert on the rebellion, Maochun Yu, states that a "unique feature of the Taiping military organization was its utilization of women soldiers in combat units. Since all men and women were regarded as brothers and sisters under God, no one was supposed to face discrimination because of their sex."[46] Such female generals as Qiu Ersao, Hong Xuanjiao, and Su Snniang emerged during this most bloody of conflicts.

Peacekeepers

At the other end of the war spectrum, there are a number of countries which have included women in their peacekeeping details seconded to the United Nations. By 2020, some 5% of United Nations "Blue Helmets" were female, serving in South Sudan, the Central Africa Republic, Darfur, Mali, and Haiti and on the India-Pakistan border. They have come from a number of countries as part of the regular army units of countries such as India, Bangladesh, Ireland, Brazil, South Africa, Nigeria, Niger, Sweden, Denmark, and Norway.

Some countries have also used this participation as a method of integrating former rebels and opponents into their national armies. These include Sierra Leone, Rwanda, and Liberia.

First of Their Kind

A great variety of women of note can be found here. Sabiha Gokcen (1913–2001) who was the adopted daughter of Mustafa Kemal and the first Turkish woman pilot as well as believed to be the first woman in air action bombing the Kurds during a punitive strike in 1937.

Or look at Ecaterina Teodoroiu (1894–1917), the Romanian woman killed in action leading Romanian troops into battle against Germans. Originally a nurse, when her brother was killed, to avenge his death she joined the 18th Infantry Regiment. Captured and wounded in action, she then became the first woman in World War I to command men in action. She was eventually killed defending a bridge with the 11th Division during the Battle of Marasesti.

Then there is Evgeniya Shakhovskaya (1889–1920), the first female aviator in Russia, who, during World War I, flew reconnaissance missions over the battlefield on the Eastern Front. Accused of spying and put in prison, she was later liberated by Bolsheviks and became a chief executioner for the Cheka.

Of note also is Susan Travers (1909–2003), an upper-class English woman raised in France. Travers joined the Red Cross in 1939 and in 1940 served with the French expeditionary force that was sent to Finland, where she was a nurse during the "Winter War." After the fall of France, she fled with the Free French to North Africa via Central Africa and the Horn and Syria. Travers then became a driver during the East African campaign and was trapped with the 1st Free French Brigade at Bir Hacheim, Libya, where she drove the commanding general in the combat breakout after the unit held off Rommel for 15 days. Travers eventually served in Italy and France and later in French Indochina as well after officially joining the Legion in 1945. Travers was the first woman to join the French Foreign Legion and she eventually received the *Medaille Militaire* and the *Legion d'Honneur*.[47]

More recently, Captain Linda Bray (1953–2011) was the first American woman to officially fight in combat. An ROTC Army MP, she led in combat some 30 male U.S. Army MPs in the 1989 invasion of Panama (dubbed "Operation Just Cause") against the Panamanian Defense Force (PDF).

And there was Nguyen Thi Dinh (1920–1990), the first female general in the Vietnam People's Army, who began by commanding an all-female force known as the "Long Haired Army" after being arrested by the French during World War II, 1940 through 1943. Nguyen subsequently helped lead insurrections in Ben Tre in 1945 and again in 1960. She was a founding member of the National Liberation Front (NLF) and was highly decorated, being awarded the Lenin Peace Prize and the Hero of the People's Armed Forces medal.

"Joan of Arcs"

There have been a number of women throughout history who have been called the "Joan of Arc" of their country. In some situations, such as that of Lady Trieu (Trieu Ba) (225–248) who is often called the Vietnamese "Joan of Arc" this is something of a misnomer because Lady Trieu was in the history books over a thousand years before there even was a French "Joan of Arc." It would be more accurate to say Joan of Arc was the "Lady Trieu of France." However, given the weight of works on the French Lady Trieu and the historical accumulation of accolades in her honor and centrality, such historical accuracy may be beside the point.

Nevertheless, there are quite a number of women who are now viewed as being heroines of their country's ultimate struggle to be free and are often referred to as the "Joan of Arc" of that country, just as a number of Chinese women are called the Hua Mulan (the legendary Chinese woman warrior) of their area, such as Han E, a.k.a. Han Guanbao (1345–1409), who is known as the "Hua Mulan of Sichuan Province."

The list of "Joan of Arcs" includes both India's Rani Lakshmibai and Arc-Veera Mangai Rani Velu Nachiyar, the Congo's Beatrice Kimpa Vita, Brazil's Maria Quiteria, Lithuania's Emilia Plater, Russia's Alena Arzamasskaia, Serbia's Sofija Jovanovic, Russia's Arzamasskaia Alena, and the Philippines' Remedios Gomez-Paraiso, "Kumander Liwayway," among others.

Others officially and unofficially also given that rubric are the North African Dihya or Al-Kahina, "The Prophetess." Born late in the 7th century, this Berber queen and military and religious leader led resistance to the Muslim conquest of the Maghreb, then known as Numidia. She and her forces fought off the Arab Islamic armies of the Umayyad Dynasty, defeating Hasan ibn al-Nu'man at the Battle of Meskiana. Hasan eventually defeated her in what is now Tunisia at the Battle of Tanarka (703 CE). In 2003, the Algerian government dedicated a statue to her, calling her the "Berber Joan of Arc."[48]

Then there was Dona Jesus Dosamentes (sometimes Dosamantes), the Mexican "Joan of Arc" who fought at the battle of Monterrey in 1846, leading a troop of lancers and earning the praise of her American opponents, one of whom described her prowess and courage: "There's an example of heroism worthy of the days of old. It has remained for Mexico to produce a second Joan d'Arc, but not, like her, successful."[49]

Slavery Revolt Participants

This category has more than its share of un- or underrepresented women. Nowhere is the devaluing of women's participation more glaring than in this cohort. Thousands of unnamed women took part in the dozens and dozens of slave revolts, resistances, and defenses, yet we have the names of only a few, and the references to them are often fragmentary or negative or both.

But exist they did and should also be of note today even as we wish we knew more about them and their companions. For example, in addition to America's Harriet Tubman, Brazil's Dandara of Palmares, Jamaica's Queen Nanny of Nanny Town, and Cuba's "La Negra Carlota" mentioned above, Haiti had Sanitte Belair (1781–1802), Victoria "Abdaraya Toya" Montou (c. 1739–1805), Dedee Bazile (?–1816) and Marie-Jeanne Lamartiniere (?). St. Croix had Queen Mary Thomas (c. 1848–1905), St. John had Breffu (?–1734) and Martinique had Fermina (dates unknown). Guadeloupe had "La Mulatresse Solitude" (c. 1772–1802) and Martha-Rose. Barbados had Nanny Grigg (dates unknown). Brazil had Filip a (sometimes Filipa) Maria Aranha (1720–1780) in Amazonia, and Zeferina (dates unknown) near San Salvador.

Guyana had Amelia, Barbara, and Pallas (last names and dates unknown) who were executed for their part in the 1763 Berbice slave uprising.

There were many more.

The sheer numbers of women executed after slave revolts in the New World suggests that they often played leadership roles in the rebellions and thus suffered the same penalties as male leaders. Unfortunately, we simply do not have their names to remember their sacrifices.

Nor do we have the names of the many women who participated in the slave revolts during their transport from Africa to Europe and the New World. It has been estimated that 1% of the total number of slaves involved—according to some estimates one hundred thousand—were killed in ship revolts and their aftermaths and judging from the numbers of female executions *after* the revolts were suppressed, women were involved in the thousands.[50]

One reason for the large number of women involved in the revolts is that on many ships they were allowed more movement than their male counterparts:

> Female slaves were rarely shackled while on board and were housed separately from men and closer to officer quarters, where they were closer to weapons and key. As they were sometimes sexually abused by crew members, women also had access to information that was essential to planning a revolt.[51]

Transgender Warriors

With the current debate about transgender and transsexual inclusion in the United States military highlighting the issue, there could also be a special category for transgender and transsexual warriors from the past and present in order to provide appropriate recognition to put their activities in this context.

The considerable outpouring of recent literature on the subject looking at warriors throughout history through this lens also argues for an exploration of this category. In general we are including persons who identified as male, not just in battle, but previously or subsequently or both, continuing to self-identify as male as well.

In our analysis of the transgender warriors below, we use "she/her" and "he/him" pronouns to mirror the pronouns used to describe the warriors in the scholarship consulted, usage which varies by exegete and era. If those sources are confusing or seemingly contradictory, we use the hybrid she/he designation. If that designation is used, it is meant neutrally and does not involve an editorial comment.

In some Native American cultures, for example, there exists a concept of two-spirit people, individuals who possess both a female and male spirit and therefore occupy a third gender or are gender nonconforming. For example, Bíawacheeitchish/Fallen Leaf/Warrior Woman and Otaki/Running Eagle of the Blackfeet Nation are characterized by some to be two-spirit (see their descriptions below).

Such a gender category would help to distinguish these warriors from women who simply dressed as men (and were thus transvestites in some sense of that term) in order to participate in battle—either not hiding their identity, such as Joan of Arc, or hiding their gender in order to pass muster with recruiting officers and subsequently with compatriots.

This category of transgender warriors would include a number of fairly well-known historical examples. Petra "Pedro" Herrera was one. Unfortunately the only truly certain date for him is 1914, when he and his band of armed 400 women took the city of Torreon in the Second Battle of Torreon, but we know he had previously joined the revolutionary movement of Pancho Villa. As Pedro, he had been accepted as a military leader, but later split with Villa and went off to war on his own with other like-minded women and fought other battles during the Mexican Revolution.

There is also the prominent case of Amelio Robles, who also fought during the Mexican Revolution. According to Gabriela Cano in his "Unconcealable Realities of Desire: Amelio Robles's (Transgender) Masculinity in the Mexican Revolution," Amelia Robles was born female, but subsequently identified as male. So Amelia became Amelio and fought with the Zapatas in a number of battles (later supporting General Álvaro Obregón) and was wounded no fewer than six times.[52] He subsequently was given the Mexican Legion of Honor and Revolutionary Merit Award.

Cano rightly notes the importance of this military self-emancipation, "As a guerilla fighter, Amelia discovered, in her words, 'the sensation of being completely free.'"[53] As the author states, "Amelio Robles made the transition from an imposed feminine identity to a desired masculinity: he felt like a man, acted like a man, and constructed a male appearance." He also didn't take kindly to bullying about his gender thereafter, allegedly shooting two men who tried to intimidate him.[54]

As Michy Martinez observes, Amelia had no interest in just being considered "only" a soldatara camp follower, as Amelio, he wanted to serve in combat.[55] It is important to reiterate that the mere fact of dressing as a man in order to join an army was of considerable importance in and of itself to some.

The liberating aspects of wearing men's clothing is a theme throughout many of the women warriors' history. For example, the cross-dressing British "Colonel" Barker put it very forthrightly:

> Trousers make a wonderful difference in the outlook on life. I know that dressed as a man I did not, as I do now I am wearing skirts again, feel hopeless and helpless. . . . Today when the whole world knows my secret I feel more a man than

a woman. I want to up and do those things that men do to earn a living rather than spend my days as a friendless woman.[56]

Another powerful example of a transgender women is Bíawacheeitchish or Fallen Leaf, also known as Warrior Woman. She was the only known woman chief among the Sioux, Arickaras, Assiniboines, Crees, and Crows. This Gros Ventre girl, captured at age 10 by the Crows, had a foster father who allowed her to pursue her passions, which included hunting, counting coup four times (which involved striking an armed opponent with a small wooden stick in the heat of battle), stealing horses, and showing great proficiency with weapons.

She gained very high stature among the Crows fighting the Blackfeet. Upon the death of her father, she assumed command of his family and participated in both warfare and tribal decision-making. In the process, she continued to act as a man and would acquire four wives before being killed, ironically enough by her original people, the Gros Ventres.[57]

Also consider Otaki or Running Eagle of the Blackfeet Nation (c. 1840–c. 1878) who entered the Braves Society and fought the Crows and others and was eventually killed in battle by the Flatheads. Born "Pitamakan" in southern Alberta Canada, her father instructed her in hunting and warcraft, and with his death, she assumed responsibility for the family and forced her way onto a raiding party despite its leader's wishes. Her subsequent vision quest and participation in the Medicine Lodge Ceremony were unusual for women. The Chief, Lone Walker, gave her the name Running Eagle, and she became a member of the Braves Society of the Young Warriors. Otaki led numerous war parties and was eventually killed by the Flatheads, who purposefully targeted her as a woman posing as a man. She continued to wear men's clothing when not going to war, and many today would put her in the transgender warrior category.

Maria van Antwerpen (1719–1781) was also an interesting if somewhat ambiguous example of transsexuality in the 18th century. She donned men's clothing and joined the Dutch army as Jan van Ant and subsequently served in a variety of locations during wars with the French. Jan courted many women and married two of them, rejoining the army in the process, not once but twice, finally "being discharged because of a 'quarrelsome nature.'"[58]

Warrior Queens

This category is probably the most widely used by those who look at war through a female lens. Here we find many of the best-known rulers who strategically (if not necessarily tactically) guided their armies and countries in significant military action. Cleopatra, Aethelflaed, Nzinga, Zenobia, Catherine the Great, Elizabeth I, Matilde, Isabella of Spain, Boudica, and Eleanor of Aquitaine are often included in most lists of "warrior queens."

In Jonathan and Emily Jordan's *The War Queens: Extraordinary Women Who Ruled the Battlefield*, a strong case is also made for more women who may not have actually been in battle per se but whose strategic imperatives guided the outcome of those wars. In this category, their examples in addition to some of the above, include the Georgian Queen and "King of Kings" Tamar, the Mongol Manduhai, Margaret Thatcher, Golda Meir, and Indira Gandhi.[59]

Intellectuals and Theoreticians

Perhaps the interesting example falling into this category is Christine de Pizan, cited above. De Pizan wrote *The Book of Deeds of Arms and of Chivalry,* an amazing document for the 15th century. Imagine how many cultural and religious barriers this early feminist writer had to overcome in order to even get her book published. Written in the 15th century by this Italian born, but French court author, *The Book of Deeds* resurrects many classical writings on war (especially Vegetius) but also provides very useful contrasts between Medieval Europe war practices and those from antiquity, including just war, siege warfare, chivalry, trickery, and "subtlety." De Pizan skillfully uses many examples from contemporary Europe as well as campaigns of Scipio, Hannibal, and Hanno. It is a truly amazing work given the time, the place, and the gender of its author.

De Pizan is also the author of *The Book of the City of Ladies*, which highlights numerous women in fact and legend, most important for our purposes, the Amazons, Zenobia, and Artemisia, who she unfortunately puts on the side of the Greeks in the Persian wars.[60]

Women Warriors Diminished by Subsequent Historical Accounts

There are some startling examples of women who played important strategic and military roles at the time but who were mostly airbrushed out of many subsequent accounts. Without the four daughters of Genghis Khan—Checheyigen, Alaqai, Al-Altun, and Yesui Khatun—there would have been no Mongol empire. The feats of the "Four Tiger Queens," suppressed by Muslim, Christian, and Chinese chroniclers and written out of subsequent histories. In the *Secret History of the Mongols*, they are all there. All four daughters played major roles in ruling and warfare during this period and kept the dynasty viable.[61]

Also the later Mongol "Queen Manduhai the Wise" or "Wolf Mother" (1449–1510) who reunited the warring Mongols, defeating the Oirats and Mings. At 45, she married Bat Monkh Dayan Khan, a direct descendant of Genghis Khan, and fought in numerous battles, often leading from the front. In one, when she was eight months pregnant, she was knocked from her horse and only saved by her loyal bodyguard. The next month she gave birth to twin boys, Ochir Bolod and Alju Bolod. She was the driving force behind the resurgence of Mongol power in central Asia.[62] Later, Queen Anu of the Dzungar Khanate (r. 1693–1696) died in battle protecting her husband in fighting against the Qings at the Battle of Jao Modo (1696). The Mongol women deserve wider attention and credit.

Likewise many Muslim women who fought in various situations over the century have tended to have faded from the accounts of later historians although there have been some attempts to renew interest in them as Moroccan author, Asma Lamrabet, whose *Women in the Qur'an: An Emancipatory Reading* provides a rereading of the Muslim Holy Scriptures from a female perspective. For example, on page 19, she quotes the Prophet describing a woman warrior, "Who else could endure all that you are suffering here Umm "Umarah?" The author says Umm was wounded 13 times in various battles including Uhud, Hudaybiyyah, Hunayn, and Al-Yamama, where she lost a hand.

Or take the example of Ahilyabai Holkar (1725–1795), Sardar of the Maratha Empire. When her husband was killed in the battle of Kumbher and her father-in-law, Malhar Rao Holkar, died in 1764, she became ruler, personally leading her troops into battle on her favorite war elephant. As the Rani of Indore, she played a key role in preventing the Mughals from taking over the Maratha Confederacy from her position in Malwa which abutted Mughal forces at Delhi. She was also in charge of the Maratha artillery in the Battle of Panipat (1761), one of the largest battles of that era, yet only belatedly has she been given full credit for her exploits in modern military annals.[63]

Modern Warfare Groupings (20th to 21st Centuries)

Regardless of how long it took for women to be recognized as warriors by large number of observers, today there are a lot of countries that accept women in that capacity—and they don't have to dress up as men to be accepted either.

At the time of this writing, women play vital roles—including actual and potential combat forces—in the armed forces of Canada, Singapore, the United States, Brazil, Cuba, China, Taiwan, Japan, South Korea, North Korea, Pakistan, South Africa, Eritrea, Sierra Leone, Iran, Rwanda, France, Great Britain, New Zealand, Australia, Canada, Germany, India, Denmark,

Finland, France, Israel, New Zealand, Norway, Sri Lanka, Sweden, Turkey, Taiwan, Norway, Poland, Lithuania, Estonia, Ukraine, Greece, Kurdistan, Latvia, Romania, Russia, Holland, Spain, Italy, Argentina, Bolivia, Ukraine, Singapore, Serbia, Thailand, South Africa, Bangladesh, Algeria, Tunisia, Czech Republic, Macedonia, Slovenia (note that in 1988, Major General Alenka Ermench became the first female chief of staff in NATO), Indonesia, and the United Arab Emirates.

By Amount of Source Material

When looking for a fit subject for interest and research among the woman warrior cohort, it is often necessary to look at how much material is available in readable or usable form. As we have indicated, there are a large number of women about whom we would like to know more, often much more.

HERE ARE SOME WAYS OF GRADING THAT SUBJECT MATERIAL

Note: It is very important to distinguish between a lot of different material versus a smaller amount of material cited by a lot of works.

Tantalizingly Brief

In some cases there are specific references to women in battle, references that intrigue and make one want more information and lament no one was paying enough attention or cared enough to write down more about them.

Who, for example, wouldn't want to know more about Maria de Jesus Dosamantes, the Mexican woman who fought as a captain with General Ampudia in his defense of Monterrey during the American invasion in the Mexican War of 1846? According to an eyewitness when she led a valiant attack with her Mexican lancers, an American officer cried out "There's an example of heroism worthy of the days of old."[64]

Or how about Giuseppa Bolognani "Peppa la Cannoniera"? She was a Sicilian woman in revolt against the restored Bourbons. Wouldn't we like to know why she acted as she did and what happened to her? In the swirl of the Italian unification struggle, there must be quite a few women like Giuseppa who joined that effort.

Even more intriguing would be additional information about the Assyrian Queen Semiramis (Shammuramat), Assyrian wife of Shamshi-Adad V (824–811 BCE). According to Diodorus, after the death of her son, she masqueraded as him and subsequently led the army he had inherited from his father, winning a number of battles as far away as India and expanding the Neo Assyrian Empire (911–605 BCE). She appears to be the only woman ever to have led the Assyrian Empire.[65]

Or Clara Camarao: wouldn't we like to know more about this woman who led tribal warriors against the Dutch invasions of Brazil during the period 1630–1637? Or Maria Estrada, who fought with Cortés in Mexico during his conquest of the Aztec and participated in a number of battles?

And what about Xi, the Tang dynasty woman who commanded a troop of women who fought against the Qidan and was given the title Mistress of Loyalty and Integrity? Or the legendary Toltec queen (c. 1116 CE) Xochitl who created a women's battalion and was killed leading it in battle?

These would all be very interesting to study if we only knew more.

We would also like to know much more about Zoia Smirnova, who left home to join the Russian Army in 1914 on the Austrian front. Despite all odds and obstacles, she was accepted as a fighter, was wounded twice, and was awarded the St. George's Cross.

Considerable: Individuals

There are a large number of women warriors about whom much has been written and the scholarship is readily available. Most of the warrior queens listed above, women such as Cleopatra, Isabella of Spain, Elizabeth I, Catherine the Great, Matilda of Canossa, Boudica, Eleanor of Aquitaine, Margaret Thatcher, Aethelflaed, and the like are all quite well represented.[66]

So too are some lesser-known (at least to most American readers) figures such as the Rani of Jhansi, Zenobia, Amina of Hausaland, Nzinga of Mbundu, Lozen the Apache, Chand Bibi, and Maria Bochkareva.

Considerable: Groups

As mentioned above, there is a lot of material on many of the resistance and partisan fighters as well as revolutionaries from a great variety of countries and ages. Women warriors operating in these spheres are quite well represented.

There is also a lot of currently available information on American women who fought or played major military roles in the Revolutionary War, the Civil War, and World War II. There is also a fairly large number of works looking at contemporary American women who have been steadily increasing their numbers fighting in the various campaigns in wars since the Reagan era.

A considerable literature has also grown up around women who fought in the Spanish Civil War, the Mexican Revolution, and especially Russian women during World War II, including those who fought in both the regular armed forces and the partisans.

In addition, there is a considerable body of material dealing with European women resistance fighters during World War II, including—but not exclusively—those in Great Britain, France, Belgium, Holland, Denmark, Norway, Poland, Yugoslavia, the Czech Republic, and Slovakia. There seems to be less available on the female resistance fighters in Asia and Africa.

Perhaps surprising to many new to this search, there is now also a substantial body of literature dealing with Native American and Indigenous women warriors, along with a considerable amount of material on the earlier Scythian and Sarmatian fighters. Twenty years ago, these would have been ignored by military writers. Now they can only be ignored at those writers' intellectual peril.

More surprising to traditional historians or casual history buffs may be the ever-growing literature on warriors housed in the LGBTQ? community. While much more needs to be done to reexamine the women throughout history who fit into this category, even a quick glance into this annotated bibliography will provide a quite amazing list of recent material in this genre. This scholarship has not only enriched and enlightened us to the specific participations from the LGBTQ? community, but it collectively points to our need to question many of our assumptions about history. Also, this new knowledge has come from a variety of genres and disciplines.

Voluminous

Joan of Arc is probably the warrior woman about whom the most has been written. There are over 20,000 works written about Joan of Arc in the Bibliothèque Nationale de France alone. There are also numerous poems, novels, essays, books, and monographs. This body of work is an astonishing amount for someone who, when her career is examined closely, really had a more important afterlife than the life she actually led.[67] In terms of volume of work, scholarly and otherwise, she is the gold standard by which biographies are compared.

By Degree of Author's Interest

Over the years, many students have been interested in which women warriors stand out in the professor's mind, either for sheer novelty or in terms of perceived impact and the degree of difficulty of their achievements. Here are a few of those favorites, for it would be hard to beat the following examples if you want to study the exciting examples of women warriors in action.

Lozen the Apache (1840–1898). Even among the most fearsome of the western Native Americans such as the Chiricahua and Mescalero Apaches, with leaders such as Cochise, Geronimo, Nana, and Victorio (her brother) in the last decades of the 19th century, Lozen stands out, treated as an equal in terms of warriorhood.

She fought with all four, leaving a reservation to fight with Geronimo, led and served as a most important leader for her people, fighting the Mexicans and the Americans as well as other tribes. As a true warrior, she must have relished her final battle, when she and her tiny band were outnumbered 7,000 to 42. As the patriarch of the Apaches, Nana, put it "Though she is a woman, there is no warrior more worthy than the sister of Victorio."[68]

War with various Apache clans turned out to be the longest in U.S. history (officially 1861–1886 but actually beginning in 1857).

Empress Zenobia (sometimes Zabbai) (240–c. 275). From Tadmor-Palmyra in what is now Syria, Zenobia led a rebellion against the Romans from 269 to 272 CE, and, for a time, she operated skillfully in the seam between Roman power and Persian power, taking advantage of their internal problems and martial competition. She led her victorious army through Egypt, Arabia, and Mesopotamia, declaring herself Queen of Egypt. But like Boudica in Britain, eventually the power of the Roman Empire came to bear, and she was eventually captured and brought to Rome as a prisoner (although some Arab sources claim she committed suicide, thereby imitating Cleopatra).[69]

Matilda of Canossa (1046–1115) was an ally of Pope Gregory VII in 1087 when she marched with her Tuscan army on Rome to fight and oust one of the anti-popes, putting one pope back in on the throne of St. Peter's, and later sustained another in office. A master strategist and military leader who waged war for 40 years defeating the Holy Roman Emperor (HRE) Henry IV when he invaded Italy.

Her military biographer calls her simply, "The most powerful woman of her time" for she denied the Holy Roman Emperor, the most powerful male leader of the period, his designs on Italy, the papacy, and especially her territory. This was an unheard-of feat for a woman in her era. It was in fact at her castle that Henry IV was so famously made to kneel in the snow in order to have his excommunication by the pope lifted. Urban II was the second pope she kept in the Holy See.[70]

Maria Bochkareva (1889–1920). Dirt poor and harmed by domestic abuse perpetrators (her drunken father, her drunken lovers, and her drunken husband), she petitioned the Czar to let her join the army. Imagine her struggles as a woman in the Czarist army of 1914, when peasant soldiers were considered to be serfs. She fought for two years in the Imperial Army, becoming a noncommissioned officer (NCO), being wounded twice, and inspiring her troops and officers to fight under very difficult situations.

When the Czar fell, she got the new government under Alexander Kerensky to let her form the Russian Provisional Government's 1st Russian Women's Battalion of Death (6,000 women) in 1917 which continued to fight against the Germans. She and her cohort of women shamed their fellow male units to fight on several occasions when they preferred to avoid combat. Later, she was captured by the Bolsheviks, met Trotsky and Lenin, and when they wanted her to integrate her female warriors into their Red revolutionary army, she fled and made it to the United States by way of Siberia. Once in the United States, she met and hectored President Wilson to intervene and fight the Reds. Frustrated when he refused, she returned to Russia to fight for the Whites. This time when she was captured by the Bolsheviks, she was shot.[71]

Njinga (Nzinga) of Ndongo and Mataba (c. 1583–1663). Ruling as regent, she killed her nephew and became the first queen of the Ndongo (Mbundu) people, successfully orchestrating a variety of campaigns and maneuvers. Her military prowess, including a decade-long stretch of successful battles both guerrilla and set-piece warfare (1624–1663), is matched only by her strategic and diplomatic efforts as she played the Portuguese, Dutch, and African tribes off against each other, even negotiating successfully with Pope Alexander VII.

Also noteworthy is her defiance of the gender, sexuality, and religious norms of her time (she took both men and women as lovers and sometimes dressed as a man but made her male lovers dress as women) and her most skillful blending of Mbundu, Impangala (Jaga), and Christian traditions to support her legitimacy, explaining to the cannibal Impangala that their religion was compatible with Christian beliefs since the Christians symbolically, at least, drank the blood and ate the flesh of Christ and were thus, at heart, cannibals. A woodcut shows her leading her troops into battle at age 73, and Ndongo survived as an independent state until 1909 when the Portuguese finally annexed it into Angola. Njinga is now rightly considered a mother of her country.[72]

What a woman. What a warrior.

CONCLUSION

Looking over the past several decades of scholarship, we find:

1. An increased examination of war, its causes, history, and extent;
2. A greater appreciation for the role women have played in war;
3. Increased and significant archaeological evidence of women warriors across the globe from the steppes of Asia to Scandinavia to Africa and Latin America;
4. Far greater recognition of the numbers, duration, and depth of importance of women warriors throughout history;
5. A huge increase in the number of scholarly works, both in journals and books, dealing with both individual women warriors, their typologies, and their influences;
6. A much-needed reexamination of many female warriors analyzed through the lenses of women's and gender studies;
7. Additional efforts to combine these new studies with a great appreciation of the warfare qua warfare in which these women fought; and
8. An ongoing recognition of the need to continue to explore the various roles played by women in war, from the foot soldiers to the strategists and a frank evaluation of the cultural, hierarchical, and gender impediments to their greater participation.

It is hoped that the annotated bibliography that follows will help stimulate these ongoing efforts across time and space, especially in getting those who come at the subject from a women's and gender studies perspective to do more to set their scholarship in a context that highlights the warfare qua warfare demands of time and place *and*, even more important, those who study military affairs from the perspective of the near totality of male domination of the subject should strive harder to examine the exceptional women who broke the barriers to participation in warfare as a subject and actor, not simply as an object or curiosity.

Also in light of the previous siloing of many academic disciplines, we seek here to integrate the work of military historians with disciplines frequently overlooked for their contributions to study of warfare, such as gender and sexuality studies, anthropology, and religious studies.

The substantial lack of communication across disciplines continues to amaze us and contributes to the marginalization of women's accomplishments in warfare. Through examining the widest ranges of scholarship in this select but wide-gauge annotated bibliography, women warriors are put in their rightful place as essential combatants, strategists, and leaders within the war space of the past, present and future.

Two final thoughts.

The first is about the nature of the scope of this inquiry. We have sought to be inclusive rather than exclusive and to define "warrior" in wide but discernable terms. We have sought to call those women who participated in wars in an active fashion as "warriors" whether as leaders or actual combatants and when in doubt have sought to adhere to a scholarly parallelism, i.e. if we consider men to be in the army (even if they are not actually in battle) as warriors, so too women belong in that category. Also, from using a weapon in combat or directing an operation of a battle or a war, the same criteria obtain.

The second concluding note has to do with the ultimate nature of war. Including women in the armed forces of a particular nation or society seems to always involve raising questions as to whether that is good or bad policy for the polity, the armed force in question, or for the individual.

Some have argued also that the inclusion of women in the realm of war in a strategic as well as a tactical sense will change the women and/or the nature of war. Some—both men and women—argue that the inclusion of women ipso facto changes either the women (making them more manlike and hence warlike) or the nature of warfare (making war itself less violent, less horrible in both intent and outcome).

For the former, we conclude that war changes men and women in similar ways if not in identical fashions. We have long argued in our *War Trilogy* that it is war that dominates humans, not humans war. There is something about the nature of war which seems to develop a life of its own, a life that overcomes individual and collective human impulses to alter it, to make it less destructive or less frequent or both. And like the COVID-19 virus that overhangs this effort, war always seems to mutate itself over and above the strictures humans try to put on it.

This overpowering nature of war cannot be disregarded, even now. In the battle of the gods, for example, throughout human history and even today Mars wins, turning pacific religions into violent ones, turning violent ones into self-justifying ones, and so on. War does the same with secular religions or ideologies such as nationalism or communism or capitalism. Regardless of economic system or political belief set, polities and societies end up tolerating and utilizing war despite all of its destructive outcomes.

War dominates.

So in that sense, we now circle back to the intent of Simone Weil, force is in and of itself a powerful determinant of human action and when war occurs, it changes the nature of men and women to suit itself.

In that sense it remains the ultimate leveler.

Women, as men, are thus war's participants, as well as its victims.

NOTES

1. Andrew Curry, "Slaughter at the Bridge," *Science*, Vol. 25, #351 (March 2016), pp. 1384–1389.

2. For background on the Sea Peoples, see Neil Silberman, "The Coming of the Sea Peoples," *MHQ: The Quarterly Journal of Military History,* Vol. 10, #2 (Winter 1998), pp. 6–13. The author indicates how the chariot, the main weapon for the Mediterranean basin for hundreds of years, was superseded by lightly armed infantry known as the Sea Peoples that swept out of the Balkans and caused the "Great Catastrophe" (although it was not a catastrophe for them) and Peter Tsouras, "Bronze Age Cataclysm: The Collapse of the Civilized Near East," *Strategy and Tactics,* #315 (March–April 2019), pp. 42–51. Silberman, an analyst at the U.S. Army's Intelligence and Threat Center in Washington, examines how the major powers of the area (with the exception of Egypt) and their reliance on chariots were swept away by the Sea Peoples and their newly specialized infantry weapons and tactics. This phenomenon shows how receptivity to innovation is the key to military success over time. Additional useful information on the Sea Peoples is also to be found in Eric Cline, "Raiders of the Lost Bronze Age," *MHQ: The Quarterly of Military History*, Vol. 28, #1 (Autumn 2015), pp. 66–75. Cline sees the Sea Peoples as perhaps initially victims turning to conquest out of desperation and hope for martial supremacy elsewhere.

3. Wayne Lee, "When Did Warfare Begin?," *MHQ: The Quarterly Journal of Military History*, Vol. 27, #2 (Winter 2015), pp. 64–71. Others take a more benign interpretation of Neanderthal/Homo sapiens interaction. See, for example, Rebecca Wragg Sykes, *Kindred: Neanderthal Life, Love, Death and Art* (New York: Bloomsbury Sigma, 2020). Perhaps we are on firmer ground with the statement of Trevor Watkins, "The origins of warfare are hidden in the mists of human prehistory, but by 1200 BC there was a long tradition of armies, campaigns, pitched battles and siege warfare" (p. 15) in his "The Beginnings of Warfare" in John Hackett, *Warfare in the Ancient World* (New York: Facts on File, 1989), pp. 15–35.

4. Nichols Longrich, "The Conversation," November 3, 2020. See also Robert O'Connell, "The Origins of War," *MHQ: The Quarterly Journal of Military History*, Vol. 1, #3 (Spring 1999), pp. 8–15.

5. *Mahabharata* (trans. By John Smith) (New York: Penguin Classics, 2009), CXXIV. Much of what we know about Aryan chariot warfare comes from the *Mahabharata*. For an examination of war during Vedic times, see Richard Gabriel, "Armies of Ancient India: Vedic and Imperial Periods," in his *The Great Armies of Antiquity* (Westport: Praeger, 2002), pp. 207–224.

6. Thucydides, *The History of the Peloponnesian War*, Book Four (3.84.1).

7. Homer, (trans. by Robert Fagles) *The Iliad* (New York: Penguin Books, 1990). See especially "The Death of Achilles."

8. James Holoka (ed. and trans.), *Simone Weil's The Iliad, or the Poem of Force: A Critical Edition* (New York: Peter Lang, 2006), p. 45.

9. Many of the arguments against war per se and the notion that it can and must be resisted can be found in Robert Gonzalez, Hugh Gusterson, and Gustaaf Houtman (eds.), *Militarization: A Reader* (Durham: Duke University Press, 2019). This work contains stimulating essays by Dwight Eisenhower, Margaret Mead, Noel Perrin, Naoko Shibusawa, Leslie Sponsel, and Robert Lifton.

10. Holoka, *op. cit*, p. 45.

11. John Keegan, *A History of Warfare* (New York: Alfred Knopf, 1993), p. 76.

12. Margaret MacMillan, *War: How Conflict Shaped Us* (New York: Random House, 2020), pp. 312, 131.

13. See his "Women of Valor: Why Israel Doesn't Send Women into Combat," *Policy Review* (Fall 1991), pp. 65–67. He amplifies these arguments in, "Armed But Not Dangerous: Women in the Israeli Military," *War in History*, Vol. 7, #1 (January 2000), pp. 82–98, "The Great Illusion: Women in the Military," *Journal of International Studies*, Vol. 29, #2 (2000), pp. 429–442, *Men, Women and War* (London: Cassell, 2001), "Warrior-Women of Dahomey," *Militärgeschichtliche Zeitschrift*, Vol. 39, #1 (2018), pp. 115–123 and *The Culture of War* (New York: Ballantine Books, 2008).

14. Nina Liza Bode, *The Imaging of Violent Gender Performances,* Master's Thesis (University of Groningen, 2014).

15. Women Peacemaker Program, *Gender and Militarism Analyzing the Links to Strategize for Peace* (Netherlands: Women Peacemakers Program, 2014), p. 9.

16. Adrian Goldsworthy, *Philip and Alexander: Kings and Conquerors* (New York: Basic Books, 2020), p. 7.

17. See especially John Lynn, *Women Armies, and Warfare in Early Modern Europe* (Cambridge: Cambridge University Press, 2008) (some of his other works in this genre include, "Women in War," *Military History* (October 2001), pp. 60–66, *The French Wars 1667–1714* (Oxford: Osprey Publishing, 2002), and "The Strange Case of the Maiden Soldier of Picardy," *MHQ: The Quarterly Journal of Military History*, Vol. 2, #3 (Spring 1990), pp. 54–56, Robert Kaplan, *Imperial Grunts* and Mark Bowden, "The Huong River Squad" in his *Hue, 1968: A Turning Point of the American War in Vietnam* (New York: Random House, 2017). With regard to Bowden's

recent book, think of the thousands of works on the Vietnam War and how few ever highlight the role of women.

18. Alexander Ingle, "Berenice II Euergetes," Pennington, *op. cit.*, p. 53. For more on her complex dynastic and marital background, see Grace Harriet Macurdy, *Hellenistic Queens: A Study of Woman-Power in Macedonia, Seleucid Syria, and Ptolemaic Egypt* (Baltimore: The Johns Hopkins Press, 1932), pp. 130–136. For a useful and more recent full-length biography that highlights her many literary and political accomplishments, see Dee Clayman, *Berenice II and the Golden Age of Ptolemaic Egypt* (London: Oxford University Press, 2014). For the political and economic background of Ptolemaic Egypt, see Andrew Monson, *From the Ptolemies to the Romans: Political and Economic Change in Egypt* (Cambridge: Cambridge University Press, 2002). Note that the term "Hellenistic" is usually defined as the period from the death of Alexander in 323 to the fall of the Ptolemaic dynasty in 30 CE even though Macedonia had long before fallen to the Romans. For a sprightly overview of the Hellenistic world, see Peter Thonemann, *The Hellenistic Age* (London: Oxford University Press, 2016).

19. Wale Ogunyemi, "Queen Amina of Zazzau," *Play* 1959. See also Philip Koslow, *Hausaland: The Fortress Kingdoms* (New York: Chelsea House Press, 1995).

20. Patrick Kagbeni Muana, "Masarico," in Pennington (ed.), *op. cit.*, pp. 285–286. For a history of the later Sierra Leone colony, see Joe Alie, *A New History of Sierra Leone* (New York: St. Martin's Press, 1990).

21. Stanley B. Alpern, *Amazons of Black Sparta: The Women Warriors of Dahomey* (New York: New York University Press, 1998), p. 207.

22. *Ibid.* Another important West Africa warrior woman of note was Orompoto, the 16th-century female Alaafin (king) of the Yoruba remembered for her skillful use of cavalry at the battle of Illayi.

23. Michael Edwardes, *Red Year: The Indian Rebellion of 1857* (London: Hamish Hamilton, 1973). See also Joyce Libra-Chapman, *The Rani of Jhansi: A Study in Female Heroism in India* (Honolulu: University of Hawaii Press, 1986).

24. See especially Sayyid Ahmad-Ullah Qadri, *Memoires of Chand Bibi The Princess of Ahmednagar* (Hyderabad: The Osmania University Press, 1939). Another Indian women who led from the front was Tarabai Bhonsale (1675–1761), a Maratha Maharani who resisted Mughal incursions and fought on horseback with a cavalry regiment.

25. Stephen Turnbull, *Samurai Women 1184–1877* (Oxford: Osprey Publishing Company, 2002), p. 37. Turnbull provides a powerful set of insights into the existence of a little-known female warrior class in this well-illustrated work. See also Royall Tyler, "Tomoe: The Woman Warrior," in Chieko Irie Mulhern (ed.), *Heroic with Grace: Legendary Women of Japan* (London: M.E. Sharpe, 1991), and "Death of Lord Kiso," excerpted from "The Tale of the Heike," *MHQ: The Quarterly Journal of Military History,* Vol. 25, #3 (Spring 2013), pp. 94–97.

26. Aunait Chutintaranond, "Suriyothai in the Context of Thai-Myanmar History and Historical Perception," in Sunait Chutintaranond and Kanokphan U-sha (eds.), *From Fact to Fiction: History of Thai-Myanmar Relations in Cultural Context* (Bangkok: Institute of Asian Studies, Chulalongkorn University, 1992), pp. 30–41, provides

a fulsome and detailed account of the battle, including her bravery and the gruesome details of Suriyothai's life-ending wounds. See also Irene Stengs, "Dramatising Siamese Independence: Thai Post-colonial Perspectives on Kingship," in Robert Aldrich and Cindy McCreery (eds.), *Monarchies and Decolonization in Asia* (Manchester: Manchester University Press, 2020), p. 274. Pamaree Surakiat, "Thai-Burmese Warfare during the Sixteenth Century and the Growth of the First Toungoo Empire," *Journal of the Siam Society*, Vol. 93 (2005), pp. 69–100 puts this war in a broader context of the rise of the Toungoo Empire. Further background is provided by Jon Fernquist, "Min-gyi-nyo, the Shan Invasions of Ava (1524–27), and the Beginnings of Expansionary Warfare in Toungoo Burma: 1486–1539," *SOAS Bulletin of Burma Research*, Vol. 3, #2 (Autumn 2005), pp. 28–35. Queen Suriyothai and her legendary sacrifice in battle continues to fascinate even today. See Amporn Jirattikorn, "Suriyothai: Hybridizing Thai National Identity Through Film," *Inter-Asia Cultural Studies*, Vol. 4, #2 (2003), pp. 296–308.

27. For an in-depth look at Maroon resistance and communities in the Spanish America, the French Caribbean, Jamaica, Brazil, and the Guianas, see Richard Price (ed.), *Maroon Societies: Rebel Slave Communities in the Americas* (Baltimore: The John Hopkins University Press, 1979) and Alvin O. Thompson, *Flight to Freedom: African Runaways and Maroons in the Americas* (Jamaica: University of the West Indies Press, 2006).

28. Polyaenus, quoted in Paul Chrystal, *Women at War in The Classical World* (Barnsley: Pen and Sword, 2017), p. 90. Cynane and her military proclivities are well sourced. Adrian Goldsworthy in his *Philip and Alexander: Kings and Conquerors* (New York: Basic Books, 2020), p. 535, for example, cites her appearances in Athenaeus, Polyaenus, and Arrian.

29. Charles Walker, *The Tupac Amaru Rebellion* (Cambridge: The Belknap Press of Harvard University Press, 2014); Leon Campbell, "Women and the Great Rebellion in Peru, 1780–1783," *The Americas*, Vol. 42, #2 (October 1985), pp. 163–196; and Lillian Fisher, *The Last Inca Revolt 1780–1783* (Norman: University of Oklahoma Press, 1966).

30. Asma Lamrabet, *Women in the Qur'an: An Emancipatory Reading* (Leicestershire: Square View Press, 2016), p. 19. Readers interested in the rise and success of the Arab armies and the implementation of light horse warfare should consult Robert Hoyland, *In God's Path: The Arab Conquests and the Creation of an Islamic Empire* (London: Oxford University Press, 2003); Tom Holland, *In the Shadow of the Sword: The Birth of Islam and the Rise of the Global Arab Empire* (New York: Doubleday, 2012); and for a broader perspective, Anthony Pagden, *Worlds at War: The 2,500-Year Struggle Between East and West* (New York: Random House, 2008). For a closer look at the Muslim armies as armies, note the trilogy by David Nicolle, *The Armies of Islam 7th–11th Centuries* (Oxford: Osprey Publishing, 1983), *Armies of the Muslim Conquest* (Oxford: Osprey Publishing, 1993) and *The Moors: The Islamic West 7th–11th Centuries* (Oxford: Osprey Publishing, 2001).

31. For some insights into Arab light horse warfare, see Gabriel, "The Arab Armies 600–850 C.E." *op. cit.*, pp. 304–314.

32. Thomas B. Marquis, *Custer on the Little Big Horn* (Algonac: Marquis Custer Publications, 1967), p. 93. See also Rosemary Agonito and Joseph Agonito *Buffalo Calf Road Woman* (Guilford, CT: TwoDot, 2006) for more on the battle and her role in it. Another Cheyenne woman warrior from this era was Ehyophsta (1826–1915). Also known as Yellow Haired Woman, she fought in the 1868 battle against the U.S. Army at Beecher's Island and later engaged the Shoshoni on Beaver Creek in 1873, counting coup and killing an opponent. She was subsequently admitted to the Crazy Dog Soldier Warrior society.

Note: For a truly magical in-depth look at Cheyenne warfare during this era, see Father Peter John Powell, *People of the Scared Mountain: A History of the Northern Cheyenne Chiefs and Warrior Societies 1830–1879*, Vol. I (New York: Harper & Row, 1981). Also interesting background on those who tried to find ways of peace between the whites and the Cheyenne can be found in Louis Kraft, "Between the Army and the Cheyenne," *MHQ: The Quarterly Journal of Military History*, Vol. 14, #2 (Winter, 2002), pp. 48–55.

33. Queen of Tahiti Niel Gunson, "Sacred Women Chiefs and Female 'Headman' in Polynesian History," *Journal of Pacific History*, Vol. 22, #3 (1987), pp. 139–172. The author believes that the role of women, both in terms of politics and standing as well as in terms of warriorhood, was submerged by missionaries and early anthropologists and needs to be revised significantly. In Polynesia, "the *mana* of a great warrior was inherited through his daughter, not a son." (p. 139). Female headmen were common in Polynesia and "Very often they were known for their prowess in warfare" (p. 142).

34. Debra Hamel, "Ancient Greeks in Drag," *MHQ: The Quarterly Journal of Military History*, Vol. 14, #4 (Summer 2002), pp. 81–89.

35. In terms of longevity of the style of warfare, it is difficult to match the horse archers of the Eurasian steppe regions. See D. V. Cernenko, *The Scythians 700–300 BC* (Oxford: Osprey Publishing, 1983) and R. Brzezinski and M. Mielczarek, *The Sarmatians 600 BC—AD 450* (Oxford: Osprey Publishing, 2002). For a closer look at this clash of war cultures in the Greek world and the differing styles, see Gabriel, *op. cit.*, "The Greek Way of War: Classical and Imperial Periods 500–323 B.C.E.," pp. 171–205.

36. https://www.newswise.com/articles/dna-reveals-2-500-year-old-siberian-warrior-was-a-woman2. Further scientific research is continuing on Scythian DNA material from 4,000 years ago.

37. Megan McLaughlin, "The Woman Warrior: Gender, Warfare and Society in Medieval Europe," *Women's Studies*, Vol. 17, #3–4 (1990), pp. 192–209. This is a seminal work providing as it does a very useful dichotomy of women at war as generals versus women as foot soldiers. Second, the author rightly looks at much of medieval warfare involving the defense of castles as "domestic warfare" and points out the advantages this type of war provides opportunities for women. See also Susan Johns in her *Noblewoman, Aristocracy and Power in the Twelfth-Century Anglo-Norman Realm* (Manchester: Manchester University Press, 2003) and Malcolm Hebron, *The Medieval Siege: Theme and Image in Middle English Romance* (London: Clarendon Press, 1997). For warfare in this era, see Philip Warner, *The Medieval Castle: Life*

in a Fortress in Peace and War (New Noble, 1971); Maurice Keen (ed.) *Medieval Warfare* (London: Oxford University Press, 1999); Brian Carey, Joshua Allfree and John Cairns, *Warfare in the Medieval World* (Barnsley: Pen and Sword, 2006); A. V. B. Norman, *The Medieval Soldier* (New York: Barnes & Noble, 1999); as well as David Nicolles's two worthwhile works, *European Medieval Tactics (1): The Fall and Rise of Cavalry 450–1250* (Oxford: Osprey Publishing, 2011) and *European Medieval Tactics New Infantry, New Weapons 1260–1500* (2) (Oxford: Osprey Publishing, 2011).

38. Elizabeth Lev, *The Tigress of Forli: Renaissance Italy's Most Courageous and Notorious Countess, Caterina Riario Sforza de 'Medici* (Boston: Houghton Mifflin Harcourt, 2011). See especially chapter 17, "Italy's Idol," pp. 216–234.

39. John Lynn, *Women, Armies and Warfare in Early Modern Europe*, p. 208. For the host of factors militating against those women and many others trying to play military roles, see Barbara Tuchman, *A Distant Mirror* (New York: Alfred Knopf, 1978).

40. Weiting Guo, "The Portraits of a Heroine: Huang Bamei and the Politics of Wartime History in China and Taiwan, 1930–1960," *Cross-Currents: East Asian History and Culture Review,* Vol. 33 (2019), pp. 6–31.

41. Loreta Velasquez, *The Woman in Battle: A Narrative of the Exploits, Adventures, and Travels of Madame Loreta Janeta Velazquez, Otherwise Known as Lieutenant Harry T. Buford, Confederate States Army* (Madison: University of Wisconsin Press, 2004, reprint of 1872 edition).

42. Nadezhda Durova, *The Cavalry Maiden: Journals of Russian Officer in the Napoleonic Wars* (Bloomington: Indiana University Press, 1988).

43. Flora Sandes, *An English Woman-Sergeant in the Serbian Army* (London: Hodder and Stoughton, 1917).

44. Jessica Trisko Darden, Alexis Henshaw and Ora Szekely, *Insurgent Women: Female Combatants in Civil Wars* (Georgetown: Georgetown University Press, 2019), p. 78.

45. See especially Tsehai Berhane Silassie, "Women Guerrilla Fighters," *Northeast African Studies*, Vol. 1, #3 (Winter 1979–1980), pp. 73–83. Documents the activities of important female guerrillas. Points out that in feudal Ethiopian society, their military leadership status depended on their existing landholdings (derived from their dead fathers or husbands). The author often helpfully quotes the women's fighting in their own words. See Jeff Pearce, *Prevail: The Inspiring Story of Ethiopia's Victory over Mussolini's Invasion, 1935–1941* (New York: Skyhorse Publications, 2014), and for Ethiopian efforts to pry themselves loose from the South Africans and British, see C. P. Potholm, *Liberation and Exploitation: The Struggle for Ethiopia* (Lanham: University Press of America, 1976).

46. Maochun Yu, "The Taiping Rebellion," in David Graff and Robin Higham (eds.), *A Military History of China* (Boulder: Westview Press, 2003), p. 143.

47. Susan Travers, *Tomorrow to be Brave* (New York: The Free Press, 2000).

48. Abdelmajid Hannoum, "Historiography, Mythology, and Memory in Modern North Africa: The Story of the Kahina," *Studia Islamica*, #85 (1997), pp. 85–130. For a fuller examination of all these issues, see Hannoum's extensive and useful work, *Colonial Histories, Post-Colonial Memories: The Legend of the Kahina North*

African Heroine (Portsmouth: Heinemann, 2001) and Benjamin Hendrickx, "Al-Kahina: The Last Ally of the Roman-Byzantines in the Maghreb Against the Muslim Arab Conquest?," *Journal of Early Christian History,* Vol. 3, #2, pp. 47–61.

49. Quoted in John Belohlavek, *Patriots, Prostitutes, and Spies: Women and the Mexican-American War* (Charlottesville: University of Virginia Press, 2017), p. 65 and elsewhere.

50. Johannes Postma, *Slave Revolts* (Greenwood Press, 2008), p. 28. Note also that in the New World from 1522 to 1865, according to Holly Norton, *Estate by Estate: The Landscape of the 1733 St. Jan Slave Rebellion* (Syracuse: Maxwell School of Citizenship and Public Affairs Dissertation, 2013), there were 135 slave revolts and the author warns that "this list is not exhaustive" (p. 318).

51. Ibid, p. 26.

52. Gabriela Cano: "Unconcealable Realities of Desire: Amelio Robles's (Transgender) Masculinity in the Mexican Revolution," in Jocelyn Olcott, Mary Kay Vaughan and Gabriela Cano (eds.), *Sex in Revolution: Gender, Politics, and Power in Modern Mexico* (Durham: Duke University Press, 2006), p. 35–56.

53. Cano, *op. cit*, p. 43.

54. *Ibid.*, p. 37.

55. Thanks also to Michy Martinez for pointing out two additional *soldaderas* who transitioned from female during the Mexican Revolution, Angel(a) Jimenez and Maria de la Luz Barrera. For more information on the differing roles (ranging from camp followers, sutlers, fighters, and even commanders) of the *soldaderas*, see Elena Poniatowska, *Las Soldaderas* (El Paso: Cinco Puntos Press, 2006).

56. Colonel Barker, The Sunday Dispatch, 31 March 1929, quoted in Julie Wheelwright, *Amazons and Military Maids: Women Who Dressed as Men in the Pursuit of Life, Liberty and Happiness* (London: Pandora, 1989), p. 50. For a further exploration of this theme, see her chapter, "Becoming One of the Boys," pp. 50ff.

57. John Koster, "The Other Magpie and the Woman Chief Were Crow Warriors of the 'Weaker Sex,'" *Wild West*, Vol 26, #1 (June 1913), pp. 24–25. Koster also highlights another Crow woman warrior as well, the companion of The Other Magpie, Finds Them and Kills Them. Finds Them and Kills Them, who is described a "neither a man nor a woman" and who helps The Other Magpie rescue Bull Snake. See also Jerry Matney and D. A. Gordon, *Woman War Chief: The Story of a Crow Warrior (*Bloomington: First Books, 2002) and Edwin Denig, "Warrior Woman," in John Ewens (ed.), *Five Indian Tribes of the Upper Missouri* (Norman: University of Oklahoma Press, 1961), pp. 195–201.

58. Rudolf Dekker and Lotte C. van de Pol, *The Tradition of Female Transvestism in Early Modern Europe* (New York: St. Martin's Press, 1989), pp. 63–69.

59. Jonathan Jordan and Emily Jordan, *The War Queens: Extraordinary Women Who Ruled the Battlefield* (New York: Diversion Books, 2020).

60. Christine de Pizan, *The Book of the City of Ladies*, eds. Sophie Bourgault and Rebecca Kingston (Indianapolis: Hackett Publishing Company, 2018) and *The Book of Deeds of Arms and of Chivalry*, ed. Charity Cannon Willard (University Park: The Pennsylvania State University Press, 1999. For an in-depth look at de Pizan's various political and social theories, see Kate Langdon Forham, *The Political Theory*

of Christine de Pizan (Hampshire: Ashgate 2002). Unfortunately, there is not much here on her military theories and writings. See also the breezy but illuminating National Geographic Profiles, "Christine de Pizan: France's First Lady of Letters," in *National Geographic History* (March/April 2020), pp. 8–11, which highlights her extraordinary life and career and points out that her portrait of Joan of Arc is the only contemporary account we have of "La Purcell."

61. *The Secret History of the Mongols: A Mongolian Epic Chronicle of the Thirteen Century*, translated by Igor de Rachewiltz (Boston: Brill, 2004). For a further examination of this fascinating subject, see Jack Weatherford, *The Secret History of the Mongol Queens: How the Daughters of Genghis Khan Rescued His Empire* (New York: Broadway Books, 2010) and especially Ruby Lal, *Empress: The Astonishing Reign of Nur Jahan* (New York: W. W. Norton, 2018). The 20th wife of the Mogul emperor, Jahangir, Nur led troops in several key battles to rescue her husband after he was captured on the way to Kashmir. While this work is mostly about the rest of her life, the battle stories are well worth a look purely from the point of her as a warrior.

62. For a brief, engaging introduction to Manduhai's rise, war-making skills and ultimate success, see Jordan and Jordan, "The Year of the Tiger" in their *War Queens, op. cit.*, pp. 84–95. For the Mongol way of war, see Gabriel, "The Mongols 1206–1294," *op. cit.*, pp. 328–344. It is important to note that the Mongols perfected a "modern" way of war which was not matched until the 19th century in Europe: Christian Potholm, *Winning At War*, pp. 21–29 and S. R Turnbull, *The Mongols* (Oxford: Osprey Publishing, 1980). To examine the founding of the Mongol empire and legacy, see Frank McLynn, *Genghis Khan: His Conquests, His Empire, His Legacy* (New York: Da Capo Press, 2015).

63. James W. Hoover, "Holkar, Anilyabhai," in Reina Pennington (ed.), *Amazons to Fighter Pilots*, two vols. (Westport: Greenwood Press, 2003), pp. 205–209.

64. Robert Johannsen, *To the Halls of the Montezumas* (London: Oxford University Press, 1988), p. 137.

65. For a helpful look at Assyrian warfare during her rule and beyond, see Richard Gabriel, *op. cit.*, "The Iron Army of Assyria 890–612 B.C.E," pp. 124–139.

66. Take, for example, Eleanor of Aquitaine who is the subject of hundreds of works. Not surprisingly, married to two kings (Louis VII of France and Henry II of England, the mother of two kings (Richard I and John of England) and the grandmother of another (Henry III), Eleanor of Aquitaine has also been the subject of many dramatic histories and novels. In many of them, the family dynamics of her life have tended to overshadow her serious political and military activities. For a succinct account of these dimensions, see Natalie Forget, "Eleanor of Aquitaine," in Pennington, *Amazons to Fighter Pilots*, pp. 140–143, which details her military activities on behalf of her son John, including hiring and leading mercenaries and later, holding out and directing troops during the siege of Mirebeau.

Note: those enjoying fiction about the medieval period will enjoy the novels of Sharon Kay Penman, especially the trilogy dealing with Eleanor and the Plantagenets: *When Christ and All His Saints Slept* (New York: Ballentine Books, 1995), *Time and Chance* (New York: Ballentine Books, 2003), and *The Devil's Brood* (New York: Putnam's, 2008). Other works about Eleanor include another trilogy of novels by

Elizabeth Chatwick, *The Summer Queen* (New York: Landmark, 2014), *The Autumn Throne* (New York: Landmark, 2000), and *The Winter Crown* (New York: Landmark, 2015) as well as the nonfiction *Eleanor of Aquitaine* by Sara Cockerill (London: Amberley Publishing, 2020), Alison Weir, *Eleanor of Aquitaine* (New York: Ballentine Books, 2001), and Marion Meade, *Eleanor of Aquitaine: A Biography* (New York: Penguin, 1991). A recent work of scholarly note is Sara Cockerill, *Eleanor of Aquitaine: Queen of France and England, Mother of Empires* (Gloucestershire: Amberley, 2019) which allows the reader to sample various conflicting sources and the author's evaluation of them.

67. Among the more recent and useful of these works include: Kelly DeVries, *Joan of Arc: A Military Leader* (London: Sutton, 1999); Mary Gordon, *Joan of Arc* (New York: Viking Penguin, 2002); Kathryn Harrison, *Joan of Arc: A Live Transfigured* (New York: Doubleday, 2014); Stephen W. Richey, *Joan of Arc: The Warrior Saint* (Westport: Praeger, 2003); Helen Castor, *Joan of Arc: A History* (New York: Harper, 2015); and Craig Taylor (editor and translator), *Joan of Arc: La Pucelle* (Manchester: Manchester University Press, 2006).

68. See Sherry Robinson, "Lozen" in her *Apache Voices* (Albuquerque: University of New Mexico Press, 2000), pp. 3–9. Lucia St. Clair Robson has also written an engaging novel about Lozen, *Ghost Warrior* (New York: Forge Books, 2012), which captures the flavor of the times and her ability to foretell upcoming battle situations.

69. Pat Southern, *Empress Zenobia: Palmyra's Rebel Queen* (London: Continuum, 2008); Agnes Carr Vaughan, *Zenobia of Palmyra* (Garden City: Doubleday, 1967); Rex Winsbury, *Zenobia of Palmyra: History, Myth and the Neo-Classical Imagination* (London: Duckworth, 2010); Yasmine Zahran, *Zenobia: Between Reality and Legend* (London: Stacey International, 2010); and Byran Nakamura, "Palmyra and the Roman East," *Greek, Roman and Byzantine Studies*, Vol. 34, #2 (1993), pp. 133–150. Nakamura most helpfully looks at Zenobia's rise to power, short reign (270–272 CE) during which she expanded and tried to hold territory in the Levant, Arabia, and Egypt and also analyzes her military forces, a mixture of heavy cavalry, light bowmen, and auxiliaries and how she was fatally hampered by her lack of a large standing army.

70. David Hay, *The Military Leadership of Matilda of Canossa 1046–1115* (Manchester: Manchester University Press, 2008) and Catherine Hanley, *Matilda: Empress Queen Warrior* (New Haven: Yale University Press, 2019).

71. Isaac Levine, *My Life as Peasant, Officer and Exile: The Life of Maria Bochkareva* (New York: Frederick Stokes, 1919).

72. Linda Heywood, *Njinga of Angola: Africa's Warrior Queen* (Cambridge: Harvard University Press, 2017).

Part II

SELECT ANNOTATED BIBLIOGRAPHY

By Author

A–D

This bibliography, while very comprehensive and unique in scope and dimension, still must be considered as "partial" because there are many other works that speak to these subjects—works that because of space limitations and redundancy could not be included, and, of course, with new material being created across a broad front, this sample, however rich, broad, and cross-cultural as it is, is but a sample.

.

Mustafa Abbasi, "The Battle for Safad in the War of 1948: A Revised Study," *International Journal of Middle East Studies*, Vol. 36, #1 (February 2000), pp. 21–47. Looks at the narrative history of the War of 1948 through the lens of the actions of the Haganah and Palmach in 1947 at the beginning of the outbreak of the war. Interesting account, but weak on the role of women on either the Israeli or Arab side.

Karen Abbott, *Liar, Temptress, Soldier, Spy: Four Women Undercover in the Civil War* (New York: Harper, 2014). An engaging tale of women at war in a variety of roles. Of special interest is Emma Edmonson, the soldier, who enlisted as Private Frank Thompson in the 2nd Michigan and fought at Fredericksburg, in the Shenandoah Valley, and at Second Bull Run before deserting and "becoming a woman again." Her memoir sold 175,000 copies, and she gave all the money to sick and wounded survivors of the Army of the Potomac.

Alexander Adams, *Geronimo: A Biography* (New York: G.P. Putnam's Sons, 1971). Captures the essence of Lozen the Apache by stating "Victorio had two unusual advisors. One was his sister Lozen, a beautiful woman who never married but fought with the warriors. She was courageous and skillful and, in the Apaches' opinion, she had magical powers. She would stand with her arms outstretched, chant a prayer and slowly turn around. By the sensations she felt in her arms, she could tell where the enemy was and how many they numbered" (pp. 208–209).

Note: The Apache wars were the longest in American history, lasting from 1849 until 1886. For an excellent introduction, see Jon Cecil, "The Apache Wars: 1849–1889," *Strategy and Tactics* #324 (Sept.–Oct. 2020), pp. 30–46. There are useful portraits of Shi-ka-She (Cochise), Goyaate (Geronimo), Biduya (Victorio), Lozen, Kas-triden (Nana), and Jlin tay I tith (Loco).

Note: For an engaging account of Victorio in action, see Robert Utley, "Victorio's War," *MHQ: The Quarterly Journal of Military History*, Vol. 21, #1 (Autumn 2008), pp. 20–29. This article contains some excellent maps showing the 1879–1880 homelands of the Warm Spring and Mescalero bands. Utley makes the claim that Victorio was actually a much more effective military leader than the more legendary Geronimo. See also his "Geronimo," *MHQ: The Quarterly Journal of Military History*, Vol. 4, #2 (Winter 1992), pp. 42–51.

Note: Robert Watt, by focusing on the Chiricahua Apaches and their military entrepreneurship and superior leadership as provided by Cochise, Mangas Coloradas, Lozen, Victorio, Nana, and Geronimo, makes a strong case that the Apaches, like the Comanches, were the most formidable opponents for the Spanish, Americans, and Mexicans in the Southwest. See his *Apache Warrior 1860–86* (Oxford: Osprey Publishing, 2014).

Asma Afsaruddin, "Early Women Exemplars and the Construction of Gendered Space," in Marilyn Booth (ed.), *Harem Histories: Envisioning Places and Living Spaces* (Durham: Duke University Press, 2010). In chapter 4, the author convincingly shows how subsequent Islamic historians and theologians altered the perceptions of early Muslim female warriors and moved them into gendered space over time, diluting the power of their early actions in the true public sphere in the age of the Prophet.

Joseph Agonito, *Brave Hearts: Indian Women of the Plains* (Helena: TwoDot, 2017). A straightforward introduction to the key players of the women warriors (female and transgender) cohort, Woman Chief, Osh Tisch, Running Eagle, and Buffalo Calf Road. Well worth reading to get a sense of the much-needed revision to the history of the West we initially encountered.

Rosemary Agonito and Joseph Agonito, "Resurrecting History's Forgotten Women: A Case Study from the Cheyenne Indians," *Frontiers: A Journal of Women Studies*, Vol. 6, #3 (1981), pp. 8–16. This article seeks to resurrect the story of Buffalo Calf Road, a Cheyenne woman who fought in numerous battles during the U.S. Army's relentless attacks during 1876–1879. Buffalo Calf Road fought against General George Crook at the Battle of the Rosebud (1876) where she saved her brother, Comes in Sight. Next she fought against General Custer and the Seventh Cavalry in the Battle of Greasy Grass (Little Big Horn). After being defeated in 1877, she and other Cheyennes were sent to Oklahoma, where, a year later, desperate to return home, they fled the reservation in September 1878 and made a 1,500-mile journey heading back to Yellowstone. On the way she fought in a number of skirmishes. Eventually recaptured, she died from diphtheria in 1879. See also their historical novel/re-creation based on solid research entitled *Buffalo Calf Road Woman: The Story of a Warrior of the Little Bighorn* (Helena: TwoDot, 2006).

Note: While most accounts of the Battle of Greasy Grass focus on the many mistakes made by Custer and his command, Robert Utley, "Last Stand," *MHQ: The Quarterly Journal of Military History*, Vol. 1, #1 (Autumn 1988), pp. 114–123, stresses the fighting ability of the Sioux and Cheyenne and the Native American leadership during the battle. Custer was simply out-generaled.

Note: For a more wide-ranging presentation of similarities and contrasts among Native American warriors and warfare, see Richard Chacon and Ruben Mendoza (eds.), *North American Indigenous Warfare and Ritual Violence* (Tucson: The University of Arizona Press, 2007). Also highly recommended is the earlier *Counting Coup and Cutting Horses: Intertribal Warfare on the Northern Plains, 1738–1889* (Lincoln: University of Nebraska Press, 1990) by Anthony McGinnis. McGinnis believes that the Cheyanne probably had more women warriors than any of the other of the Plains Native Americans.

Miranda Aldhouse-Green, *Boudica Britannia* (Edinburgh: Pearson Education Limited, 2006). Gives a good background on the causes of Boudica's uprising and the impact it would later have on Roman Britain.

Note: For a cogent image of Boudica in action, see Barry Cunliffe, *The Ancient Celts*, Second Edition (London: Oxford University Press, 2008) "and the large bulk of Boudica, with her harsh voice and mass of red hair falling to her knees, resplendent in a gold torc and bright cloak, remains a lasting image of Celtic female power" (p. 23).

Note: A broad-gauge introduction to the Celtic way of war is Daithi O Hogain, *Celtic Warriors: The Armies of One of the First Great Peoples in Europe* (New York: St. Martin's Press, 1999).

Peter Aleshire, *Warrior Woman: The Story of Lozen, Apache Warrior and Shaman* (New York: St. Martin's Press, 2001). Lozen spent 40 years fighting, a true warrior even among the likes of Cochise, Geronimo, and Victorio in "a war dominated culture." Finding her "a great exception" to the normal sexual hierarchy, the author marvels at her skill, steadfastness, and vision-skills in seeing the enemy. A good source for her whole life.

Note: For extensive background on the Chiricahua way of war, see Robert Watt, *Apache Warrior 1860–85* (Oxford: Osprey Publishing, 2014). Goes to considerable lengths to indicate just how special Lozen really was.

Svetlana Alexiyevich, *War's Unwomanly Face* (Moscow: Progress Publishers, 1985). Despite its title and propaganda intent, this work manages to become a most powerful paean to women at war. Eight hundred thousand Russian women answered their country's call during World War II, either as members of the regular armed forces or partisan bands, or both. The Germans feared the female partisans, calling them *Flintenweiber* ("War Women"). Moving, poignant, and insightful, it captures the many faces of women in battle, including frontline soldiers. Ordinary women do extraordinary things as comrades in arms, declaring "What do you mean, girls—they're soldiers." They were.

Miranda Alison, "Women as Agents of Political Violence: Gendering Security," *Security Dialogue,* Vol. 25, #4 (December 2004), pp. 447–463. Looking at women warriors in the contexts of Northern Ireland and Sri Lanka, the author concludes that "liberatory" forms of nationalism provide greater ideological and practical "space" for women to engage in combat then do "loyalist" counterinsurgent governments and groups.

Ilhem Allagui and Abeer Al-Najjar, "From Women Empowerment to Nation Branding: A Case Study From the United Arab Emirates," *International Journal of Communication*, Vol. 12 (2018), pp. 68–85. This article looks at the way the government of the United Arab Emirates used the photos and story of the first female F-16 pilot, Major Mariam Al Mansouri, bombing ISIS targets to "rebrand" the image of the country to counter criticisms of its "backward traditions" and also to build a sense of nationhood.

Antoinette Tidjani Alou, "Niger and Sarraounia: One Hundred Years of Forgetting Female Leadership," *Research in African Literatures,* Vol. 40, #1 (Spring, 2009), pp. 42–56. Reaffirms that women warriors have existed throughout history, but male historians have submerged their role and diminished their accomplishments, often ghosting them out of existence. Focusing on Sarraounia Mangou and the 1899 Battle of Lougou and the subsequent successful Azna Hausa guerrilla movement against the French, the author documents these processes clearly and cogently.

Stanley B. Alpern, *Amazons of Black Sparta: The Women Warriors of Dahomey* (New York: New York University Press, 1998). An interesting and multifaceted look at Dahomey's Amazons with particular attention to their battles at Abeokuta against the Egba in 1851 and 1854, and later against the French in 1890 and 1892. With some questioning their battle worthiness (see the van Creveld review below), it is worth quoting one of the French Legionaries who fought them.

> These warrioresses fight with extreme valor, always ahead of the other troops. . . . They are outstandingly brave . . . well trained for combat and very disciplined." (p. 207)

And Major Grandin, who published a two-volume work in 1895, concluded:

> The valor of the amazons is real. Trained from
> childhood in the most arduous exercises,
> constantly incited to war, they bring to battle a
> veritable fury and a sanguinary ardor . . . inspiring by
> their courage and their indomitable energy the other troops
> who follow them. (p. 207)

Ave Altius and Joel Raveloharimisy, "Women's Access to Political Leadership in Madagascar: The Value of History and Social Political Activism," *Journal of International Women's Studies,* Vol. 17, #4 (2016), pp. 132–142. Pointing out that Madagascar was ruled by women in the Merina dynasty during most of the 19th century and thus there are significant female role models, the authors suggest that access to education and knowledge about these precedents are vital. This work contains their amusing anecdote that Queen Ranavalona. I found it strange when her communications with her contemporary Queen Victoria were always answered by men.

Susan Amatangelo (ed.), *Italian Women at War: Sisters in Arms from the Unification to the Twentieth Century* (Madison: Fairleigh Dickinson Press, 2016). A wide-ranging series of essays covering 100 years of Italian women in action. The sections on Italian unification women warriors in the 1860's are truly outstanding.

Stefan Amirell, "Female Rule in the Indian Ocean World (1300–1900)," *Journal of World History*, Vol. 26, #3 (2016). Recent scholarship has identified 227 female rulers in the area from Madagascar to the Comoros to Indo-nesia and Malaya. The author finds that in this space during this time period, these female rulers were accepted "with relative ease—although it rarely seems to have been the preferred solution" (p. 470).

Margaret Poulos Anagnostopoulou, "From Heroines to Hyenas: Women Partisans during the Greek Civil War," *Contemporary European History,* Vol. 10, #3 (2001), pp. 481–501. The author argues convincingly that the huge contribution Greek women made to the resistance movement during World War II was turned on its head during the civil war that followed and the eventual success of the right-wing government.

Note: For background on the Civil War itself, see David Close (ed.), *The Greek Civil War, 1943–1950* (London: Routledge, 1995), especially "The Military Struggle," pp. 97–128.

Anonymous (edited by Volundr Lars Agnarsson), *The Saga of Erik the Red* (New York: CreateSpace Independent Publishing Platform, 2012). According to this saga, in the 10th century CE, Fredis Eiriksdottir, a shieldmaiden, sees her menfolk losing a battle to the Skraelings or Native Americans. Although pregnant, she bares her breasts and appears to be sharpening her sword on them as she attacks the Skraelings. They flee. A cautionary tale about the chance encounter between two cultures as well as the extent to which women warriors in history have been subordinated to their male counterparts.

Note: See also Margaret Elphinstone, *The Sea Road* (Edinburgh: Canongate, 2000) (F) for the saga of Gudrid of Iceland, who traveled to Vineland, bore a son, and witnessed the battles (and misunderstandings) with the Skraelings, and who also seemed to see alternatives to fighting.

Jekila Antony Raj and P. Barathi, "Queen Velu Nachiyar: First Women Against British," *InfoKara,* Vol. 9, #3 (June 2020), pp. 891–897.

Engaging account of Velu Nachiyar (1730–1796) who led opposition to the English East India company and commanded her troops in battle. Her Udaiyall Woman Army recaptured Sivaganga in 1772.

Teena Apeles, *Women Warriors* (Emeryville: Seal Press, 2003). A breezy and superficial account, but one that leaves the correct impression that there were a fair number of women warriors who have always existed across a variety of societies, from Vietnam and China to Russia to Mexico and among many Native American tribes, including the Apache, Cherokee, Blackfeet, and Gros Ventre. A few bridges too far: Mia Hamm, Buffy the Vampire Slayer, and Madeleine Albright, to name but a few.

Marie Arana, "Glory Over the Mountains," *MHQ: The Quarterly Journal of Military History,* Vol. 25, #3 (2013), pp. 39–43. Examines Simón Bolívar's military and political talents as he won various battles, including that of Boyacá, which ended Spanish rule in Colombia, declaring, "A weak man requires a long fight in order to win. A strong one delivers a single blow and an empire vanishes" (p. 43). Precious little about Manuela Saenz (1797–1856), *La Libertadora del libertador,* however.

Nerea Aresti, "The Gendered Identities of the 'Lieutenant Nun': Rethinking the Story of a Female Warrior in Early Modern Spain," *Gender and History*, Vol. 19, #3 (November 2007), pp. 401–418. An engaging article that looks at this Spanish woman who, after fleeing her life in a convent, won battle honors serving the Crown in Peru and Chile and when outed, presented herself as a virgin and thus worthy of consideration, which was granted by both Philip II and Pope Urban VII. A truly exceptional story of gender-bending across the ages as many generations used her as examples of their changing views of gender identity.

Joanna Arman, *The Warrior Queen: The Life and Legend of Aethelflaed, Daughter of Alfred the Great* (Gloucestershire: Amberley, 2017). Concluding that Aethelflaed was "the greatest female leader of her time" (p. 205), the author does a good job of separating fact from fiction and clearly putting her subject in the forefront of women warriors of her era. See especially, "Shield Maiden 916–918" (pp. 183–205). Commanding her army on horseback, she recaptured much of the Kingdom of Mercia from the Danes, including retaking Derby, Leicester, and York. Arman puts her on horseback, leading her army successfully.

   Note: For an in-depth look at the cultural, religious, and political forces working against women as warriors, see Christine Fell, *Women in Anglo Saxon England* (London: Basil Blackwell, 1984).

   Note: For much-needed background on how Aethelflaed came to be in a position to achieve her greatness, see Normal Kotker, "Arthur, Artorius," *MHQ: The Quarterly Journal of Military History*, Vol. 7, #1 (Autumn 1994), pp. 102–109.

Lauren Arrington, *Revolutionary Lives: Constance and Casimir Markievicz* (Princeton: Princeton University Press, 2016). See especially chapter 10, "The Markieviczes at War," pp. 111–137. Arrington gives a good account of the slapdash flavor of the Easter Rising and suggests that Constance may not have known she killed a constable, thinking she had only wounded him by shooting him in the arm (the bullet actually went through the arm and hit him in the lungs, killing him later).

Note: Anne Marreco in *The Rebel Countess: The Life and Times of Constance Markievicz* (Philadelphia: Clinton Books, 1967) has a good chapter on the day of the Rising, "A Terrible Beauty Is Born," pp. 190–208, while Lindie Naughton (ed.) has complied Countess Markiewicz's own thoughts in her *Markievicz: Prison Letters and Rebel Writings* (Newbridge: Irish Academic Press, 2018).

Ruth Ashby and Deborah Ohrn, *Herstory: Women Who Changed the World* (New York: Viking, 1995). A wide-ranging listing of many important women, including the warriors from the Trung sisters through Sultana Razia, including seldom-mentioned ones such as Phung Thi Chinh (Chinese) and Trieu Au (Vietnamese).

Note: The especially long arc of interest in the Trung sisters is captured in Lisa Long, "Contemporary Women's Roles through Hmong, Vietnamese, and American Eyes," *Frontiers*, Vol. 29, #1 (2008), pp. 1–36.

Kathryn J. Atwood, *Women Heroes of World War II* (Chicago: Chicago Review Press, 2011). A breezy introduction to women who risked their lives in the war, featuring examples from Poland, Denmark, France, Great Britain, Holland, Belgium, the U.S., and Poland. See especially the inclusion of Nancy Wake and Pearl Witherington. Unfortunately, no Russian women are included.

Note: See Terry Crowdy, *SOE Agent: Churchill's Secret Warriors* (Oxford: Osprey Publishing 2008) for an excellent introduction to the training of all SOE agents with a case study of Pearl Witherington.

Albert Azell, *Russia's Heroes* (London: Robinson, 2001). Luckily given the concerns about Atwood's book cited above, there is this volume. Breezy and an easy read but worth consulting for the amazing story of Nadechda "Nadya" Popova, the Russian woman pilot who flew over 1,000 missions during World War II beginning in October 1941 and going to the end of the war. "Yes, the Germans called us 'Night Witches.' Yes, we practiced our 'witchcraft' almost from the first to the last days of the war."

Anni Baker, "Daughters of Mars: Army Officers' Wives and Military Culture on the American Frontier," *Historian,* Vol. 67, #1 (Spring, 2005), pp. 20–42. Army wives in the 1870s and 1880s in the American West identified with their husband's army and its cultures and traditions. The author believes these women developed the "Cult of Army Womanhood," "incorporating military and masculine characteristics into their behavior, even explicitly rejecting some values of civilian women."

Lolita Baldor, "Few Army Women Want Combat Jobs," *Portland Press Herald*, February 26, 2014, A-5. Only 7.5% of women in the U.S. Army at the time of this survey said they were interested in combat positions (including field artillery and combat engineers), but an overwhelming number of that 7.5% wanted to be a Night Stalker (elite special operations helicopter pilots, navigators, and gunners). Note the comparison with the "Night Witches" of World War II Soviet women.

David Balfour, "'A Formidable Sight,'" *Medieval Warfare*, Vol. 4, #2 (2014), pp. 13–18. This delightful piece puts the story of Sichelgaita (1040–1090) in historical context and perspective. She was a Lombard princess of Salerno and the second wife of Robert Guiscard, Duke of Apulia. She commanded Lombard troops in her own right and helped Robert win the Battle of Dyrrhachium (1081), where she was wounded (although this Norman second son adventurer eventually lost the territory on the Adriatic). Later she and Robert returned to Italy to defend Pope Gregory VII against the Emperor Henry IV and on Robert's second campaign against the Byzantines, where he died at Kefalonia. Called "a formidable sight" and "the closest approximation history has ever produced of a Valkyrie" by contemporaries, Sichelgaita brought her own armies to these adventures, directed sieges in Robert's absences, and was a formidable campaigner.

Guillermo Baralt, *Slave Revolts in Puerto Rico: Conspiracies and Uprisings, 1797–1873* (Princeton: Markus Wiener Publishers, 2007). Argues against the previously held belief that Puerto Rican slaves were primarily docile, the author documents 40 instances of slave resistance and revolt and believes that the nearby example of Haiti and the subsequent freeing of slaves in the other European territories in the Caribbean contributed to the unrest. Unfortunately for the purposes of this volume, there is little focus on the role of women in the revolts and no index.

Juliet Barker, *Conquest: The English Kingdom of France 1417–1450* (Cambridge: Harvard University Press, 2012). See especially "Jehanne D'Arc," (pp. 93–171). As Barker puts it, the story of Jehanne, the Pucelle or Maid, is "extraordinary almost beyond belief. Her youth, her sex, her background, all militated against what she became: the companion of princes, inspirational military leader, martyr for faith and country" (p. 102). All of those and then some.

J. Neilson Barry, "Ko-Come-Ne Pe-Ca, The Letter Carrier," *The Washington Historical Quarterly,* Vol. 20, #3 (1929), pp. 201–203. From a tiny fragment of a tale comes this article, celebrating the life and times of Ko come ne Peca, a Kootenay woman who against the modesty of her sex and culture became a warrior and became noted for her bravery. She obtained a wife and many horses as she played a variety of roles in what is now Washington State.

Gretchen Bataille and Laura Lisa (eds.), *Native American Women* (New York: Routledge, 2001). This is a grand listing of many Native American women from poets and ballerinas to warriors. Some useful examples of Native American warriors include: (a) The Other Magpie (p. 309), who rode with the Crow Wolves, scouted for the U.S. Army, and counted coup four times against the Lakota in the Battle of the Rosebud (1876) crying "See my spirit is my armor"; (b) Running Eagle (p. 258) of the Blackfeet Nation, who entered the Braves Society and fought the Crows and others and was eventually killed by the Flatheads; as well as (c) Dahteste (p. 83), an Apache warrior who fought with Geronimo and Lozen and her two husbands against the U.S. Army and later served with them as a scout.

Note: For this latter point, see Philip Burnham, "Unlikely Recruits: Indians Scouting for America," *MHQ: The Quarterly Journal of Military History*, Vol. 11, #3 (Spring, 1999), pp. 78–85. This work gives some useful insights into the crosscurrents working on individual Native Americans. Especially interesting is the life and times of Wooden Leg, a Cheyenne who would fight at both the Little Bighorn (known as "Greasy Grass" to the Native Americans) and Wounded Knee, but on different sides.

Note: Interesting background on those who tried to find ways of peace between the whites and the Cheyenne can be found in Louis Kraft, "Between the Army and the Cheyenne," *MHQ: The Quarterly Journal of Military History*, Vol. 14, #2 (Winter, 2002), pp. 48–55.

Judy Batalion, "The Women of the Jewish Resistance," *New York Times*, Sunday, March 21, 2021, p. B4. Taken from her book *The Light of Days: The Untold Story of Women Resistance Fighters in Hitler's Ghettos*, the author underscores the many brave Resistance fighters who confronted the Nazis from 90 ghettos.

———, *The Light of Days: The Untold Story of Women Resistance Fighters in Hitler's Ghettos* (New York William Morrow, 2021). It is a powerful, illuminating, very important account of the many brave Jewish (and other) partisans who fought the Nazis in their occupation of Poland. This human cruelty described in this work is breathtaking, but so is the courage of the

Jewish women who, against all odds, struck blows for freedom and revenge. Should be required reading for all those seeking to understand Poland during World War II.

Jelnea Batinic, *Women and Yugoslav Partisans: A History of World War II Resistance* (New York; Cambridge University Press, 2015). Declaring that the Communists under Tito in Yugoslavia made the best use of female *partizankas* during World War II, the author puts their number at over 100,000 and compares this total with an estimated 55,000 who fought in Italy, and 8,000 in Poland (pp. 260–261).

D. N. Beach, "An Innocent Woman, Unjustly Accused? Charwe, Medium of the Nehanda Mhondoro Spirit, and the 1896–97 Central Shona Rising in Zimbabwe," *History in Africa*, Vol. 25 (1998), pp. 27–54. Looks at the important—but not singular—role played by Charwe in the rising of the Ndebele and Shona people against the British in the 1890s in what is now Zimbabwe. He concludes that other valley leaders such as Hwata, Chidamba and Chiweshe also were influential even though Charwe was to become the central symbolic referent for that resistance movement.

Note: Some authors have argued that the overdependence on symbolic traditional ancestors is inimical to modern democratic forms and thus pejorative. See, for example, Zorodzai Dube, "The Ancestors, Violence, and Democracy in Zimbabwe," *Verbum et Ecclesia,* Vol. 59, #1 (2014), pp. 1–8.

Bessie Beatty, "The Battalion of Death" from her *The Red Heart of Russia* (1918) published in *MHQ: The Quarterly Journal of Military History*, Vol. 23, #2 (Winter 2020), pp. 78–81. A firsthand contemporary account of Maria Bochkareva and the 1 Russian Women's Battalion of Death written by a reporter for the *San Francisco Bulletin*, which sent her to Russia during the Russian Civil War. Beatty concluded in 1917, "Women can fight. Women have the courage, the endurance, even the strength, for fighting."

Note: Another Russian woman, Zoia Smirnova, was one of hundreds of other women who joined the Russian armed forces and fought during World War I. Smirnova was involved in numerous battles, was wounded twice, and eventually received the St. George's Cross.

Note: A much-needed set of contexts for the Women's Battalion of Death can be found in Laurie Stoff, "They Fought for Russia: Female Soldiers of the First World War," in DeGroot and Corinna Peniston-Bird, *op. cit.*, pp 66–82.

Note: For a lively introduction to the Russian Civil War, see David Bullock, *The Russian Civil War 1918–1922* (Oxford: Osprey Publishing, 2008). It has many good pictures and timelines as well as straightforward text. For an overview of the leadership of Czar Nicholas, see George Feifer, "The Last Czar as Leader," *MHQ: The Quarterly Journal of Military History,* Vol. 11, #1 (Autumn 1998), pp. 18–27. It is not a flattering portrait. More standard works include W. Bruce Lincoln, *Passage Through Armageddon: The Russians in War and Revolution* (New York: Simon & Schuster, 1986) and also his *Red Victory: A History of the Russian Civil War* (New York: Simon & Schuster, 1989), Evan Mawdsley, *The Russian Civil War* (New York: Pegasus Books, 2008) and the classic by Richard Pipes, *The Russian Revolution* (New York: Alfred Knopf, 1990).

Hilary Beckles, *Natural Rebels: A Social History of Enslaved Black Women in Barbados* (New Brunswick, NJ: Rutgers University Press, 1989). Looks at the slave revolts of 1675, 1692, and 1816 shows the odds against a successful rebellion on such a small island and one with such economic significance for the planter class.

Kelly Bell, "Werewolves of Aachen," *Military History,* Vol. 34, #2 (July 2017), pp. 22ff. Presents a surprising account of the last-ditch SS resistance assassins who include a woman named Ilse Hirsch.

Judith Bellafaire, *Women in the United States Military: An Annotated Bibliography* (New York: Routledge, 2001). This is quite a compendium of books, articles and notes on women in the military ranging from "Early Patriots" to "The All-Volunteer Force and the War on Terror." Many seldom-cited articles are mentioned here. A very useful resource.

John Belohlavek, *Patriots, Prostitutes, and Spies: Women and the Mexican-American War* (Charlottesville: University of Virginia Press, 2017). A great deal of useful information about the many roles of women during the Mexican War, both Mexican and American, can be found here. See especially "Women in Combat," pp. 63–67.
    Note: Robert Merry puts the Mexican-American War in a much-needed broader perspective. See especially his *A Country of Vast Designs: James Polk, The Mexican War*, and the *Conquest of the American Continent* (New York: Simon & Schuster, 2009).

Joyce Benneson with Henry Markovits, *Warriors and Worriers: The Survival of the Sexes* (London: Oxford University Press, 2014). The author, a professor of psychology, argues that men and women are fundamentally different, which explains why women do not make good warriors:

Warfare provides a context that combines better than most:

"a man's predilections for play fighting, enemy targeting, and direct competition, along with his respect for physically tough and emotionally cool and confident fellow males who follow rules and demonstrate expertise. . . . Girls and women don't demonstrate these traits." (p. 122)

Barbara Benton, "Friendly Persuasion: Women as War Icons 1914–1945," *MHQ: The Quarterly Journal of Military History*, Vol. 6, #1 (Autumn 1993), pp. 80–87. Captures the essence of women as icons in, and of, war when used by men to achieve particular goals, whether buying war bonds or supporting the country's armed forces. It also contains an interesting array of the actual posters used by a number of countries.

Carol Berkin and Clara Lovett (eds.), *Women, War and Revolution* (New York: Holmes and Meier Publishers, 1980). A set of essays covering situations (ranging from France in 1789 to Cuba, Italy, and World War I) in which women played a role seeking peace as well as war. Wide-ranging account with many interesting dimensions presented.

Jennifer Berry, "Free Greece!," *MHQ: The Quarterly Journal of Military History,* Vol. 24, #3 (Spring 2012), pp. 66–71. The struggle for Greek independence from the Ottoman Empire took place from 1821 to 1832 and required the support of Britain, France, and Russia. One participant was Laskarina "Bouboulina" Pinotsis, a Greek naval commander. When her first husband was killed in battle against Algerian pirates, she took over his fortune and trading company and built additional ships, including a large warship, the *Agamemnon.* She took that ship into action in 1821 under the Greek flag and led it and other Greek ships in various naval battles. Eventually she was on the wrong side of a Greek internal split and was killed in a family argument. Tsar Alexander I of Russia granted her the honorary title of "Admiral" after her death, as did the Greek government in 2018.

Shabnam Bharti, "An Analytical Study: Political Role of Women During Medieval Period," *International Journal of Research in Social Sciences*, Vol. 8, #1 (2018), pp. 150–159. While this article briefly touches on the careers of Chand Bibi and Razia Sultana, its principal utility is putting their activities in the broader context of the many women who played important political roles during this era.

Tanya Biank, *Undaunted: The Real Story of America's Servicewomen in Today's Military* (New York: NAL Caliber, 2013). Since 9/11, over 250,000 women have served in Iraq and Afghanistan and more than 140 have been killed in action. Biank looks at a brigadier general in the Marines, a drill instructor in the Marines, an army major, and an army MP. The author also gives a very good set of insights into what life in the military is really like for today's women.

Eliza Billings, *Female Volunteer, or The Life and Adventures of Miss Eliza Allen, a Young Lady of Eastport Maine* (Unknown binding, 1851). This delightful little romance cum memoir is in Bowdoin's Rare Book Collection. It purports to be "a truthful and well-authenticated narrative" and has vivid descriptions of the author's military service, especially her participation in, and wounding at, the Battle of Corro Gordo.

Note: Although there is some question as to the authenticity of this particular memoir of women fighting in the (1846–1848) war, other works cite examples of both American and Mexican women in action. See especially Allan Peskin (ed.), *Volunteers: Mexican War Journals (*Kent State: Kent State University Press, 1991); Tom Reilly and Manley Witten, *War with Mexico* (Lawrence: University Press of Kansas, 2010); and Robert Johannsen, *To the Halls of the Montezumas* (London: Oxford University Press, 1988). Johannsen in particular gives us tantalizingly brief references to such American and Mexican *soldaderas* (who did cooking, nursing, foraging, and providing companionship but in some cases fought in battle). See especially his portraits of Maria de Jesus Dosamantes and Sarah Borginnis. Borginnis (or Boundetteo) was also known as "Great Western" for her size and courage. She became the "Heroine of Ft. Brown" and served in the Battle of Buena Vista. For her part, Dosamantes (sometimes Dosamentes) commanded a company of Mexican lancers at the Battle of Monterrey, and her courage in battle provoked an American officer who witnessed it to cry "There's an example of heroism worthy of the days of old" (p. 137). Another women in that war was the American Elizabeth Newcome, who served with the Missouri Volunteer Infantry.

Note: Maria de Jesus Dosamantes fought in what was one of the hottest engagements of the entire Mexican War, an assertion buttressed by recent scholarship. See Noah Trudeau, "An American Fandango in Monterrey," *MHQ: The Quarterly Journal of Military History*, Vol. 26, #33 (Summer 2014), pp. 34–41. The five-day battles made for high casualties, and one division commander declared, "I do not believe that, for downright, straightforward, hard fighting, the battle of Monterey has ever been surpassed" (p. 41).

Phyllis Birnbaum, *Manchu Princess, Japanese Spy: The Story of Kawashima Yoshiko, the Cross-Dressing Spy Who Commanded Her Own Army* (New York: Columbia University Press, 2015). While it is perhaps stretching things to label her a true warrior, given her position in Manchukuo and her only loose command of the "helter skelter part-time band, the Ankoku Army," during the battle of Rehe, this account of Yoshiko is diverting, albeit a tad bizarre.

Jane Blair, *Hesitation Kills: A Female Marine Officer's Combat Experience in Iraq* (Lanham, MD: Rowman & Littlefield, 2011). A strong woman warrior who rises through the ranks in the U.S. Marine Corps sees action in Iraq in the 26-day war and part of the occupation, and certainly shows that women have been assets in combat if allowed to participate. A very insightful portrait of one female "Devil Dog," who remarks, "Once you kill, you can't take it back" and "Our only certain destiny was killing or being killed."

Deanne Blanton and Lauren Cook, *They Fought Like Demons: Women Soldiers in the Civil War* (New York: Vintage Books, 2002). This is an in-depth look at the broader (many more than the normally quoted 250–400) range of women who fought in the Civil War, beginning with First Bull Run and ending with Appomattox and including the Peninsula campaign, 2 Bull Run, Antietam, Fredericksburg, Chancellorsville, Gettysburg (Pickett's Charge!), Vicksburg, the Wilderness, Cold Harbor, Red River, Shiloh, Petersburg, and Sherman's March to the Sea. Also examines the many motivations for enlisting, including patriotism, love of freedom, desire to be with one's spouse, father, or brother, spirit of adventure, economic advancement, and desire to escape the confines of womanhood in the mid-19th century.

Mia Bloom, *Bombshell: Women and Terrorism* (Philadelphia: University of Pennsylvania Press, 2011). Arguing that women have pressured the leadership in Sri Lanka, the Irish Republic, and Palestine to let them participate in warfare, including suicide bombings, the author nevertheless hopes for pathways for women to exit those terrorist organizations. See especially her chapter "The Black Widow Bombers," pp. 35–67. Looking at the pattern of female suicide bombers, she looks at the historical, religious, and cultural imperatives motivating the women (as well has harsh training and the threat of family reprisals if missions are not carried out). Good short summary of the 2002 seizure of the Moscow Dubrovka House of Culture.

James Blythe, "Women in the Military: Scholastic Arguments and the Medieval Images of Female Warriors," *History of Political Thought*, Vol. 22, #2 (Summer 2001), pp. 242–269. Blythe analyzes the arguments for and against women in war in the political treatises of Ptolemy of Lucca (1236–1347) and Giles of Rome (1243–1316). Opposes not only their "medieval misogyny" but their echoes among the arguments of some "difference feminists" who use the same arguments against women in combat today.

Melissa Lukeman Bohrer, *Glory, Passion and Principles: The Story of Eight Remarkable Women at the Core of the American Revolution* (New York: Atria Books, 2003). Featuring the likes of Molly Pitcher, who fought at the Battle of Monmouth in 1778, Deborah Sampson who served 18 months before being discovered as a woman, and Nancy Ward, the Cherokee "Honored Woman" and slave owner whose prowess in battle led her to be included in the Cherokee War Council.

Jayne Boisvert, "Colonial Hell and Female Slave Resistance in Saint-Domingue," *Journal of Haitian Studies*, Vol. 7, #1 (2001), pp. 61–76. The description of horror of the lives of African slaves in Haiti before the revolution will stay with you for a long time. Hell indeed, for its harshness, cruelty, and desecration of humanity, including branding, forced abortions, maiming, and summary executions. Slave resistance in Africa, on the journey from Africa, and once in Haiti are all also ably described. Uses contemporary sources to illuminate numerous instances of women engaged in the fluid combat of guerrilla and set-piece warfare on the island from 1791 to 1804.

   Note: For background, a short, free-flowing account of the Haitian Revolution can be found in Jeremy Popkin, *A Concise History of the Haitian Revolution* (London: Wiley Blackwell, 2011).

   Note: The uniqueness of the Haitian Revolution is underscored by the fact that in the 200 years before the American civil war there were 250 attempted slave revolts and only the Haitian one was successful.

Laudomia Bonanni, *The Reprisal* (Chicago: University of Chicago Press, 2013). (F) This powerful novel captures the essence of the "warrior woman" with her "fury-like power" and feminine qualities (her heroine, "La Rossa," the red haired revolutionary, is pregnant and not killed by the Fascist partisans until after giving birth). Takes place in Italy during the waning months of World War II when Germans, Fascists, and partisan bands of various political hues roamed the land in a Hobbesian "all against all struggle."

Neal Bonenberger, "The Forgotten Crusaders—A Comparative Analysis of the Role of and Effect on Christian Women in the West and the East during the Crusading Era," *Journal of History,* Vol. 15, pp. 1–13. Concludes that women in the East play larger and more important roles than their counterparts in the West, including in actual fighting and political warfare direction.

Mark Bowden, "The Huong River Squad" in his *Hue, 1968: A Turning Point of the American War in Vietnam* (New York: Random House, 2017), pp. 5–11. See especially the important roles played by female Viet Cong and

NVA warriors such as Che Thi Mung and Hoang Thi No in leading the assault on the Imperial city of Hue during the 1968 Tet offensive.

Kate Bowen, *Close Quarters* (Sheffield: Crucible Lyceum Studio, 2018). A look at three young women who successfully join and excel in the British infantry, passing physical standards only 5% of female soldiers can achieve.

Laura Brady, *Essential and Despised: Images of Women in the First and Second Crusades, 1095–1148* (University of Windsor, Master's Thesis, 1992). Using contemporary examples, the author covers the wide range of female roles played during the First and Second Crusade and concludes that knowledge about those roles helps to move women from the despised to the essential with regard to both the idea and the actuality of that service.

Note: For a good, short introduction to the differing martial cultures of the Christians and Muslims, see Norman Kotker, "The First Crusade," *MHQ: The Quarterly Journal of Military History*, Vol. 2, #2 (Winter 1990), pp. 24–37. A far more disturbing account is found in Jay Rubenstein in this "A Time to Kill," *MHQ: The Quarterly Journal of Military History,* Vol. 25, #2 (Winter 2013), pp. 41–47. Rubenstein argues that even by the standards of medieval times, "the atrocities were unprecedented" as "fearing the apocalypse was near, Thomas of Marle and the knights of the First Crusade unleashed holy hell on Jerusalem" (p. 42).

Anthony Brandt, "Lessons of the Vendée," *MHQ: The Quarterly Journal of Military History*, Vol. 27, #3 (Spring 2015), pp. 46–53. The bloody counterrevolution that convulsed the Vendée region of France in the aftermath of the French Revolution was one of the bloodiest suppressions of the period with between 40,000 and 600,000 dead caused by the insurrection itself and the "hell columns" that accompanied its defeat. "God the king" became the chief slogan of the counterrevolutionaries, and the author asks, "Was it the first modern genocide, an attempt to destroy an entire region and its population?" (p. 53). One very interesting woman warrior was Renée Bordereau, "L'Angevin" (who lived from 1766 to 1824) of the Vendean Insurrection, who fought against the central government and its forces in 200 battles. She was eventually captured by the French government but later freed when Louis XVIII was restored to power. Other women who fought against the revolutionaries include Marie-Louise Victorine de la Rochejaquelein and Jeanne Robin.

Note: For a broader perspective, see Marilyn Yalom, *Blood Sisters: The French Revolution in Women's Memory* (New York: Pandora, 1995), especially chapter 10, "The Women of the Vendée," pp. 191–208.

Martin Brayley, *World War II Allied Women's Services* (Oxford: Osprey Publishing, 2001). This is a richly illustrated work providing insights into the British, American, Canadian, Australian, South Africa, Burmese, New Zealand, French, and Soviet women who played a vital role during World War II, providing "human power" (in the case of Americans, equal to 15 male divisions).

———, *World War II Allied Nursing Services* (Oxford: Osprey Publishing, 2002). The first fully illustrated study of the U.S., British, Commonwealth, and other nursing organizations who saved so many lives, sometimes at the cost of their own.

Bridget Brereton, "Searching for the Invisible Woman: Slavery and Resistance in Jamaica," *Slavery & Abolition: A Journal of Slave and Post-Slave Studies,* Vol. 13, #2 (1992), pp. 86–96. An engaging look at the emerging scholarship around "the invisible woman," the female slave in the Caribbean.

Lucy Brewer, *The Female Marine* (Boston: Shaw & Shoemaker, 1817). This melodramatic account has all the tales of her in her own words. A fascinating look at her life and times and the war of 1812 as she imagined them. For a literary criticism of the novel as novel, see Alexander Medlicott, Jr., "The Legend of Lucy Brewer: An Early American Novel," *The New England Quarterly*, Vol. 39, #4 (December 1996), pp. 461–473. Medlicott argues that nothing about the work is true per se and that the U.S. Marine Corps should have checked her story out *before* they made her a legend and only later found nothing verifiable. The author puts her in the genre of "fringe fiction" of the late 18th and early 19th centuries, what "Herbert Ross Brown has aptly labeled 'The pseudo-biographies of prostitutes and pirates, actresses and adulteresses'" (p. 462). Yet Medlicott concludes "Among the heroines of early American fiction, Miss Lucy offered her new nation a most refreshing breath of salt air" (p. 473). And the U.S. Marines in the 21st century kept her very mixed legacy alive, using it to infuse their long and glorious tradition with a new, feminine dimension!

Claire Brewster, "Women and the Spanish-American Wars of Independence: An Overview," *Feminist Review,* #79 (2005), pp. 20–35. While this work has an unfinished, choppy quality to it and seems bent on including references to much of the literature in question, it does end up naming a number of important Latina warrior women, including those of the Tupac Amaru Rebellion (1780–1783), Francesca Zubina Bernales, Teresa Corneja, Rosa Canelones,

Juana Azurduy, Petronila Carrillo de Albarnaz, Maria Simona de Guisla, and others in Colombia, Mexico, Peru, Argentina, Bolivia, etc.

Note: A more clotted and denser look at the context of South American independence is provided by Catherine Davies, Claire Brewster, and Hilary Owen, *South American Independence: Gender, Politics, Text* (Liverpool: Liverpool University Press, 2006).

Jamila Brijbhushar, *Sultana Raziya: A Reappraisal* (New Delhi: Manohard, 1990). Indian-sourced, this is an in-depth work that covers the whole of her reign and administration. Particularly interesting are pp. 50–54 on her army. This Muslim ruler was bedeviled by the disloyalty of her Turkish nobles, many of the Hindu princes, and the lurking Mughals to the north. Concludes, "A study of Raziya's reign gives no indication of the fact that her sex was any real hardship to her."

Anne Broadbridge, *Women and the Making of the Mongol Empire* (Cambridge: Cambridge University Press, 2018). An in-depth, highly detailed, and well-researched study of the important roles women played in the rise of the Mongol empire beginning with their dominance at home, which enabled the Mongols to field such huge armies relative to their population. Wide-ranging examination of the various political roles played by numerous women at various stages of the empire's development.

Lisa Brooks, *Our Beloved Kin: A New History of King Philip's War* (New Haven: Yale University Press, 2018). The tantalizing fragmentary account of the diplomatic and military ("A potent military leader") role of the Wampanog Squa-Sachem, Weetamoo, in peace and war ending in her death at the hands of the English colonists. The author clearly delineates how settler land hunger was the major root cause of the war waged by her brother-in-law, Metacom. King Philip's War remains the costliest war in American history based on a percentage of military and civilian deaths and deportations.

Note: For putting her life and times in Wampanoag perspective, a useful work is David Silverman, *This Land is Their Land: The Wampanoag Indians, Plymouth Colony, and the Troubled History of Thanksgiving* (New York: Bloomsbury Publishing, 2019).

Note: Squa-Sachem Weetamoo appears less prominently in Christine DeLucia's *Memory Land: King Philip's War and the Place of Violence in the Northeast* (New Haven: Yale University Press, 2018), although her serial marriages and the rapaciousness of the English colonists remain constant.

Note: At the risk of overpraising both the authors and the work, we would direct those interested in the holistic context of Squa-Sachem Weetamoo's world to Julie Fisher and David Silverman, *Ninigret, Sachem of the Niantics and the Narragansetts* (Ithaca: Cornell University Press, 2020). This is an outstanding source for understanding the extremely complex and ever-shifting world of 17th-century New England faced by the sachems and squa-sachems of the period. For her part, Weetamoo is portrayed in sympathetic but fleeting terms (see pp. 177–123) as the main focus is on Ninigret, a prominent sachem within the greater Narragansett peoples and the leader of the Niantics. Faced with the increasing encouragments of the United Colonies of New England, Ninigret forged alliances with the Mohawks, the Pocumtucks, and the Dutch colony of New Netherlands (whom Ninigret found far less rapacious than the English), and then he successfully avoided taking sides in what became King Philip's War of 1675–1676. The authors feel that had he sided with the Wampanoags against the English along with the rest of the Narragansetts, he would have prevented the Pequots and Mohegans from so actively assisting the English and reduced their chances of success. Ultimately, of course, the increasing population of the English settlers (and various sachems' willingness to sell Native land) reduced the Narragansetts' room for maneuver. The life story of Ninigret thus provides the interested reader with an ever-changing kaleidoscope of power and trade, and in the case of this author, no doubt enhanced by the fact that as a 10-year-old living in East Lyme, Conn., he learned to hunt and fish with the last of the Niantics, Livy Huntley. See C. P. Potholm, *Tall Tales from the Tall Pines* (Camden: Down East Books, 2015) (F).

Note: There is an additional portrait of Ninigret in Michael Johnson, *Indian Tribes of the New England Frontier* (Oxford; Osprey Publishing, 2008, plate B), and one of a typical Narragansett and Niantic warrior in Michael Johnson, *American Woodland Indians* (Oxford: Osprey Publishing, 1990, plate A).

Note: In order to appreciate what the Native Americans were up against generally, it is important to move beyond the "guns, germs, and steel" paradigm and focus on two other elements of great impact: disunity among the tribes, and the European/colonial emphasis on "sustained ruthlessness." See especially James Warren, "Total War Comes to the New World," *MHQ: The Quarterly Journal of Military History*, Vol. 11, #1 (Autumn 1998), pp. 28–39 and C. P. Potholm, "Sustained but Controlled Ruthlessness," in *Winning at War* (Lanham, MD: Rowman & Littlefield, 2010), pp. 69–102. Metacom's war is covered in much greater detail in Nathan Philbrick, *Mayflower* (New York: Viking, 2006). For a broader context, see Ian Steele, *Warpaths: Invasions of North America* (London: Oxford University Press, 2000), especially "Plymouth, New England and the Wampanoag 1620–1677," pp. 80–109. The most important (and at the time revisionist) analysis of warfare between the Europeans and Americans against the Native Americans remains Dee Brown, *Bury My Heart at Wounded Knee* (New York: Holt Rinehart and Winston,

1970). For an in-depth look at the ferocity of King William's War, see John Grenier, "New England's Mournful Decade," *MHQ: The Quarterly Journal of Military History,* Vol. 28, #2 (Winter 2016), pp. 35–43.

Frederick Brown, "The Battle for Joan," in *The Embrace of Unreason: France, 1914–1940* (New York: Alfred Knopf, 2014), pp. 76–91. This work provides an incisive look at the continuing fascination with "the Maid." She not only was beatified in 1909, but she also became the patron saint of Vichy France so that "the archenemy was no longer Germany but England."

O'Brien Browne, "Revolution Unleashed," *MHQ: The Quarterly Journal of Military History*, Vo. 15, #2 (Summer 2011), pp. 78–87. This work features quite a bit of text on Zohra Drif and her initial bombing (including a picture of her), but then goes on to do a most useful analysis of what the French and the revolutionaries did right and what they did wrong and emphasizes the importance of de Gaulle being elected as the savior of French Algeria and his ultimate role in its departure, much to the disgust of the *pied noires.*

————, "Honor, Oil and Blood," *MHQ: The Quarterly Journal of Military History*, Vol. 26, #1 (Autumn 2013), pp. 30–43. A very good introduction to the Yom Kippur War of 1973, highlighting the strategic decisions of Prime Minister Golda Meir, declaring "She was firm and wise during the darkest days of the October War, but was strongly criticized for the military's unpreparedness" (p. 43).

Patrick Brugh, *Gunpower, Masculinity, and Warfare in German Text, 1400–1700* (Rochester: Rochester University Press, 2019). A wide-ranging look at armor, cannons, and gunpowder during the period in question. Also examines the depiction of women warriors in the literature, most notably Hans Jakob Grimmleshausen's *Courasche* and Eberhard Werner Happel's *Mandorell*, seeing in them considerable threats to the perceived virtues of masculinity during the era.

James S. Brust, "John H. Fouch: First Post Photographer at Fort Keogh," *Montana: The Magazine of Western History*, Vol. 44, #2 (1994), pp. 2–17. The author reproduces a number of photographs taken by John Fouch, who was the first to capture images of the Little Big Horn battlefield and the Nez Perce Chief Joseph. Of interest for our study, he also took the first and only known picture of Osh Tisch, also known as Finds Them and Kills Them, as well as who was probably The Other Magpie. Calling their picture "Squaw Jim and his Squaw," Brust is thus said to have captured the only (?) image of the *berdache* or *bote*, describing her as "a male homosexual who was afforded distinctive social and ceremonial status within the tribe" (p. 10).

Note: The term berdache seems to have a variety of usages and meanings. See Walter Williams, *The Spirit and the Flesh: Sexual Diversity in American Indian Cultures* (Boston: Beacon Press, 1992), which contains major sections on "The Character of the Berdache" and "Changes in the Berdache Tradition Since the Coming of the Europeans."

R. Brzezinski and M. Mielczarek, *The Sarmatians 600 BC–AD 450* (Oxford: Osprey Publishing, 2002). The authors claim that Sarmatian women fought in battle and were either (a) not able to marry before killing an enemy in battle or at least (b) not able to marry unless facing an enemy in battle. In any case, they were doing actual fighting against many enemies. Good pictures of women in action so many eons ago. Many excavated graves show Sarmatian warrior women buried with their weapons. A very useful introduction to these horse archers who used the talents of women in battle for a long, long time.

Kimberly Moore Buchanan, *Apache Women Warriors* (El Paso: University of Texas at El Paso Press, 1986). Believes that women were allowed into male activities with "high prestige" in many Native American societies (among them the Pawnee, Mandan, Gros Ventres, Crow, and Sioux) and gives specific examples such as Bowdash (Water Sitting Grizzly) of the Kutenai, Running Eagle of the Blackfeet, Ehyophsta and Mutsimiuna of the Cheyenne, the Ghigau Society of the Cherokee, and Chief Earth Woman of the Ojibwa. See especially chapter 6, "Women Warriors: Forgotten Gladiators." The author gives a number of reasons women went to war: (1) revenge of a loved one (such as Running Eagle of the Blackfeet), (2) love (such as Chief Earth Woman of the Ojibwa), and (3) rescue (such as Ehyophsta of the Cheyenne). Very good map of Apache clan groups and their location on p. 6.

Note: Some good background material on the war-making habits and customs of the Plains Native Americans can be found in Michael Johnson, *Tribes of the Sioux Nation* (Oxford: Osprey Publications, 2000) as well as his *North American Indian Tribes of the Great Latkes* (Oxford: Osprey Publications, 2011) and Jason Hook, *The American Plains Indians* (Oxford: Osprey Publications, 1985).

David Bullock, "Women in the Russian Civil War," in *The Russian Civil War 1918–1922* (Oxford: Osprey Publishing, 2008), pp. 107–113. The author documents with many concrete examples his statement that "Women, in fact, served in every army on every front in every phase of the Russian Civil War." Some women warriors depicted include Baron Fredericks, Varvara "The

White Angel of the White Army," Marina Yurlova and Pavlina Ivanovna Kuznetsova.

Lauren Cook Burgess (ed.), *An Uncommon Soldier* (Pasadena: the Minerva Center, 1994). Letters of Sarah Rosetta Wakeman, a.k.a. Pvt. Lyons Wakeman, of the 153 Regiment, New York Volunteers, whose members signed up for $152, a year's wages. Three million joined the colors and hundreds of thousands of letters were written without censorship. Wakeman served from 1862 to 1864, and during the Red River campaign in Louisiana came down with chronic diarrhea, dying after a month in the hospital, during which time her female status was never discovered.

Alex Burghart, "Aethelflaed: Iron Lady of Mercia," *BBC History Magazine,* Vol. 12, #8 (2011), pp. 60–63. Answers the question "Where is a woman's place?" with the answer "A woman's place is on the throne" or "in the saddle leading her troops successfully against the Welch and the Norsemen."

Richard Burton, *A Mission to Gelele, King of Dahomey* (New York: Praeger, 1966). In this book, Burton goes to many places, including Mecca, and he is quite impressed with the Amazons and describes their practices, weapons, dress, and many other aspects of their military lives. Suspect now as anthropologists have had difficulty corroborating some of his findings, but at the same time, his descriptions portray warrior abilities and capabilities, which are much verified.

Barbara Bush, "Defiance or Submission? The Role of the Slave Woman in Slave Resistance in the British Caribbean," *Immigrants & Minorities: Historical Studies in Ethnicity, Migration, and Diaspora,* Vol. 1, #1 (1982), pp. 16–38. Makes a strong and well-documented case for her central argument that women "contributed positively to slave resistance at all levels and in so doing presented a strong challenge to the slave system and all that it represented" (p. 32).

————, *Slave Women in Caribbean Society, 1650–1838* (London: James Currey, 1990). This book-length study is rich with detail and analysis, concluding:

> Evidence presented here suggests that women were active at all levels of resistance from everyday non-cooperation to active participation in slave revolts, where they showed as much, if not more courage than men, and were equally prepared to die. (p. 81)

Note: Women continued to play important roles in the post-Emancipation according to Gad Heuman, "Post-Emancipation Resistance in the Caribbean: An Overview," in Karen Olwig (ed.), *Small Islands, Large Questions: Society, Culture and Resistance in the Post-Emancipation Caribbean* (London: Frank Cass, 1995), pp. 123–134.

Pierce Butler, "Jeanne de Montfort," in *Women of Mediaeval France* (Philadelphia: The Ritten House, 1907), pp. 285–305. Marguerite, Countess to Jeanne Montfort of Britany (also known as "La Flamme") took over defense of his realm when he was captured. She led her mounted knights to destroy the camp of the besieging French and burned their tents and wagon train, hence her nickname. She later fought at sea with the English against the Genoese (Jeanne de Montfort had pledged allegiance to Edward III), and later her husband escaped his captivity. Their son was eventually recognized as Duke of Brittany. This is a real warrior's warrior.

Note: Another woman warrior of the period, and a good example of "Medieval Domestic Warfare" is Ermengarde of Narbonne (c. 1130–1194) who led troops into battle against her feudal overlords, the counts of Toulouse, in support of the French King Louis VIII and again in 1172–1173, when the nobility of Aquitaine revolted against King Henry II of England.

Kevin Cahillane, "The Women of West Point," *New York Times Magazine*, September 7, 2004, pp. 46–59. A contemporary look at how women were being prepared for combat missions beginning in 1976. From 1802 to 1976, there were no women, since then almost 4,200 have enrolled. In 2015, they made up 22% of the incoming class.

D'Ann Campbell, "Women, Combat, and the Gender Line," *MHQ: The Quarterly Journal of Military History*, Vol. 6, #1 (1993), pp. 88–97. Indicates that a U.S. World War II study proved that female soldiers were ready to serve under fire and examines the reasons the U.S. did not adopt that strategy.

Gwyn Campbell, "The Adoption of Autarky in Imperial Madagascar, 1820–1835," *Journal of African History*, Vol. 28, #3 (1987), pp. 395–411. Argues that the Merina monarchy's move toward autarky did not start with Queen Ranavalona but with her predecessor of Radama I 1826–1835.

Leon Campbell, "Women and the Great Rebellion in Peru, 1780–1783," *The Americas*, Vol. 42, #2 (October 1985), pp. 163–196. Goes into considerable detail focusing on the women such as Micaela Bastidas, Thomasa Titu Condemaita, Quispicanchis, Cecilia Escalera, Tupac Amaru, Bartola Sisa, and Gregoria Apasa in this last Inca rebellion against Spanish rule in Peru. Micaela Bastidas was a strategic leader and organizer along with her husband Tupac Amaru. Eventually crushed by the Spanish, Micaela, her husband, and her son Hipolito were all executed and have become folk heroes in Peru. He concludes "In sum the total activities of women during the Great Rebellion in Peru in 1780 makes it clear that these were primarily familial undertakings and that females participated fully in both advisory and combatant roles" (p. 190). The author provides detailed descriptions of dozens of these women and their contributions.

Note: For a fuller exploration of the 1780–1783 rebellion and Micaela Bastidas's role in it, see Lillian Fisher, *The Last Inca Revolt 1780–1783* (Norman: University of Oklahoma Press, 1966). It is very clear from this narrative that the Incas, from the time of the arrival of the Spanish, had great, even overwhelming, grievances and that the revolt, however unsuccessful, was warranted and did result in some changes in administration. But the central finding of this work is worth noting, i.e., a description of its scope:

Little has been written concerning the importance and extent of this uprising in South America. It stretched from Tucuman to Colombia and Venezuela through Peru, Bolivia, northwestern Argentina, and part of Ecuador, covering a larger territory than that of our war for independence on the North American continent, our own Civil War, and even most of the European conflicts preceding the world wars. It was the greatest Indian revolt in the Americas and fully taxed the resources of Spain and the genius of military officials to put it down. (p. ix)

Note: For what is the currently definitive account of the Tupac Amaru rebellion, see Charles Walker, *The Tupac Amaru Rebellion* (Cambridge: The Belknap Press of Harvard University Press, 2014). Carefully researched and balanced in tone, it does justice to the 1780–1783 rebellion, the largest in the history of the Spanish control in the Americas. Adopting the Inca royal name Tupac Amaru, Jose Gabriel Condorcanqui and his wife Micaela Bastidas defeated the Spanish in many battles and eventually occupied major portions of Peru, Chile, Bolivia, and Argentina. Micaela Bastidas's extensive role in the war is well documented. The military advantages of the Spanish are covered in Terence Wise, *The Conquistadores* (Oxford: Osprey Publications, 1980).

Rick Campbell, *Empire Rising* (New York: St. Martin's Press, 2015). (F) In the near future, China invades Taiwan *and* Japan and sinks the U.S. Pacific Fleet, but eventually loses due to computer malware inserted by the U.S. via a SEAL Team into Beijing led by National Security Advisor Christine O'Connor, who is twice as smart as any man and better with a gun. A new superhero emerges. Oddly enough, neither side uses tactical or strategic nuclear weapons in this strange creation.

Gabriela Cano, "Unconcealable Realities of Desire: Amelio Robles's (Transgender) Masculinity in the Mexican Revolution," in Jocelyn Olcott, Mary Kay Vaughan, and Gabriela Cano (eds.), *Sex in Revolution: Gender, Politics, and Power in Modern Mexico* (Durham: Duke University Press, 2006), pp. 35–56. The fascinating story of a brave warrior who made herself a male (without surgery or hormones). Amelia Robles became Amelio Robles and fought with the Zapatas, being wounded six times. "As a guerilla fighter, Amelia discovered, in her words, 'the sensation of being completely free.'" (p. 43) As the author puts it "Amelio Robles made the transition from an imposed feminine identity to a desire masculinity: he felt like a man, acted like a man, and constructed a male appearance." He also didn't take kindly to bullying about his gender, allegedly shooting two men who tried (p. 37).

Thomas Cardoza, "'Habits Appropriate to Her Sex': The Female Military Experience in France during the Age of Revolution," in Karen Hagemann, Gisela Mettele, and Jane Rendall (eds.), *Gender, War and Politics: Transatlantic Perspectives, 1775–1830* (London: Palgrave Macmillan, 2010), chapter 9, pp. 188–205. This is a very important addition to our knowledge of women at war during the Age of Revolution, revealing as it does that "Thousands of women served with French military units between 1775 and 1820" (p. 188), making France, under the Ancient Regime, the First Republic, the First Empire and the restoration of the monarchy, the country which used the most women in its war-making efforts. These included *femmes soldats* (soldiers), *blanchisseuses* (laundresses), and *vivandieres* (sutlers). Of these, the *vivandieres* were the most numerous and most important as they often constituted major portions of the supply chains. The author also indicates how *vivandieres* quite often participated in battles, defending themselves, and were often rewarded for their actions.

Ann Baumgarten Carl, *A WASP Among Eagles: A Woman Military Test Pilot in World War II* (Washington: Smithsonian Books, 1999). Declaring "This is what I was made for," the author serves her country as an outstanding test pilot. And indeed she was, flying and testing a vast number of American (and other countries') warbirds, including the Douglas Dauntless, the Curtis Helldiver, B-25, B-24, B-26, B-17, B-29, P-38, P-40, P-51, and P-47 as well as British Mosquitos and Spitfires and German J-88s. She was also the first U.S. woman to fly a jet, the Bell YP-59A. Quite a résumé.

Elizabeth D. Carney, "Women and Military Leadership in Pharaonic Egypt," *Greek, Roman, and Byzantine Studies*, Vol. 42 (2001), pp. 25–41. Shows that while women acting militarily in the ancient world were rare, several prominent Egyptian examples, including Ahhotep and Hatshepsut, exist. The author argues that "The rulers of the 17 dynasty transformed themselves into national kings by leading their armies into successful battles against foreign and domestic enemies. They fought from the newly arrived war chariots and wore a blue war-helmet crown" (p. 36).

Roger Carpenter, "Womanish Men and Manlike Women," in Sandra Slater and Fay A. Yarbrough (eds.), *Gender and Sexuality in Indigenous North America* (Columbia, SC: University of South Carolina Press, 2011), pp. 141–110. Looks at the Native American Two-spirit or "berdache" as warrior in a number of Plains societies such as the Anishinabe, Hidatsa, Dakota, Osage, Flathead, and Crows. Gives a number of historical examples, such as Woman Chief, Strikes-two, and Qanqon, concluding, "Many Native American societies recognize that gender had a permeable quality about it and embraced the berdache—whether for their spiritual or military prowess—as an essential component of warfare. *Berdaches*, or two-spirits, remained important persons in many native communities until the late nineteenth and early twentieth centuries" (p. 161). Three hundred years of cultural acceptance, the author maintains, were then overridden by Christian missionaries and government educators who imposed European notions of gender norms on Native societies.

Luke Carroll, "Raising a Female-Centric Infantry Battalion: Do We Have the Nerve?," *Australian Army Journal*, Vol. 11, #1, pp. 34–55. The author, a colonel in the Australian army, argues that piecemeal and incremental intro-duction of women into the Australian armed forces will not have the desired effects and that a more holistic approach is required. He concludes that mean-ingful change requires courage.

Brenda Carter, Kevan Insko, David Loeb, and Marlene Tobias (eds.), *A Dream Compels Us: Voices of Salvadoran Women* (Boston: South End Press 1989). A number of participants in the Salvadorian revolution including a most poignant account by Ileana, commander of the all-women's unit, the "Companera Silvia Women's Platoon," pp. 161–167. This unit attacked the military headquarter in San Vicente, the taking of San Ilfonso and San Se-bastian, and the blowing up of the Quebrada Seca bridge. Ileana was killed in action in the spring of 1984.

Victoria Cass, *Warriors, Grannies and Geishas of the Ming* (Lanham, MD: Rowman & Littlefield, 1999). A wide-ranging account and analysis of "the Great Ming" (1368–1644). See especially chapter 4, "Warriors and Mystics," pp. 65–85, as the author examines a number of women warriors and legendary female archetypes in battle. Quite a group of disrupters, both of their societies and the myths about "submissive" women.

Sophie Cassagnes-Brouquet and Michèle Greer, "In the Service of the Just War: Matilda of Tuscany (Eleventh-Twelfth Centuries)," *Clio* (English Edition), #29 (2014), pp. 35–52. This extremely perceptive article puts Matilda at the heart of the Investiture Conflict (1075–1122) and shows that her military activities as a "female Mars" on behalf of the Church caused Catholic theologians to confront and ultimately, after some substantial canonical gyrations, confirm a positive answer to the question "Can a woman truly be involved in a Just War?"

Note: For a recent and in-depth scholarly overview of the Crusades, please consult Thomas Asbridge, *The Crusades* (New York: Harper & Row, 2010).

Helen Castor, "The Real Joan of Arc Is Every Bit as Extraordinary as the Myth," *BBC History Magazine,* Vol. 15, #10, pp. 50–51. The title says it all, and its content is well introduced by the telling phrase, "In many ways, then, her story is a life told backwards."

———, *Joan of Arc: A History* (New York: Harper, 2015). Perhaps the best of all her biographies in putting "La Pucelle's" story in the truce context of the existing power struggles between and among the English, the Burgundians, and the House of Valois. She tells the story from the beginning of the period (with great detail) to the exact story of the Maid. Very good on the military side of Joan. Her religious fervor, native sense, and personal courage eventually brought her triumph, but all of these were eventually subsumed by the medieval intrigue of the day—at least in the short term.

———, *She-Wolves: The Women Who Ruled England before Elizabeth* (New York: Harper, 2015). Vilified for their "usurpation" of men's roles and rules, these women—such as Matilda, Eleanor, Isabela, and Margaret—paved the way for Queen Elizabeth. Smooth-flowing stories will intrigue the reader.

E. V. Cernenko, *The Scythians 700–300 BC* (Oxford: Osprey Publishing, 1983). These horse archers held sway for 400 years and spawned an immortal legend of women warriors. See page 24D for drawing of a Scythian noblewoman, 4th century BCE. During their centuries of glory, the Scythians defeated the Babylonians, Medes, Persians, Assyrians, and Urartus. A dominant warrior culture in which women played an important role in battle.

Note: See also Shareeen Blair Brysac, "The Scythian Scourge," *MHQ: The Quarterly Journal of Military History*, Vol. 16, #2 (Winter 2004), pp. 6–13.

Note: Putting the horse archers in every broader perspective, consult Antony Karasulas, *Mounted Archers of the Steppe 600 BC–AD 1300* (Oxford: Osprey Publications, 2004) and also Cam Rea, "Scythian Horse Archer Swarms," *Strategy and Tactics,* #328 (May–June 2021), pp. 72–79.

Note: Some recent scholarship has focused on the Scythians as not simply a nomadic people, but one with important trading centers, winter quarters and royal tombs. See Renate Rolle, "The Scythians: Between Mobility, Tomb Architecture, and Early Urban Structures," in Larissa Bonfante (ed.), *The Barbarians of Ancient Europe: Realities and Interactions* (Cambridge: Cambridge University Press, 2011), pp. 107–131.

Note: Although portrayed by Herodotus and other Greeks as bloodthirsty barbarians, in fact the Scythians were military innovators and very successful warriors over a long period of time, Shareen Brysac, "The Scythian Scourge," *MHQ: The Quarterly Journal of Military History*, Vol. 16, #2 (Winter 2004), pp. 6–13.

Richard Chacon and Ruben Mendoza (eds.), *Latin American Indigenous Warfare and Ritual Violence* (Tucson: The University of Arizona Press, 2007). A wide-ranging—the Caribbean to Patagonia—look at warfare among the Indigenous Peoples before, during and after the coming of the European. See also their similar type of work on North American Native American warfare patterns, *North American Indigenous Warfare and Ritual Violence* (Tucson: The University of Arizona Press, 2007) reviewed above.

Note: For an insightful look at the low-violence and ritualized warfare among the Aztecs and the subsequent disadvantage that it caused when they confronted the Spanish invaders, see Ross Hassig, "Aztec Flower Wars," *MHQ: The Quarterly Journal of Military History*, Vol. 9, #1 (Autumn 1996), pp. 8–21. Also John Pohl, *Aztec, Mixtec and Zapotec Armies* (Oxford: Osprey Publications, 1991) for their differing war styles.

Satish Chandra, *History of Medieval India* (800–1700) (Hyderabad: Orient Blackswan, 2007). See especially pp. 78–80, "Raziya," which stresses the preparation for rule she received from her father Iltutmish before he died, the forces constantly arrayed against her, and her bravery in action.

Vibha Chauhan, "Lakshmibai and Jhalkaribai: Women Heroes and Contesting Caste and Gender Paradigms and Histories," *South Asian Review*, Vol. 37, #2 (2016), pp. 81–96. The author seeks to explain the different handlings by various Indian authors and historians of these two women warriors concluding, "the negotiation going on between Lakshmibai and Jhalkaribai in many ways unsettles the older concepts of nationhood and forces us to look afresh at the existing diversities of castes, class, communities, gender, language, region and much else" (p. 95). Also points out that Jhalkaribai benefited from an unusual husband who allowed, even encouraged, her to practice using weapons such as the pistol, sword, and spear as both husband and wife would join the queen's army and fight to the death together.

Nadia Maria El Cheikh, *Women, Islam, and Abbasid Identity* (Cambridge: Harvard University Press, 2015). See especially her seminal chapter, "Hind bint 'Utba: Prototype of the Jahiliyya and Umayyad Woman," pp. 17–37, which firmly and cogently shows the rewriting of early Muslim history to feminize and de-warriorize women who fought at the side of the Prophet.

Note: Calling her "a famously ferocious woman," Justin Marozzi in his *Islamic Empires* (New York: Pegasus Books, 2019), pp. 17–18, describes in considerable detail that ferocity, especially with regard to her resistance to Muhammad and Islam before eventually converting.

Fan Pen Li Chen, *Chinese Shadow Theatre: History, Popular Religion, and Women Warriors* (Montreal: McGill-Queen's University Press, 2007). See especially chapter 4, "Women Warriors in Shadow Play" which asserts, "Since Chinese historians were inherently prejudiced against these groups, the few such women recorded in the Chinese histories likely represent the tip of the iceberg" (p. 117).

Aleksandr A. Cherkasov, Michal Smigen, and Violetta S. Molchanova, "The Glorification of Underage Volunteers in Russian Military Service during World War I," *Propaganda in the World and Local Conflicts*, Vol. 5, #1 (2016), pp. 4–11. The author demonstrates the extent to which the Czarist regime glorified the service of underage "volunteers" and even cites the example of Kira Bashkirova, a fifth grader of the Highest Marlinsky Vilen School who was awarded the St. George's Cross for her combat actions. She had enlisted as the boy "Nicholas Popov."

Peter D. Chimbos, "Women of the 1941–44 Greek Resistance Against the Axis: An Historical and Sociological Perspective," *Atlantis: Critical Studies in Gender, Culture & Social Justice*, Vol. 28, #1 (2003), pp. 28–35. The author clearly demonstrates how central women were to the Greek Resistance and the National Resistance Movement and how the winners of the civil war which followed altered the perceptions about those women and often demonized their very contributions.

Norma Stoltz Chinchilla, *Women in Revolutionary Movements: The Case of Nicaragua* Working Project #27 (Michigan University Press, 1983). Explores the many contributions women made to the successful revolution and its "prolonged people's war."

Paul Chrystal, *Women at War in the Classical World* (Barnsley: Pen and Sword, 2017). An extensive, nearly exhaustive look at reports of women warriors from the early Greek to late Roman periods. Zenobia, Artemisia, and other favorites are here, but so are interesting generic groups such as the Ambrones. Many examples and an excellent combing of ancient texts illuminate the author's conclusion: "War, as Homer said, may be man's work, but it is, at the same time, the curse of many a woman."

Aunait Chutintaranond, "Suriyothai in the Context of Thai-Myanmar History and Historical Perception," in Sunait Chutintaranond and Kanokphan U-sha (eds.), *From Fact to Fiction: History of Thai-Myanmar Relations in Cultural Context* (Bangkok: Institute of Asian Studies, Chulalongkorn University, 1992), pp. 30–41. A fine introduction to the details of the battle in which Suriyothai rode to her husband's defense on a war elephant, one that provides a fulsome and detailed account of the battle, including gruesome details of Suriyothai's life-ending wounds.

John Clark, "Jennie Iren Hodgers in the American Civil War," *Strategy and Tactics*, #254 (Jan/Feb 2009), pp. 35–37. She enlisted as Albert Cashier in the 95 Illinois and fought at Vicksburg, the Meridian and Red River campaigns, Nashville, and Mobile. Never wounded nor discovered, she was also not outed until 1911, when she was in an automobile crash.

Tim Clarkson, *Aethelflaed: The Lady of the Mercians* (Edinburgh: John Donald, 2018). In dry pose and with specific sourcing, the author establishes how this queen, "a queen by title, but in deeds a king" expanded the kingdom of Mercia, established defensive fortresses (burhs) as she enlarged Mercia, and reduced the power of the Norse, Danes, and others to her north.

Notes: Interested students will enjoy the popularization of her story in the *Saxon Stories*, the series of novels written by Bernard Cornwell and tarted up for TV by Netflix, there known as *The Last Kingdom* the story of Uhtred, who loves and champions Aethelflaed.

Elsa Clavé, "Silenced Fighters: An Insight into Women Combatants' History in Aceh (17th–20th c.)," *Archipel*, Vol. 87 (2014), pp. 273–306. The author argues that the mythology surrounding the 18th-century Aceh resistance against the Dutch has obscured the more widespread and more accurate women warriors in the 1976–2005 struggle of Aceh against the Indonesian central government. She urges further study of contributions of the Potjut Baren regiment of the Rencong Division, especially those who fought in the Division Tengku Cik Paya Bakong.

   Note: Sher Banu Khan provides a fascinating introduction to the Sultanahs of Aceh, 1641–1699 in *Sovereign Women in a Muslim Kingdom* (Ithaca: Cornell University Press, 2017) while Matthew Davies looks at the modern war in Aceh. See his *Indonesia's War Over Aceh: Last Stand on Mecca's Porch* (London: Routledge, 2006). Also, Peter Hamburger provides background to the Aceh war in "Song of the Holy War," *MHQ: The Quarterly Journal of Military History*, Vol. 18, #4 (Summer 2002), pp. 32–41.

   Note: For a brief but broader look at Dutch counterinsurgency efforts, see Benjamin Welton, "A Method to His Madness," *Military History* (January 2021), pp. 32–41.

Tessa Cleaver and Marion Wallace, *Namibia Women in War* (London: Zed Books, 1990). Despite the title and the information about the war's impact on women, unfortunately there is precious little about the women warriors of SWAPO. Pity.

Carol J. Clover, "Maiden Warriors and Other Sons," *Journal of English and Germanic Philology*, Vol. 85, #1 (1986), pp. 35–49. A challenging reassessment of the old Norse and Germanic accounts of women warriors, shield maidens, and the like, looking at examples from Iceland and Albania to argue that "In the end, these tales tell us less about daughters than they do about sons, and less about female volition than about the power, in Norse society, of the patrilineal principle to bend legend and life to its intention" (p. 49).

Cynthia Cockburn and Zubravka Zarkove, *The Postwar Moment: Militaries, Masculinities and International Peacekeeping Bosnia and the Netherlands* (London: Lawrence and Wishart, 2002). This collection of essays explores the notion that peace is but "a continuum of conflict" with war. Moreover since war may threaten masculine-dominated society, "After war, the traditional militarized gender regime endows men with the power in politics and locates women's importance within the family." The authors are justly disdainful of the "soft yet armed, masculinity," of the Dutch peacekeepers who turned over male Bosnian Muslims to the Bosnian Serbs during the siege of Srebrenica. In fairness to "masculine-dominated societies," few male or female warrior cultures would ever exonerate the Dutch peacekeepers for their performance here, for it was pathetic by any standards of warriorhood. Various contributors comment on the "gendered nature of war" and one, Cynthia Enloe, declares, "Nationalism typically has sprung from masculinized memory, masculinized humiliation and masculinized hope" while Stefan Dudink argues that "War and the military have always been major forces in the making of modern Western masculinity." The "heightened masculinity" of the radial Salafists would make an interesting comparative study since that particular strain is more than 1,200 years old.

———— (ed.), *Women and Wars* (Cambridge: Polity Press, 2013). A wide-ranging set of essays that operate through "a gender lens" on such diverse topics as "Sexual Violence and Women's Health in War" and "Women and the Peace Process" and "Women 'After' Wars." A very extensive bibliography is included. Strangely, given the title of the work, there is almost nothing about women warriors or war leaders especially in combat qua combat throughout history, although Cohn argues that "all wars are deeply gendered."

Sara Cockerill, *Eleanor of Aquitaine: Queen of France and England, Mother of Empires* (Gloucestershire: Amberley, 2019). Of all the hundreds of book about Eleanor, this is one that allows the reader to sample various conflicting sources and the author's evaluation of them. It is comprehensive, fair, balanced, and scholarly, even lawyerly, but somehow doesn't seem to capture the excitement of the women in question.

Marthe Cohen with Wendy Holder, *Behind Enemy Lines: The True Story of a French Jewish Spy Behind German Lines* (New York: Three Rivers Press, 2002). An amazing story of a Jewish girl from Alsace whose "Nordic" looks and sheer courage enabled her to deeply penetrate German positions at the end of World War II (especially during "Operation Nordwind") while attached to the *Commando d'Afrique*.

Carol Cohn, "Sex and Death in the Rational World of Defense Intellectuals," *Signs*, Vol. 12, #4 (Summer 1987), pp. 687–718. If one can get by the truly bizarre fascination (of both the author and the subjects of her study) with the male phallus as images of the atomic bombing of Nagasaki and nuclear craters as "feminine," the article ends with some commonsense suggestions concerning nuclear deterrence leading to "creating compelling alternative visions of possible futures."

Vanessa Collingridge, *Boudica: The Life of Britain's Legendary Warrior Queen* (Woodstock: The Overlook Press, 2006). A long, lingering (a hundred pages of pre-Boudica and many post-Boudica), meandering look at the reality and the legend, concluding that she was "A Queen for All Seasons."

Helen Collinson (ed.), *Women and Revolution in Nicaragua* (London: Zed Books, 1990). Contains a telling map showing FDA incursions which begin the book, and there are many essays dealing with the women, especially "Fighting for Peace." Quite a worthwhile look through the prism of revolutionary fervor. One of the authors admits to being "stunned" by the "Right-wing" UNO victory at the polls in 1992 as a union of 14 parties defeated the Sandinista Front for National Liberation, but she does not believe that victory will turn back the clock on the revolution.

Note: For the important background on the importance of Augusto Sandino, see Terrance Co, "Sandino's War in Nicaragua 1927–32," *Strategy and Tactics*, #325 (Nov.–Dec. 2020), pp. 44–51. A most cautionary tale about U.S. counterrevolutionary activity in the Caribbean and how it turned out.

Dan Connell, *Against All Odds: A Chronicle of the Eritrean Revolution* (Trenton: Red Sea Press, 1993). A must-read as it highlights all the ways in which women served in the revolution against Ethiopia and the extent to which this Red Sea country leveled the playing field for women in combat. However, many women justly claim that after victory, they were not given the credit and equality they felt they deserved. The double helix is alive and well in the Horn of Africa.

Sarah Corbett, "The Women's War," *New York Times Magazine,* March 18, 2007, pp. 41ff. Some insightful glimpses into women in today's armed forces. Shows how close to actual combat many women have come and how some have been in combat, no matter how rigorously that is defined by those not wanting to admit it.

Pearl Witherington Cornioley, *Code Name Pauline* (Chicago: Chicago University Press, 2013). Edited by Kathryn Atwood, this is the story of a most modest heroine: "I don't like blowing my own trumpet. I find it really difficult but at the same time I want people to know what really happened." What really happened is that this English woman brought up in Paris (acquiring "a perfect Parisian accent") escaped to England and then parachuted back into France to assist the Resistance for the SOE from September 1943 to September 1944. She developed and led a Maquis unit of 2,000 and engaged in sabotage, greatly helping the Allied cause. Unfortunately, this account is perhaps overly modest and irritatingly skimpy on details of major operations. Does make a good point about the Germans surrendering only to the Americans, however, concluding, "Armies prefer to deal with armies."

Bernard Cornwell, *The Empty Throne* (New York: Harper, 2014). (F) Set in the early 10th century in what is now England, this is the fictionalized account of how Aethelflaed, daughter of Alfred of Wessex and widow of Aethelred, Lord of Mercia, ruled Mercia. A very capable woman who "proved herself to be more of a warrior than her brother." A good read and one which also provides valuable insights into the shield wall form of warfare practiced by the Vikings and Saxons (among others) and how men would follow a woman in battle if she had the right birthright *and* warrior skills.

Note: See also Terence Wise, *Saxon, Viking and Norman* (Oxford: Osprey Publications, 1979) for comparable and opposing views.

Imogen Corrigan, "'Put That Light Out!' The 93 Searchlight Regiment Royal Artillery," in Celia Lee and Paul Strong (eds.), *Women in War: From Home Front to Front Line* (Barnsley: Pen and Sword, 2012), pp. 78–86. Following the quite amazing story of the 93, conceived in 1935 and actualized in 1941 when Churchill approved women in combat. As General Frederick Pile wrote, "The girls lived like men, fought their fights like men and, alas, some of them died like men. Unarmed, they often showed great personal bravery. They earned decorations and they deserved more. As a partial solution to our manpower problems, they were grand. But, like all good things, they were in short supply" (p. 85).

James Corum, "Chaco War: Battle in the Barrens," *MHQ: The Quarterly Journal of Military History*, Vol. 21, #4 (Summer 2009), pp. 52–65. Bolivia fought Paraguay from 1932 until 1935 in a little known but predictor of World War II with its use of airplanes, tanks, and armored warfare.

Note: This war is well covered and interpreted as well as being lavishly illustrated in Antonio Sapienza and José Paláez, *The Chaco War 1932–1935: Fighting in Green Hell* Latin America War Series, War #20 (Warwick: Helion and Company, 2020).

Kazimiera Cottam, *Women in War and Resistance: Selected Biographies of Soviet Women Soldiers* (Nepean, Canada: New Military Publishing, 1998).

Provides a wide range of biographies of 92 Soviet women including air-women, infantry and tank troops, partisans and scouts, and combat political officers. Rich in detail and broad in scope.

Kathryn Coughlin, "Women, War and the Veil: Muslim Women in the Resistance and Combat," in DeGroot and Corinna Peniston-Bird (eds.), *op. cit.*, pp. 223–239. Introduces the reader to some understudied concepts and individuals, such as the Algerian Jamilah Buhrayd, the Palestinians Fatmeh Ghazzal, Rashida Obeida, and Leila Khalid, and the Moro Filipina Farouza, and points out that here and there in the Islamic worlds there have been some "striking gender role reversals" over the last 50 years (p. 239).

Chris Coulter, "Female Fighters in the Sierra Leone War: Challenging the Assumptions?," *Feminist Review*, #88 (2008), pp. 54–73. Based on extensive interviews with former Sierra Leone female rebels, this intriguing examination of them concludes that many were both victims and subsequently perpetrators of violence during the very brutal Sierra Leone civil war from 1998 to 2006. Ironically, a number of these women warriors were later reintegrated in Sierra Leone society as part of its military, and some were sent to Somalia as UN peacekeepers from 2013 to 2014.

Alison Leigh Cowan, "They Fought and Bled for Liberty," *New York Times*, July 3, 2019, C1ff. Newly discovered diaries from the Civil War underscore Deborah Sampson's shifting narrative but confirm her central story.

Camillia Cowling, "'As a Slave Woman and as a Mother': Women and the Abolition of Slavery in Havana and Rio de Janeiro," *Social History,* Vol. 36, #3 (2011), pp. 294–311. Looks at how women during the last stages of legal slavery used the system to make gains but it was not easy.

Eugene A. Coyle, "The Belcamp Park Story: The Swift-Grattan-Markievicz," *Dublin Historical Record*, Vol. 63, #1 (Spring 2010), pp. 54–67. This is a delightful account of how Constance Markievicz, fearing the imperialist propaganda of the Boy Scouts, created (briefly) the Fianna, which instructed young men in the use of firearms and insisted that they be "willing to work for the independence of Ireland" (p. 63).

Brian Crim, "Silent Partners: Women and Warfare in Early Modern Europe," in Gerard DeGroot and Corinna Peniston-Bird (eds.), *A Soldier and a Woman: Sexual Integration in the Military* (London: Longman, 2000), pp. 3–17. Points out how women dressing as men in order to join the armies of the world shows how militaries were gendered. Also gives a number of examples showing how some politics break "the combat taboo" when the situation demands (Soviet Union in World War II) but that societies seem to fear that women will grow used to their power and thus become a threat to them.

Note: The DeGroot and Peniston-Bird book contains many fine essays, and other than the two volumes of Pennington, *Amazons to Fighter Pilots*, the widest scope of women warriors encountered in this study. It is a fine work and very stimulating.

Robin Cross and Rosalind Miles, *Warrior Women: 3000 Years of Courage and Heroism* (New York: Metro Books, 2011). This breezy, well-illustrated, and engaging account rounds up the usual suspects (Amina, Nzinga, Zenobia, etc.), but also brings focus to Deborah, Laskarina Bouboulina, Harshepsut, and Christina "Mother Ross" Davies, among others.

Terry Crowdy, *SOE Agent* (Oxford: Osprey Publishing, 2008). Interesting take on one Special Operations Executive (SOE) operative, Pearl "Pauline" Witherington, who fought with the French Resistance during World War II and was nominated for the military cross for her activities, but since she was a "civilian," she had to settle for an Order of the British Empire.

Roger Crowley, *Empires of the Sea: The Siege of Malta, the Battle of Lepanto, and the Contest for the Center of the World* (New York: Random House, 2008). A fascinating work containing an important reference to a female warrior on the Christian leader's ship. "And on Don Juan's flagship was one particularly fresh-faced Spanish arquebusier. Her name was Maria la Bailadora (the flamenco dancer), she had disguised herself to accompany her soldier lover to the wars" (p. 262). The huge victory of the Venetians and Spanish at the Battle of Lepanto Gulf (1571) was widely heralded as a great Christian victory although strategically, it did not do as much to check the Turkish outreach as it did to boost subsequent Christian morale after Cyprus had fallen.

Azad Cudi, *Long Shot: The Inside Story of the Snipers Who Broke ISIS* (New York: Atlantic Monthly Press, 2018). The defense of Kurdish Tobani with all its Stalingrad-in-miniature dimensions features portraits of the women's YPG (Yekineyen Parastina Gel) from Generals Medua and Tolin to snipers Arin, Yildiz and Nasrin, where equality runs the front lines. The role of women in the defeat of ISIS and the assumptions it validates about gender equality in wartime would make an excellent research project.

Lani Cupchoy, "Fragments of Memory: Tales of a Wahine Warrior," *Frontiers: A Journal of Women Studies*, Vol. 31, #2 (2010), pp. 35–59. And what a tale this is. Manono II (c. 1780–1819, a Hawaiian warrior woman, died with her husband fighting for the traditional religion at Battle of Kuamo'o in 1819. They were defending the traditional *Kapu* system, which kept women and men from eating together and prohibited women from eating certain foods. When this was abolished by Liholiho (as King Kamehameha II), her husband Kekuaokalani gathered a force of warriors and fought, only to be killed along with Liloliho. The author captures all the pathos and ironies of the situation and yet is able to find nobility in losing one's life over dietary restrictions. Who knew?

Don Cutler, "Your Nations Shall Be Exterminated," *MHQ: The Quarterly Journal of Military History*, Vol. 22, #3 (Spring 2010), pp. 46–53. This article is excellent background for the study of our star, Colestah the Yakama, in the 1858 Battle of Spokane Plains. After her husband was badly wounded by artillery fire, Colestah raced into battle using a stone ax, eventually rescuing her husband and nursing him back to health. In an attempt to pacify the Northwest Indian warriors, Col. George Wright fought with terror tactics and the hangman's noose to subjugate the Northwest Indians, killing 700 horses and destroying many villages. This "ignominious" campaign against the Nez Perce, Yakama, Palouse, and Walla Wallas was deadly and punitive.

   Note: Useful background on the Native Americans in the wider region is contained in Elizabeth von Aderkas, *American Indians of the Pacific Northwest* (Oxford: Osprey Publications, 2005). See also Kurt Nelson for the broken treaties and promises that ended freedom for the Native Americans of the Northwest in his *Treaties and Treachery: The Northwest Indians' Resistance to Conquest* (Caldwell, Idaho: Caxton Press, 2011).

Princess Kati Dadeshkeliani, *Princess in Uniform* (London: G. Bell, 1934). This woman from Georgia in the Caucasus joined the Russian army as "Djamal" and ended up in the Tartar Regiment of the "Savage Division" commanded by Grand Duke Michael. Wounded several times and receiving two St. George Crosses, she saw action on the Austrian front and barely escaped death during the Russian Civil War, finally leaving via Batum and Constantinople, ultimately settling in France.

Stella Dadzie, "Searching for the Invisible Woman: Slavery and Resistance in Jamaica," *Race & Class*, Vol. 32, #2 (1990), pp. 21–38. Gives a wide-ranging account of the miseries of being a female slave in the Caribbean and the many ways they resisted and persevered.

William Dalrymple, *The Last Mughal: The Fall of a Dynasty: Delhi, 1857* (New York: Alfred Knopf, 2006). A highly sympathetic and in-depth analysis of the Great Indian Rebellion of 1857, with an extraordinary richness of characters and background. See especially the author's take on Rani Lakshmi Bai, who led her Jhansi troops against the British during the Sepoy Rebellion of 1857–1958. She called on her troops to die in battle if necessary and is now regarded as one of the pioneers for Indian independence a hundred years later.

Francine D'Amico and Laurie Weinstein (eds.), *Gender Camouflage: Women and the U.S. Military* (New York: New York University Press, 1999). Very informative collection of essays divided into "Women in the Military," "Women *with* the Military," and "Outsiders: Women and the Military." Basically argues that the military always puts men first and that great change is necessary to liberate women *and* men from the core gender hierarchy that overpowers all.

Jessica Trisko Darden, "Assessing the Significance of Women in Combat Roles," *International Journal,* Vol. 70, #3 (September 2015), pp. 454–462. Provides a useful overview of women in combat roles in 43 rebel armed forces, ranging from El Salvador and Colombia to Sierra Leone and Uganda, including a number in the Middle East. Sees socioeconomic, generational, and communal differences as being variables in their participation.

Jessica Trisko Darden, Alexis Henshaw, and Ora Szekely, *Insurgent Women: Female Combatants in Civil Wars* (Georgetown: Georgetown University Press, 2019). An expanded study of the above with case studies from the Ukraine, Kurdistan, and Colombia. One useful thread linking all three is the notion that female presence in command, control, and recruitment processes enhances the likelihood of women wanting to become warriors.

Sonia d'Artois (nee Sonia Esmee Florence Butt), "I, Spy," *MHQ: The Quarterly Journal of Military History*, Vol. 31, #1 (Autumn 2018), pp. 44–53. Fast-moving account by a woman member of Britain's Special Operations Executive (SOE) who parachuted into occupied France and fought the Germans on the ground in the Resistance nine days before the Allied landings at Normandy, June 6, 1944. Amazingly casual account.

Jessica Davis, "Evolution of the Global *Jihad*: Female Suicide Bombers in Iraq," *Studies in Conflict and Terrorism*, Vol. 36, #4 (2013), pp. 279–291. Analyzes a spike during 2008 in the use of female suicide bombers from a modest beginning in 1978 and argues for a closer look at the reasons that motivate these women, because they seem to foreshadow more imitators in the future.

————, "Gendered Terrorism: Women in the Liberation Tigers of Tamil Eelam (LTTE)," *Minerva Journal of Women and War,* Vol. 2, #1 (April 2008), pp. 22–38. Davis suggests that women who become Liberation Tigers are set apart from other women and have more status and autonomy but when they return to civilian life, they are often remanded to their previous state. Thus, she concludes that LTTE has not changed Tamil society. Interestingly, from a counterterrorism perspective, the author argues that women are often overlooked as agents of terror.

Jeannine Davis-Kimball, *Warrior Women: An Archaeologist's Search for History's Hidden Heroines* (New York: Warner, 2002). Breezy and personal account of the author's discoveries among the Saka, Scythian, and Sarmatian graves from Kazakhstan, Russia, and China focusing on women in various cultures who were warriors. A useful *tour de horizon.*

Kristine Dawkins-Wright, "Francoise Marie Jacquelin De La Tour," in Pennington, Amazons *op. cit.*, p. 121. Dawkins-Wright describes Francoise Marie de La Tour (1602–1645) who, French born, in 1625 goes to Nova Scotia, marries Charles de La Tour, and helps build Fort La Tour. She wars with Jesuit Seigneur d'Aulnay Charnise and assumes the role of military commander when her husband is away. She uses their three ships to fight Charnise off, but later he returns and captures the fort, putting her soldiers to death and her in prison at Port Royale, where she dies.

   Note: For background on the discovery and wars of New France and the struggles with and among the settlers, the various Indigenous Peoples, and eventually during the Seven Years' War, the English and the French, see the magisterial *Champlain's Dream* by David Fischer (New York: Simon & Schuster, 2008), Robert Leckie, *"A Few Acres of Snow," The Saga of the French and Indian Wars* (New York: John Wiley, 1999) and especially John Keegan, *Fields of Battle: The Wars for North America* (New York: Alfred Knopf, 1996). Michael Johnson provides much-needed background on the war fighting of the Iroquois in his *Tribes of the Iroquois Confederacy* (Oxford: Osprey Publications, 2003).

Wilfred Deac, "We Will Fight You Forever," *MHQ: The Quarterly Journal of Military History*, Vol. 7, #1 (Autumn 1994), pp. 58–73. A very fine introduction to the warfare of the Maori and the British. A wonderful opportunity to examine the warfare of the era of Heni Te Kiri Karamu (1840–1933), a Maori woman warrior from northern New Zealand. Normally in Maori society women warriors were not encouraged to take part in battle except in exceptional circumstances. Heni's clan, the Koherki, joined the Nga Te Pangi group, which was being hard pressed by the British. Their defensive *pa* (fortified trench and dugout) was under attack and Heni went in action during the battle. Ironically, she is best remembered in Britain for giving water to wounded British soldiers before the Koherki retreated rather than for having fought against them.

Richard Deacon, "Feminine Exploits in World War II," in *A History of the British Secret Service* (London: Frederick Muller, 1969). A most sobering portrait of the actions of the British Special Operations Executive (SOE) during World War II. Of 53 women sent into action (many with only minimal training or support), 12 were executed and 29 were either arrested or died in captivity.

Daniel Defoe, *The Life and Adventures of Mrs. Christine Davies Commonly Called Mother Ross* (London: Peter Davies, 1928). This great story needed a great author to tell it, and the writer of *Robinson Crusoe* did just that. Very enjoyable and entertaining account of "Kit" Ross, who survives multiple husbands and multiple wars. Fighting with the Duke of Marlborough at Landen, she is first wounded at Namar, then wounded again at Schellenberg, fights at Blenheim, and finally is seriously wounded in the head at Ramilles in 1706. This ends her combat career with the prestigious Scots Greys. A most remarkable woman who showed great courage and valor in battle and was indomitable in life. A wonderful read.

Rudolf M. Dekker and Lotte C. van de Pol, "Republican Heroines: Cross-dressing Women in the French Revolutionary Armies," *History of European Ideas*, Vol. 10, #3 (1989), pp. 353–363. Rose Barreau (even pregnant!), Olympe de Gouges, Reine Chapuy, Julien Sophie, Theroigne de Maricourt, and 30 women in all are identified as cross-dressing soldiers who contributed to the success of the Revolution. The author also shows the celebration of these women warriors in a vast array of contemporary short stories, novels, plays, and puppet shows. Not cross-dressing was Marie Charpentier, who was involved directly in the storming of the Bastille jail in 1789 or Marie-Barbe Parent, Theroigne de Mericourt, Marie-Henriette Heiniken Zaintrailes, and Anne Quatsault, who fought during the French revolutionary wars.

Note: Those interested in the broader women's movement(s) at the heart of the French Revolution, see Dominique Godineau, *The Women of Paris and the French Revolution* (Berkeley: University of California Press, 1998).

————, *The Tradition of Female Transvestism in Early Modern Europe* (New York: St. Martin's Press, 1989). A more inclusive study looking at Europe in general. See especially their examples of Maria van Antwerpen (subsequently Jan van Ant), Hannah Snell, Ann Mills, "Mother Ross," Geertruid ter Brugge, Genevieve Premoy, and Christine de Meyrak.

Edwin Denig, "Warrior Woman," in John Ewens (ed.), *Five Indian Tribes of the Upper Missouri* (Norman: University of Oklahoma Press, 1961), pp. 195–201. Calling Woman Chief the only woman chief among the Sioux, Arickaras, Assiniboines, Crees, and Crows, the author outlines her fascinating history. This Gros Ventre girl, captured at age 10, had a foster father who allowed her to pursue her passions, which included hunting, counting coup, stealing horses, and proficiency with weapons. Upon his death, she assumed command of his family and participated in both warfare and tribal decision-making and would acquire four wives before being killed by her own people, the Gros Ventres.

Gouri Desai, "The Historical Projections of Maharani Tarabai," *Student Research Journal of Arts and Science* (2017–2018), pp. 67–75. The author shows how different historical accounts of her military prowess and strategic sense was valued (by Mughal historians) and devalued (by British ones) across time and how even some positive Indian sources accent her "manliness" as a way to devalue her accomplishments as a woman.

Linda Grant DePauw, *Battle Cries and Lullabies; Women in War from Prehistory to the Present* (Norman: University of Oklahoma Press, 1998). A wide-ranging and very comprehensive look at thousands of years of female participation in the military, including the 100 Year's War, the Napoleonic wars, and the French and Indian wars. Good section on African women leaders in combat.

Christine de Pizan, *The Book of Deeds of Arms and of Chivalry.* An amazing document for the 15th century, written by an early feminist. Imagine how many cultural and religious barriers she had to overcome to even get her book published. Written in the 15th century by this Italian-born but French court author, *The Book of Deeds* resurrects many classical writings on war (especially Vegetius) but provides very useful contrasts between medieval Europe war practices and those from antiquity, including just war, siege warfare, chivalry, trickery, and subtlety. Many examples from contemporary Europe as well as the campaigns of Scipio, Hannibal, and Hanno. A truly amazing work given the time, the place, and the sex of its author. Belies the notion that women did not appreciate war in the Middle Ages but were only interested in court romance and jewelry.

————, *The Book of the City of Ladies* (New York: Penguin 1999). A fine translation of an extraordinary book first written in 1405. Utterly charming, this work uses the device of "a city" peopled by women to destroy many myths of the day concerning women. Among her warrior choices are pagan Queen Semiramis (who married her son as the only man worthy of her, and who conquered Babylon and led an expedition into Ethiopia), the Amazons of Scythia, Queen Thamiris (who defeated and decapitated Cyrus the Great), Queen Penthesilea of Amazon fame, and Queen Fredegunde of France. Although wrong about Queen Artemisia (who de Pizan has fighting Xerxes instead of with him), the author shows a powerful and courageous inclination to fight against the "literary misogyny of the mediaeval period." Honestly, who would not want to live in this marvelous metaphoric city? The answers were, and are, telling. The author was a most unusual woman herself, earning her livelihood by writing in an age when few women tried or succeeded in doing so.

Note: For an in-depth look at de Pizan's various political and social theories, see Kate Langdon Forham, *The Political Theory of Christine de Pizan* (Hampshire: Ashgate 2002). Unfortunately, there is not much here on her military theories and writings.

di Joyce De Vries, "Caterina Sforza: The Shifting Representation of a Woman Ruler in Early Modern Italy," *Lo Sguardo,* Vol. 13, #3 (2013), pp. 165–181. This article looks at the various ways people over time have portrayed Caterina Sforza concluding, "Caterina Sforza has simultaneously been a woman doing her duty and a woman violating expectations' exemplary and notorious' normative and exception" (p. 183).

Note: For his part, Machiavelli seems to have been central to the rewriting and reinterpretation of her career and shows his disdain for her in his *Discourses on Livy* (Mineola: Dover Publications, 2012):

> Certain conspirators, after murdering their lord, Count Girolamo of Forli, made prisoners of his wife and of his children who were still very young. By thinking they could not be safe unless they got possession of the citadel, which the governor refused to surrender, they obtained a promise from Madonna Caterina, for so the Countess was named, that on their permitting her to enter the citadel

she would cause it to be given up to them, her children in the meantime remaining with them as hostages. On which undertaking they suffered her to enter the citadel. But no sooner had she got inside, than she fell to upbraid them from the walls with the murder of her husband, and to threaten them with every kind of vengeance; and to show them how little store she set upon her children, told them scoffingly that she knew how others could be got. In the end, the rebels having no leader to advise them, and perceiving too late the error into which they had been betrayed, had to pay the penalty of their rashness by perpetual banishment. (p. 421)

Note: Julia L. Hairston, "Skirting the Issue: Machiavelli's Caterina Sforza," *Renaissance*, Vol. 53, #3 (2000), pp. 687–712 shows how Machiavelli's various interactions with Caterina in his writing has led to something of a cottage industry on this subject. Hairston argues that "Machiavelli takes a perspicacious political move on her part" and "turns it into an empty, histrionic gesture" (p. 709).

Note: For a more through look at the military explanation of the role of the condottiere, see David Murphy, *Condottiere 1300–1500* (Oxford: Osprey Publishing, 2009).

For an older but still interesting overview of the Sforza family, see L. Collison Morley, *The Story of the Sforzas* (New York: Dutton, 1934).

Note: For a more thorough look at the military explanation of the role of the condottiere, see David Murphy, *Condottiere 1300–1500* (Oxford: Osprey Publishing, 2009) and for a more holistic overview of their place in Renaissance history, see Geoffrey Trease, *The Condottieri: Soldiers of Fortune* (New York: Holt, Rinehart & Winston, 1971). Unfortunately, there is little mention of Camilla Rodolfi and other female condottieri in these two works.

Kelly DeVries, *Joan of Arc: A Military Leader* (London: Sutton, 1999). Easy to read and understand, this is the best book I have read focusing on her military accomplishments, concluding "She had completed her mission and sealed it with her blood." Gives "the Maid" credit for turning around the French military situation (with her successes in the Loire Valley, Reims, and Patay) and blames the newly crowned Charles II for a failure to keep using her and her tactics both at Paris and beyond. "Joan of Arc was a soldier plain and simple." Not too clear on how this farmer's daughter acquired the skills of warfare, however, leaving us wanting more information. Men in that era literally took years—if not decades—to learn how to fight effectively in medieval warfare.

Nidia Díaz, *I Was Never Alone: A Prison Diary from El Salvador* (Melbourne: Ocean Press, 1992). Wounded and captured by an American mercenary, a "Yankee," Nidia Dias (Maria Marta Valladares), a member of the urban underground leadership of the FMLN, was eventually exchanged to the kidnapped daughter of President Duarte of El Salvador. This is her unvarnished story written with verve and excitement and pride.

Note: The "Yankee" was Felix Rodriguez, a.k.a. Max Gomes, whose own book, *Shadow Warrior: The CIA Hero of a Hundred Unknown Battles* (New York: Simon & Schuster, 1989) claims that his personal war trophies include Che Guevara's pipe and Nidia Díaz's bra. Too much information perhaps, but it does capture his mindset.

Nguyen Thi Dinh, *No Other Road to Take*, Data Paper #107 (Ithaca: Cornell University, 1976). Gives the reader a firsthand account of a woman revolutionary in South Vietnam, letting her tell her story about the formative stirrings against the French and later the Americans. A key female player of the Viet Minh and National Liberation fronts.

Sara Dissanayake, "Women in the Tamil Tigers: Path to Liberation or Pawn in a Game?," *Counter Terrorist Trends and Analyses,* Vol. 9, #8 (August 2017), pp. 1–6. Argues that although the use of female suicide bombers defied traditional gender stereotypes and caused considerable casualties to the Sri Lankan Army and Indian Peace Keeping Force (PKF), that use did not result in gender equality within the Tamil Eelam. States that 30–40% of suicide bombers were women and they were used in 15 out of 23 attacks against high-value targets.

Nicole Dombrowski (ed.), *Women and War in the Twentieth Century: Enlisted with or without Consent* (New York: Garland Publishing, 1999). Although this wide-ranging group of essays could definitely have used a strong conclusion to tie together its many disparate threads, there are some interesting essays on Japanese women in action in Saipan as well as Peru and Guatemala.

Lan Dong, *Mulan's Legend and Legacy in China and the United States* (Philadelphia: Temple University Press, 2011). A wide-ranging look at the various images, interpretations, and commercial uses of the tale(s) of Mulan from premodern China to the Disney films of today.

Kirstin Downey, *Isabella: The Warrior Queen* (New York: Doubleday, 2014). An in-depth look at "the woman who governs the world from her bed" (i.e., dying of cancer) whose will united Spain, defeated Portugal, recaptured the Emirate of Granada, launched the Inquisition, and bankrolled Columbus and led an empire which took $1.5 billion in gold and silver out of the Americas.

Isabella was a devout Catholic who turned back the Muslim tide, was beloved by her people, and who forced her husband Ferdinand to excel in battle and to do her bidding even when he tried to demur. "Isabella's influence on the New World cannot be underestimated." She truly was "a warrior queen." See especially the chapter "The Queen's War," detailing her ramrodding the Christians to victory in the Reconquest, pp. 180–203.

Laurent Dubois, *Avengers of the New World: The Story of the Haitian Revolution* (Cambridge: Harvard University Press, 2004). Although millions of Africans in Eritrea, Mozambique, Guinea-Bissau, Zimbabwe, Namibia, and South Africa might well be startled and take issue with the author's statement that Haiti was "a unique example of successful black revolution" (p. 6) and unfortunately makes no mention of others, this work nevertheless is useful in providing context and a smoothly flowing narrative of the various other dynamics of the struggle for Saint Dominque from 1791 to 1804. It is also quite good in showing the implications for the United States—had Napoleon easily subdued the revolt, he would not have so easily and cheaply sold the territory of the Louisiana Purchase.

———, "Solitude's Statue: Confronting the Past in the French Caribbean," *Outre-Mers*, Vol. 93, #350–351 (2006), pp. 27–38. The reality and myth of Solitude's role in the Guadeloupian revolt sparks ongoing controversy and frustration at the fragmentary nature of the accounts and the very existence of her statue.

Nora Duff, *Matilda of Tuscany* (London: Methuen and Company, 1909). This loving, lush portrait from an earlier era outlines the importance of Matilda and her relevance to the Italy of her day. Calling her "the Warrior Mind of the Holy Church," the author points out her early weapons training, her two suits of armor, and her military acumen were all special, as was her protection of the papacy from the designs of the Holy Roman Emperor. Duff also believes Matilda is most worthy of her inclusion in St. Peter's Basilica and Dante's Canto 28 "Guardian of the Earthly Paradise."

Laura Sook Duncombe, *Pirate Women* (Chicago: Chicago Research Press, 2017). Arguing that female pirates and privateers upset the male world, she nevertheless lists a lengthy array of said creatures, from Anne Bonny and Maria Cobhum to Mary Read, Flora Burn, Maryann Townsend and Cheng I. Sao.
    Note: Ironically, A. Kenstam and D. Richman in *Pirate: The Golden Age* (Oxford: Osprey Publishing, 2011) argue that Bonny and Read were not hung when captured only because they were women and pregnant (p. 51).

Note: Interestingly enough, recent scholarship on the history of piracy introduces the notion that the Bronze Age Sea Peoples were the first massive waves of pirates and their action culminated in "The Great Catastrophe" of 1200 BCE. See Steven Johnson, *Enemy of All Mankind* (New York: Penguin, 2020), especially pp. 19–25.

Note: For background on the Sea Peoples, see Neil Silberman, "The Coming of the Sea Peoples," *MHQ: The Quarterly Journal of Military History,* Vol. 10, #2 (Winter 1998), pp. 6–13. The author indicates how the chariot, the main weapon for the Mediterranean basin for hundreds of years, was superseded by lightly armed infantry known as the Sea Peoples, swept out of the Balkans and caused the "Great Catastrophe" (although it was not a catastrophe for them). Peter Tsouras, an analyst at the U.S. Army's Intelligence and Threat Center, in "Bronze Age Cataclysm: The Collapse of the Civilized Near East," *Strategy and Tactics,* #315 (March–April 2019), pp. 42–51, examines how the major powers of the area (with the exception of Egypt) and their reliance on chariots were swept away by the Sea Peoples and their newly specialized infantry weapons and tactics. Shows how receptivity to innovation is the key to military success over time. Additional useful information on the Sea Peoples is also to be found in Eric Cline, "Raiders of the Lost Bronze Age," *MHQ: The Quarterly of Military History,* Vol. 28, #1 (Autumn 2015), pp. 66–75. Cline sees the Sea Peoples as perhaps initially victims turning to conquest out of desperation and hope. Longer studies of these phenomena include: N. K. Sandars, *The Sea Peoples: Warriors of the Ancient Mediterranean 1250–1150 BC* (London: Thames & Hudson, 1978); Alfred Brandford, *With Arrow, Sword, and Spear: A History of Warfare in the Ancient World* (Westport: Praeger, 2001); Robert Drews, *The End of the Bronze Age: Changes in Warfare and the Catastrophe ca. 1200 BC* (Princeton: Princeton University Press, 1993); Eric Cline, *1177 B.C. The Year Civilization Collapsed* (Princeton: Princeton University Press, 2014); and Raffaele D'Amato and Andrea Salimbeti, *Sea Peoples of the Bronze Age Mediterranean c. 1400 BC–1000 BC* (Oxford: Osprey Publishing, 2015).

Shannon Dunn, "The Female Martyr and the Politics of Death: An Examination of the Martyr Discourses of Vibia Perpetua and Wafa Idris," *Journal of the American Academy of Religion,* Vol. 78, #1 (March 2010), pp. 202–225. A rather odd pairing on the surface, but the author works hard to link these two martyr narratives despite Perpetua taking her own life in 203 CE and Wafa Idris blowing herself up in 2002, killing one and wounding 100, would seem to have different intents. She does make a strong point, however, that militant Muslims such as Hamas make it clear that certain situations call on women to fight along with men and that martyrdom for such a purpose is acceptable.

Fidelis P. T. Duri, "Presentism, Contested Narratives and Dissonances in Zimbabwe's Liberation War Heritage: The Case of Joyce Muhuru," in Munyaradzi Mawerc and R. Mubaya (eds.), *Colonial Heritage, Memory and Sustainability in Africa* (Cape Town: Langaa RPCIG, 2015), pp. 11–31. The ZANU freedom fighter and the changing images of her legacy are explored. Numerous other women fighters are mentioned.

Nadezhda Durova, *The Cavalry Maiden: Journals of a Russian Officer in the Napoleonic Wars* (Bloomington: Indiana University Press, 1988). Delightful reminiscences of the Russian girl from the Urals who, disguised as a boy, joins the Imperial Army and becomes a lancer in the Polish Regiment and later the Mariupol Hussars, seeing action in 1807 and again in 1812–1814 in the struggle against Napoleon. "What a life! What a full joyous, active life! . . . Every day and every hour now I live and feel alive" (p. 171) she says of being a soldier. She fights at Smolensk and Borodino and on the Moscow front. A true warrior and a highly decorated one (Cross of St. George) who writes in a most engaging fashion. Do not miss this one. Also, see the career of Virginie Ghesquiere who served in the Napoleonic wars from 1806–1812, but on the French side.

   Note: While there are a multitude of books on Napoleon, several recent ones are worth noting: Andrew Roberts, *Napoleon: A Life* (New York: Viking, 2014) and Adam Zamoyski, *Napoleon: A Life* (New York: Basic Books, 2018). Students interested in substantial accounts of warfare in that age should consult Russell Weigley, *The Age of Battles: The Quest for Decisive Warfare from Breitenfeld to Waterloo* (Bloomington: Indiana University Press, 1996); Tim Blanning, *The Pursuit of Glory: Europe 1648–1815* (New York: Viking, 2007); and for the run-up to the Napoleonic era, Lauro Martines, *Furies: War in Europe 1450–1700* (New York; Bloomsbury, 2013).

   Note: Perhaps the most useful examination of the role played by Russia in the eventual defeat of Napoleon is Domini Lieven, *Russia against Napoleon* (New York: Viking, 2009). Finally Russia gets its well-deserved credit for being the sine qua non in his eventual defeat. Durova even gets a mention in this magisterial work (pp. 151–152).

E–K

Frances Early and Kathleen Kennedy (eds.), *Athena's Daughters: Television's New Women Warriors* (Syracuse: Syracuse University Press, 2003). These essays argue that the television portrayal of such female characters as Xena the Warrior Princess, La Femme Nikita, and Buffy the Vampire Slayer help to liberate today's girls and women by empowering them to imagine true female power.

Richard Eaton, "Tarabai (1675–1761): The Rise of Brahmins in Politics," in his *A Social History of the Deccan, 1300–1761* (Cambridge: Cambridge University Press, 2005), pp. 177–202. The author calls her "one of the most remarkable women in Indian history" (p. 177) and notes especially her strategic sense in warfare dealing with the anti-Mughal resistance and the rise of the new Maratha state.

   Note: A much more detailed early history of the rise, zenith, and eventual fall of the Maratha state can be found in James Duff, *A History of the Mahrattas* 2 vols. (London: Oxford University Press, 1921).

Meredith E. Ebel, *My Body is a Barrel of Gunpowder: Palestinian Women's Suicide Bombing in the Second Intifada*, Honor's Thesis (Carnegie Mellon University, 2012). Argues that Palestinian female suicide bombers are not failed or disgraced members of society, are not doing it for equal rights, but simply that they are driven by the same nationalist motivations as male Palestinian suicide bombers.

Robert B. Edgerton, *Warrior Women: The Amazons of Dahomey and the Nature of War* (Boulder: Westview, 2000). The most scholarly and inclusive account of the Amazons of Dahomey, accenting their small unit cohesion, their vigorous training, their in-group bonding, and their elite status as warriors without sex. If one became pregnant, she was tortured until she revealed the cause and both were then killed. Covers their participation in the slave trade and as worthy opponents of the French Foreign Legion as late as the 1890s.

Susan Edgington and Sarah Lambert (eds.), *Gendering the Crusades* (New York: Columbia University Press, 2002). An exciting reappraisal of the role of women during the crusades which finds them far more central to the process than heretofore acknowledged. See especially, Karen Caspri-Reisfeld "Woman Warriors during the Crusades, 1095–1254." Despite church policy, women played extensive roles in sieges, invasions, looting, and other warrior aspects, including as archers. Much evidence from Muslim sources in various battles from Antioch to Acre makes this an excellent and provocative source.

Michael Edwardes, *Red Year: The Indian Rebellion of 1857* (London: Hamish Hamilton, 1973). Interesting account of the role played by the Rani of Jhansi in the uprising and quotes the general who defeated her in battle, Sir Hugh Rose, who called her "the bravest and best of the military leaders of the rebellion" after she was killed in action during the Battle of Gwalior.

Louise Edwards, "Women Warriors and Amazons of the Mid Qing Texts Jinghua Yuan and Honglou Meng," *Modern Asian Studies,* Vol. 29, #2 (May 1995), pp. 225–255. The author writes convincingly and in depth about the depiction of women warriors in various Ming dynasty novels including Qin Liangyu, Liang Hongyu, and Thirteenth Sister.

————, "The Transformation of the Warrior Woman Hua Mulan," *Nan Nu,* #12 (2010), pp. 175–214. Like Joan of Arc this Chinese legendary female warrior has spawned poems, plays, operas, and films, all in the service of some cause.
  Note: The 2020 film *Mulan* has come under fire not for its representation of her, but for the human rights abuses in the area where its credits lie. See Isaac Stone, "Why Disney's New 'Mulan' Is a Scandal," *Washington Post*, September 7, 2020, p. C 6.

Marian Eide, "Maeve's Legacy: Constance Markievicz, Eva Gore-Booth, and the Easter Rising," *Éire-Ireland*, Vol. 51, #3&4 (2016), pp. 80–103. Two sisters, one a pacifist and one a revolutionary, find their lives inextricably linked to the Easter Rising, and their artistic efforts reflect that.

Konrad Eisenbichler, "The Women in the Siege of Siena," in Pennington, *op. cit.* pp. 499–403. Provides much-needed details and context about the role women played in the siege and especially the role of Laudomia Forteguerri in the losing effort against the Spanish imperial forces.

Elizebeth A. Eldredge, "The 'Mfecane' Revisited," *Journal of African History*, #33, pp. 1–35. A devastating critique of the previous revisionist arguments concerning the Mfecane. Very germane background for any study of the rise of Mmanthasatsi (sometimes Manthatisi) and her "Horde." For a more traditional explanation of the Mfecane and some of the subsequent literature about it, see Leonard Thompson, "The Zulu Kingdom and the Mfecane," in *A History of South Africa* (New Haven: Yale University Press, 2001), pp. 80–87. Note, in Sesotho, Mfecane is translated "Difaqane." This study also provides a broader examination of Manthatisi, whose Tolokwa clan of the Sotho people formed the basis of her horde.

Note: Elsewhere, Thompson makes the point that there were actually three "hordes" operating at the same time for some of this period. See Leonard Monica Wilson and Leonard Thompson (eds.), *The Oxford History of South Africa*, Vol. I (London: Oxford University Press, 1964), pp. 391–405.

Note: For an in-depth look at the military revolution created by the Zulus and the subsequent Mfecane, see Donald Morris, *The Washing of the Spears—A History of the Rise of the Zulu Nation Under Shaka and Its Fall in the Zulu War of 1879* (New York: Simon & Schuster, 1986). The depths and extent of that revolution are also highlighted in C. P. Potholm, *Winning at War: The Seven Keys to Military Victory Throughout History* (Lanham, MD: Rowman & Littlefield, 2010), pp. 32–24. Ian Knight does a fine job in outlining the Zulu military structure in his well-illustrated *The Zulus* (London: Osprey Publishing, 1989) and Angus McBride explains how the Zulus defeated the British in the 1879 Battle of Isandlwana, *The Zulu War* (London: Osprey Publishing, 1976).

Note: More recent scholarship has accented the importance of the royal women of the Zulus in the running of their polity's affairs: Maxwell Z. Shamase, "The Royal Women of the Zulu Monarchy through the Keyhole of Oral History: Queens Nandi (c.1764–c.1827) and Monase (c.1797–c.1880)," *Journal of Humanities and Social Sciences*, Vol. 6 (2014), pp. 1–14.

Meir Elran and Gabi Sheffer, *Military Service in Israel: Challenges and Ramifications* (Tel Aviv: Institute for National Security Studies, 2006). See especially the chapter "What is the Appropriate Model for Female Service in the IDF?" by Pnina Sharvit Baruch (pp. 77–92). The author points out the continuing difficulties of women finding what they take to be proper status in the Israeli Defense Force because their motivation to serve is conditioned on the way in which they are treated.

Jean Elshtain, *Women and War* (New York: Basic Books, 1987). Focusing on the "seduction" of war, she sees women as "the ferocious few and the non-combatant many" and men as "the militant many and the pacific few." Argues that women do not belong in combat (or men either if she had her druthers).

Cynthia Enloe, "Paying Close Attention to Women Inside Militaries," in her *Globalization and Militarism: Feminists Make the Link* (Lanham, MD: Rowman & Littlefield, 2007), pp. 63–92. This work serves as a counterbalance to the assumptions of both Bowdoin graduates, Sage Santangelo and Katie Petronio (cited above), that service in the military is ipso facto liberating if women are treated as equals within it. In fact, Enloe argues that "a less militarized military would be one less imbued with an institutional culture of masculinized violence" and instead would (and should) place as more emphasis on rescuing civilians from natural disasters worldwide.

———, *Globalization and Militarism: Feminists Make the Link* (Lanham, MD: Rowman & Littlefield, 2007). Based on her Tokyo lectures on the eve of the U.S. invasion of Iraq, the author uses the device of "a feminist curiosity" to declare a link between globalization and militarization. She also argues that the woman soldier should not simply be a globalized version of the "modern woman," but should instead push for "a less militarized military (which) would be less imbued with an institutional culture of masculinized violence."

———, *Does Khaki Become You? The Militarization of Women's Lives* (London: South End Press, 1983). Although much of this work is quite dated in terms of specifics and, one could argue, shows a complete misreading of the reasons for the original Amazon legends (the Greeks rightly feared their style of warfare as well as their gender); nevertheless, some of the chapters such as "The Military Needs Camp Followers" and "Some of the Best Soldiers Wear Lipstick" raise important issues. Still, one wonders whether one of her core statements, "Women are being used by militaries to solve their nagging problems of manpower availability, quality, health, morale and readiness" might be made even more relevant by changing or adding "and men" to the quote. Unfortunately, there is almost nothing here on women warriors qua warriors.

————, *Maneuvers; The International Politics of Militarizing Women's Lives* (Berkeley: University of California Press, 2000). Noting that "Women *in* the military has never been an easy topic," the author argues it shouldn't be. "Sexism, patriotism, violence and the state—it is a heady brew," the author looks at the many impacts of war on many different women—prostitutes, rape victims, mothers, wives, nurses, and feminist activists. Concerned about masculinity and militarism, her chapter 7, "Filling the Ranks," shows how and when women are recruited.

————, *Bananas, Beaches and Bases: Making Feminist Sense of International Politics*, 2nd edition (Los Angles: University of California Press, 2000). A wide-ranging set of chapters dealing with the international dimensions of feminism and the need to make common cause globally to combat human trafficking, exploitation of local women by the military, NGOs, etc., all built around a common theme of "the personal is global; the global is gendered."

Elizabeth Ewan, "Agnes of Dunbar," in Pennington, *op. cit.,* pp. 7–9. Agnes Randolph (1300–1369). According to the author, she "Defended Dunbar Castle, Scotland during the Second Scottish War of Independence, 1332–1341." She held out for five months before surrendering to the English.

John Ewers, "Deadlier than the Male," *American Heritage*, Vol. 16, #4 (1965). Despite its hyperbolic and inaccurate title, this work is a short, pithy article introducing Elk Hollering in the Water, the Blackfeet woman warrior, The Other Magpie, the Crow, and Woman Chief of the Gros Ventre (but raised as a Crow), and Running Eagle, the Blackfeet. Suggests that female participation in war and raids was more widespread than previously understood or acknowledged. Young brides, for example, often went with their new husbands on raids. Note also how Running Eagle was thought to have been killed because she violated her oath of celibacy, a widespread projection of male values upon even women warriors, as obviously no similar prohibition existed for male warriors.

Jacqueline Fabre-Serris and Alison Keith (eds.), *Women and War in Antiquity* (Baltimore: John Hopkins Press, 2015). Although most of these essays deal with aspects of women and war, Violaine Cuchert, "The Warrior Queens of Caria" (pp. 228–246) stands out by highlighting four actual female warriors of the 4th and 5th centuries, including Artemisia II, Artemisia I, and Ada I.

Leslie Feinberg, *Transgender Warriors: Making History From Joan of Arc to RuPaul* (Boston: Beacon Press, 1996). A highly personal account linking cross-dressing and transgender figures such as Joan of Arc, Catalina de Erause, and Angelique Bruion to the present struggles for gender rights and self-fulfillment.

Ilene R. Feinman, *Citizen Rites: Feminist Soldiers and Feminist Antimilitarists* (New York: New York University Press, 2000). According to the author, feminist anti-militarism relies on the fundamental connection between patriarchy and war, while feminist egalitarian militarism accents the notion that women can be as good as men in the "be all you can be" ethos of the military. Declaring that "War is no longer a dick thing," she argues that "women have fought long and hard for inclusiveness and respect in the realm of martial citizenship" and also that liberal feminists hope to democratize the military.

Yael S. Feldman, "Hebrew Gender and Zionist Ideology: The Palmach Trilogy of Netiva Ben Yehuda," *Prooftexts*, Vol. 20, #1&2 (Winter/Spring 2000), pp. 139–157. A strangely written piece that does seem to capture the essence of Netiva Ben Yehuda, "The Yellow Devil," who in the name of Zionism wrote poetry, exalted Hebrew as a language, and earned the enmity of the Arabs for her commanding the first successful Jewish ambush of an Arab bus early in 1948.

Lorry Fenner and Marie deYoung, *Women in Combat: Civic Duty or Military Liability* (Washington: Georgetown University Press, 2001). Two articulate authors give the pros and cons for American women being used in combat. They both have extensive military experience. Fenner is an Air Force intelligence officer and favors opening up all aspects of military service to women while deYoung, an Army chaplain, opposes this on many grounds, arguing the recent surge for their use is based purely on political correctness, not a dispassionate examination of all of its dimensions.

Laura K. Ferguson, *Resilience: Stories of Montana Indian Women* (Helena: Montana Historical Society Press, 2016). Covers some interesting female warriors including Kauzuma Nupika, A Kootenai, Kwilqs, a Pend d'Oreille, and a woman chief of the Gros Ventre known as Pine Leaf, who was captured by and eventually became a Crow and was ironically later killed by the Gros Ventre.

Nic Fields, *Boudicca's Rebellion AD 60–61* (Oxford: Osprey Publishing, 2011). Fine details and maps of the rebellion and some good commentary. He ends asking us the question "Why do men fear women warriors so much?" and puts Boudica's rebellion in the long line of such sentiments going back to the original "Amazonian" concerns of the ancient Greeks. If you are interested in why Boudica attained so much and then lost it all, this analysis will help you understand.

Note: A useful background work on the diversity within the wider Celtic world can be found in Barry Cunliffe, "In the Fabulous Celtic Twilight," in Larissa Bonfante (ed.), *The Barbarians of Ancient Europe: Realities and Interactions* (Cambridge: Cambridge University Press, 2011), pp. 190–210 and Stephen Allen, *Celtic Warrior 300 BC–AD 100* (Oxford: Osprey Publishing, 2001).

Halina Filipowicz, *Taking Liberties: Gender, Transgressive Patriotism and Polish Drama 1786–1989* (Athens: Ohio University Press, 2014). Notes that "gender is recoded over and over again, depending on whether it stamps unpatriotic men as effete, equates soldiering with masculinity, stigmatizes female soldiering as trespassing on male territory, brands women soldiers as defeminized, apotheosizes them as ethereal perfections, or identifies women's exceptional patriotic service as a claim or gender equality" (p. 278). Relevance for many, many societies beyond Poland.

Alan Forrest, Karen Hagemann, and Jane Rendall (eds.), *Soldiers, Citizens, and Civilians: Experiences and Perceptions of the Revolutionary and Napoleonic Wars, 1790–1820* (London: Palgrave Macmillan, 2008). See especially David Hopkin, "The World Turned Upside Down: Female Soldiers in the French Armies of the Revolutionary and Napoleonic Wars," pp. 77–95. Hopkin argues persuasively that as many as 80 women can be documented as having fought in the ranks of the Revolutionary and Napoleonic armies. Far from unique, he shows this was a pattern duplicated in both Holland and England. But Hopkin also points out that there are 44 cases of French female soldiers from the Old Regime so the revolution qua revolution does not alone explain their presence. Interestingly enough, the revolutionary fervor diminished by 1793, when women were no longer encouraged to join the military. This switching of attitudes in mid-war is also notable in the Spanish Civil War of 1936.

Note: A sampling of Dutch women who, dressed as men, served in the armed forces of the 18th century including Geertruid ter Brugge, Maria ter Meetelen, Maria Meening, Johanna Bennius, Elisaeth Huyser, Maria van Antwerpen, Gertruid van Duiren, Maria Stording, Jochem Wiesse, Anna Spiesen, Margareta Reymers, Maria van Spanje, Lena Wasmoet, and Anna Maria Everts.

Marie-Madeleine Fourcade, *Noah's Ark* (New York: Dutton, 1974). Truly extraordinary story of a one-legged British woman who parachuted into France during World War II and established a major Resistance network named "Noah's Ark." Told in the first person, the tale captures the stress and danger of life on the run. The chapter "Bar of Freedom" about her escape through iron bars after being captured by the Gestapo is worth the price of admission, as is her dictum, "Resisting torture was undoubtedly what Resistance meant" (p. 333).

Will Fowler, *Eastern Front: The Unpublished Photographs 1941–1945* (St. Paul: MBI Publishing, 2001). One of the best collections of primarily Soviet photographs of the war (although it contains some pictures of Germans and Romanians as well). Many shots of the wide-tracked T-34 and other Soviet equipment (even a shot downed American B-17). There is also a much-needed emphasis on often-overlooked battles such as the Crimea and Oder campaigns as well as women and partisans in battle (in these cases closely watched by the NKVD). The shots of women in wartime action on behalf of the Soviet Union are most engaging and show their centrality to the war effort. Taken in context, they provide stunning evidence of women warriors in daily combat during World War II.

Heath Fowler-Salamini and Mary Kay Vaughan (eds.), *Women of the Mexican Countryside 1850–1990* (Tucson: University of Arizona Press, 1994). See especially Elizabeth Salas, "The Soldaderas in the Mexican Revolution," pp. 93–105. Salas also identifies Gertrudis Bocanegra (1765–1818) as fighting against the Spanish during the Mexican War of Independence against Spain (1810–1823). See her "Bocanegra, Gertrudis," Pennington, *op. cit.*, p. 60.

Amaryllis Fox, *Life Undercover: Coming of Age in the CIA* (New York: Alfred Knopf, 2019). Engrossing and a quick read. This warrior woman penetrates, at length, the world beyond the classroom and spends a lot of time in harm's way. She concludes, "It's our cover and not our weapon that keeps us from being killed" (p. 125). Words to ponder.

Linda Bird Francke, *Ground Zero: The Gender Wars in the Military* (New York: Simon & Schuster, 1997). This book looks at the ways in which an element of society and the military tried to restrict the role of women in the military, but how over time the stereotypes of males as protectors and women as caregivers lost some of their power.

Antonia Fraser, *The Warrior Queens* (New York: Alfred Knopf, 1990). Well written, erudite, and entertaining, with a kaleidoscope of historical, psychological, and sociological references. Queen Boadicea, Elizabeth I, Catherine the Great, and the Rani of Jhansi all are colorfully described. Who says women cannot be as ruthless as men, in battle as well as elsewhere? Not this author. Contains interesting subthemes about the role of sexuality in the depiction of warrior queens. They are depicted either as voracious breakers of norms or virginal upholders of them depending on one's perspective.

————, *The Weaker Vessel* (New York: Alfred Knopf, 1984). A charming exploration of the ways women were/are regarded as being "weaker." See pp. 168–184 for an interesting take on the variety of women who played military and quasi-military roles during the English Civil War of 1642–1651. Especially interesting are the activities of the highborn women on both sides during sieges.

Ronald Fraser, *Napoleon's Cursed War: Popular Resistance in the Spanish Peninsular War* (London: Verso, 2008). A fine, comprehensive—even definitive—account of the Peninsular War (1807–1814) sometimes known as the "Spanish Ulcer" for its strategic significance in the eventual downfall of Napoleon. Good use of sources and the roles of ordinary people, including those women who fought at the sieges of Saragossa, Valencia, and Gerona as well as the Madrid uprising.

Andrés Reséndez Fuentes, "Battleground Women: Soldaderas and Female Soldiers in the Mexican Revolution," *The Americas*, Vol. 51, #4 (April 1995), pp. 525–553. Suggests that the wide variety of female participation in the Mexican insurrection of 1910–1917 makes it difficult to generalize about women warriors in that conflict (or series of conflicts). He cites the various groups and their differing approaches to employing women in war as well. The author also provides the examples of Rosa Bobadilla, Clara de la Rodia, Petra "Pedro" Ruiz, Carmen Parra viuda de Alaniz, Maria Martinez, Angela Jimenez, La Guerra Carrasco, Carmen Velez and Chiquita of the Federal Army, Enriqueta Martinez, and Maria de la Luz Espinoza Barrera to make this point, although he concludes that most of the actual women fighters came from the middle and upper classes of Mexico.

Note: Disregarding the depressingly tiny references to the *soldaderas* themselves, Frank McLynn does provide the overarching dynamics of the various personalities of the Mexican Revolution and their interactions in his *Villa and Zapata: A History of the Mexican Revolution* (New York: Carroll & Graf Publishers, 2000).

Alberto Fujimori, "Terror, Society, & Law: Peru's Struggle Against Violent Insurgency," *Harvard International Review*, Vol. 20, #4 (Fall 1998), pp. 58–61. The author argues cogently that terrorism must be confronted with changes in the law that allow for the just persecution of the terrorists. He feels that the "North American terrorist" Lori Berenson and her comrades in arms planned and executed terrorist acts that resulted in the deaths of a number of innocent people and therefore should not be treated as "tourists" but be held accountable for the acts within the framework of the local legalities.

Harcourt Fuller, "Commemorating an African Queen: Ghanaian Nationalism, the African Diaspora, and the Public Memory of Nana Yaa Asantewaa, 1952–2009," *African Arts,* Vol. 46, # 4 (Winter 2014), pp. 58–71. A marvelous example of an African female warrior whose legendary war-making earned her the praise of the British general who eventually vanquished her and the extensive afterlife she enjoyed as various modern political groups have gravitated toward her courage and nationalism.

Alison Gaines, *Mary Edwards Walker* (New York: Cavendish Square, 2018). A doctor who advocated new outfits for women (pants plus knee-length skirts) and other feminist advances, she petitioned the army repeatedly to enlist in the U.S. Army, but was denied. Served as surgeon civilian contractor at Antietam, Fredericksburg, and Chickamauga. Captured by the Confederates and exchanged four months later, she received the Congressional Medal of Honor in 1865, only to have it revoked in 1917 and then reinstated in 1977.

George Gatzoflias, *Λεοντόκαρδες Γυναίκες: The Story of Two Women in the Greek War of Independence* (Cardiff University). From the origins of the Greek Revolution on March 25, 1821 at the monastery in Kalamata, the author traces the accounts, poems, songs, and other sources validating the contributions of two women warriors who fought at sea, adding to and leading portions of the Greek fleet from Hydra, Spetses, and Psara. Mando Mavrogenouse and Bouboulina Laskarina, who commanded men in battles such as Phocis and Nafplio, have not gotten proper credit for their contributions, the author makes clear.

Deborah Gera, *Warrior Women: The Anonymous Tractatus de Mulieribus* (Leiden: E. J. Brill, 1997). Based on six pages of an anonymous tract depicting 14 outstanding women from the 5th and 4th centuries BCE, the author expands on these "Women intelligent and Courageous in Warfare" including Zarinara (Parthian), Rhodegyna (Persian), Pheretine (Cynane), Tomyris (Massagetae), and Artemisia (Halicarnassian).

Note: Then there is Cynane (357–323 BCE). Half sister of Alexander the Great (and daughter of Philip II and the Illyrian Audata), Cynane was a warrior princess in her own right. Illyrian women often were fighters, and Cynane had considerable military training. She fought in a number of early battles with Alexander, according to Polyaenus. For an overview of warfare during the dominance of the Macedonians, see Arrian, *The Campaigns of Alexander* (New York: Penguin Books, 1957); Peter Green, *The Greco-Persian Wars* (Los Angeles: University of California Press, 1997); Michael Wood, *In the Footsteps of Alexander the Great* (Los Angles: University of California Press, 1997); and especially Adrian Goldsworthy, *Philip and Alexander: Kings and Conquerors* (New York: Basic Books, 2020).

Caitlin Gillespie, *Boudica: Warrior Woman of Roman Britain* (London: Oxford University Press, 2018). Sifting through archaeological evidence, contemporary Roman and other sources, and extensive background material, the author rightly concludes, "Boudica was a proud mother and fierce warrior, masculine leader and feminine moralist, non-Roman freedom fighter and harsh avenger. No matter where her image appears, she continues to demand attention."

Florance M. Gillis, "Matilda, Countess of Tuscany," *The Catholic Historical Review,* Vol. 10, #2 (1924), pp. 234–245. From an unlikely early 20th-century source comes high praise for the warrior Matilda: "The intrepid soul of the maiden yearned for the courage and the liberty of a man that at the head of her troops she might ride forth to battle for the right. . . . Ere four years had elapsed she was to don the armor of a man and at the head of her troops commence that campaign against the foes of the Church that was to end only with her death" (p. 236). Very good on the inner workings of Catholic papal and Holy Roman Empire policy of the time.

Daniela Gioseffi (ed.), *Women on War* (New York: The Feminist Press at the City University of New York, 2003). A wide-ranging collection of authors, celebrating not female warriorhood but female Cassandrahood. Many women from various cultures decry war and exploitation in all its forms.

Philippe Girard, "Rebelles with a Cause: Women in the Haitian War of Independence, 1802–04," *Gender and History*, Vol. 21, #1 (April 2009), pp. 60–85. Excellent description of the various roles women played in the Haitian Revolution and provides context on the huge size of the French expedition sent by Napoleon in 1801 to suppress it. Shows how the situation of revolutionary warfare itself reduced the taboos on female war-making, especially for the insurgents (and conversely their harsh, often lethal treatment if captured). Numerous instances of unnamed women warriors working for the revolution are well documented by contemporary sources, as are some specific ones such as Dedee Bazile and Marie-Jeanne Lamartiniere.

Tore Gjelsvik, *Norwegian Resistance 1940–1945* (Montreal: McGill-Queen's University Press, 1979). A personal account of a major resistance operation that confronted between 300,000 and 400,000 German occupiers or 10% of the total population of Norway at the time. Precious little on the Battle of Hegra Fort, however.

Osire Glacier, *Political Women in Morocco* (London; Red Sea Press, 2013). A breezy introduction to many Moroccan women from poets to sages to political leaders. Also included are some short sketches of women warriors such as Princess Fammu Bent Omar Ben Yintan, Al-Kahina, and Sayyida Al-Hurra Hakimattetouan.

Alexander Gogun, *Stalin's Commandos: Ukrainian Partisan Forces on the Eastern Front* (London: I.B. Tauris, 2016). Describes in detail the various forces involved and the degree of Soviet control over the different units. Reading the chapter on NKVD after-action reports of women pressed into services as "wives" or simply raped gives one a sense that women partisans must have highly prized their weapons and rarely let them out of hand or sight.

Nancy Loring Goldman (ed.), *Female Soldiers—Combatants or Noncombatants* (Westport: Greenwood Press, 1982). Gives the reader portraits of women in war (Germany, Russia, Yugoslavia, Vietnam, and Israel) and as noncombatants (Greece, Japan, Denmark, Sweden), ending with an argument for women in combat (Mandy Seal) and against (Jeff Tuten). These last two essays are somewhat overridden by events, but well worth perusing for historical context and values.

J. S. Goldstein, *War and Gender: How Gender Shapes the War System and Vice Versa* (Cambridge: Cambridge University Press, 2001). It is estimated that 8% of Soviet armed forces were women as were approximately 40% of doctors in the Soviet armed forces, many of whom served in combat. According to Goldstein's estimates, approximately 1% of all warriors throughout history have been women, with an overall total of hundreds of millions of fighters worldwide. This is not an insignificant number. The author also highlights the "cross-culture consistency of gender roles in war" and looks at women in all-female, mixed-gender, and individual situations. Appreciated his emphasis on often-overlooked women military leaders such as Semiramis (Assyrian), Tomyris (Maggagetae), Tamara (Georgia), and Nzinga (Angola).

Note: For an examination of the Assyrian army at the time of Semiramis, see Mark Healy, *The Ancient Assyrians* (Oxford: Osprey Publications, 1991). For a broader global perspective on war in the ancient world, see Alfred Bradford, *With Arrow, Sword and Spear: A History of Warfare in the Ancient World* (Westport: Praeger, 2001).

R. James Goldstein, "The Women of the Wars of Independence in Literature and History," *Studies in Scottish Literature*, Vol. 26, #1 (1991), pp. 271–282. The author laments that "Most of these women are too obscure, socially too marginal, to interest modern historians, who tend to focus on the public events of the war, which are by definition conducted almost entirely within a male sphere" (p. 281). He urges more in-depth study of the role of women in the Scottish Wars of Independence.

Adrian Goldsworthy, "Rome's Disgrace at Adrianople," *MHQ: The Quarterly Journal of Military History,* Vol. 22, #2 (Winter 2009), pp. 36–43. A good introduction to the battle of Adrianople. This huge defeat for Rome also illuminates the appearance of Mavia who ruled (r. 375–425) in what is now Syria, reigning over the Tanukhid Arabs, who had fled the advancing Persians south from northern Arabia. Mavia launched a massive revolt against the Romans in 378, leaving Aleppo and going into the desert. She had succeeded her husband al-Hawari when he died in 375. Like Zenobia, she led her armies into battle and won numerous battles in Palestine and Phoenicia. They even defeated a large Roman force sent against them. Emperor Valens then sued for peace, and she subsequently married her daughter to the head of the Roman army and even sent units to fight with Valens at the disastrous battle of Adrianople in Thrace against the Goths. The Tanukhids would later revolt against the Romans and their new emperor Theodosius I in 373.

Note: For a good account of the Battle of Adrianople, see Adrian Coombs-Hoar, *Eagles in the Dust: The Roman Defeat at Adrianople AD 378* (Barnsley: Pen and Sword, 2015).

Robert Gonzalez, Hugh Gusterson, and Gustaaf Houtman (eds.), *Militarization: A Reader* (Durham: Duke University Press, 2019) which contains essays by Dwight Eisenhower, Margaret Mead, Noel Perrin, Naoko Shibusawa, Leslie Sponsel, and Robert Lifton. Plus wide-ranging looks at women in economy and war, the military and masculinity and war, culture and counterinsurgency.

Bob Gordon, "The Quiet Heroine," *Military History,* Vol. 37, #2 (Summer 2020), p. 16. The amazing story of the French woman who worked with the Resistance from 1941 to 1945, earning the French Legion d'Honneur, the British George Medal, and the U.S. Distinguished Service Cross. A remarkable heroine who, captured by the Gestapo and interrogated for three months, never cracked, and, when released, went to London and parachuted back into France on behalf of de Gaulle's Free French Forces.

Mary Gordon, *Joan of Arc* (New York: Viking Penguin, 2002). Although she made none of the major decisions of the various campaigns in which she fought, and although she was eventually convicted and burned alive on a charge of being a transvestite, "Is it possible to say that she fought like a knight but otherwise didn't behave like one?" The author answers this question in the affirmative.

William Gotterman, "Zenobia," in *Improbable Women: Five Who Explored the Middle East* (Syracuse: Syracuse University Press, 2013). A most breezy introduction to Zenobia, who is oddly yoked to five other women who came to the Middle East from afar. Strange business this.

Julie Gottlieb, *Feminine Fascism* (London: I. B. Tauris, 2000). This interesting study is determined to give "women their due as autonomous historical agents" by looking at "a polyphony of women." Puts a spotlight on some understudied women. Useful appendix.

Nimmi Gowrinathan, "The Committed Female Fighter: The Political Identities of Tamil Women in the Liberation Tigers of Tamil Eelam," *International Feminist Journal of Politics,* Vol. 19, #3 (2017), pp. 327–341. Looks at a number of case studies of actual Tamil fighters and concludes that their attitudes going forward are shaped by their individual experiences with militarization.

Dale Torston Graden, *From Slavery to Freedom in Brazil: Bahia, 1835–1900* (Albuquerque: University of New Mexico Press, 2006). Asserts that "The involvement of Bahian women in the overthrow of slavery in the province of Bahia is one of many hidden histories that merits future study" (p. 227).

David Graff and Robin Higham (eds.), *A Military History of China* (Boulder: Westview Press, 2002). See their introduction, which decries "the understudied subject of women in Chinese warfare" and especially Maochun Yu's fine account "The Taiping Rebellion: A Military Assessment of Revolution and

Counterrevolution," pp. 135–151. Yu maintains that women were widely used in combat units because the ideology of the rebels proclaims men and women as strict equals and attacked Confucianism, which had women staying indoors and far from military affairs. He also asserts that women of the Hakka minority did not practice foot binding and were therefore more useful in combat, giving evidence of their importance to the key battles at Guilin and Changsha.

Note: For further in-depth accounts of the Taiping Rebellion which lasted from 1850 to 1864 and resulted in 20 million deaths, see Stephen Platt, *Autumn in the Heavenly Kingdom* (New York: Alfred A. Knopf, 2000) and Chin Shunshin's long historical novel, *The Taiping Rebellion* (London: M. E. Sharpe, 1982).

Alison Graham-Bertolini, *Vigilante Women in Contemporary American Fiction* (New York: Palgrave Macmillan, 2011). See especially her chapter "Women Warriors and Women with Weapons," which concludes, "In sum, contemporary stories of women warriors traverse racial boundaries, class boundaries and boundaries that prescribe gender and sexuality for women."

Saxo Grammaticus, *The History of the Danes* (Lanham, MD: Rowman & Littlefield, 1979). This reprint of the 13th-century work (which is notorious for mixing myth and reality) does provide accounts of Viking woman warriors, the subsequent proof of which is now attested to by archaeological findings of the graves of Scandinavian women buried with weapons.

Anat Granit-Hacohen, *Hebrew Women Join the Forces: Jewish Women from Palestine in the British Forces during the Second World War* (London: Vallentine Mitchell, 2017). An enlightening look at the many Jewish women who participated in World War II in this fashion, some of whom later fought with the Hagenah in the struggle for the establishment of the state of Israel.

Note: For a short introduction to the war that created the modern state of Israel, see Benny Morris, "Lashing Back," *MHQ: The Quarterly Journal of Military History*, Vol. 21, #3 (Spring 2009), pp. 30–41. Morris ranks Jewish unity and Arab disunity as major factors in the eventual success of the Jewish forces in establishing their own state.

Susan R. Grayzel, "The Role of Women in the War," in Hew Strachan (ed.), *First World War* (London: Oxford University Press, 2011), pp. 149–163. Looking at both individuals and groups, the author highlights the important work done by them in a variety of venues, including industrial production (40% of Russian, 33% of French) and especially the impact of the war in giving women the vote in Austria, Belgium, Britain, Latvia, Hungary, Lithuania, Germany, Denmark, Netherlands, the United States, and Czechoslovakia, among others.

Miranda Green, *Celtic Goddesses: Warriors, Virgins and Mothers* (New York: George Braziller, 1996). Argues that for the Romans "only a primitive society would entertain the ideas of involving women as participants in battle and even as warrior-rulers" (p. 28) and in her chapter "Goddesses of War," she quotes Ammianus, Arrian, Plutarch, Tacitus, and Caesar to set a context then looks at the ferocity of Celtic women in, near, and around battles despite these Roman prejudices.

Janny Groen and Annieke Kranenberg, *Women Warriors for Allah: An Islamist Network in the Netherlands* (Philadelphia: University of Pennsylvania Press, 2010). Using the Hofstad group as a case study, the authors probe the motivations and actions of the women of jihad, finding that many have even more radical views than their male counterparts.

Monika Gronke, *Iran: A Short History* (Princeton: Marcus Wiener Publishers, 2006). While this brief introduction to the Arab conquest of Persia does not mention the women warriors by name, its opening chapter describes the reasons for the largely abortive uprisings against the first four caliphs despite the efforts of such Persian women warriors as Apranik, Negan Azad Deylami, Banu, and others. A much more in-depth study of the Arab conquest of Persia is found in Peter Crawford, *The War of the Three Gods: Romans, Persians and the Rise of Islam* (New York: Skyhorse Publishing, 2014). See especially "Stealing Roman Bread and Persian Heart," pp. 167–195. An excellent map of Arab conquest routes in Persia can be found on page 193.

   Note: A good introduction to the revolts of Babak Khorramdin and other from 816–837 is Koveh Farrokh, "An Overview of the Historical Circumstances that led to the Revolts of Babak Khorramdin," *Persian Heritage*, Vol. 19, #74 (Summer 2014), pp. 21–23. A fuller account can be found in Khodadad Rezakhani, "The Rebellion of Babak and the Historiography of the Southern Caucasus," in H. Berberian and T. Daryaee (eds.), *Reflections of Armenian Identity in History and Historiography* (Irvine: University of California Jordan Center for Persian Studies, 2010), pp. 55–70. For an older, more comprehensive narrative of the history of the broader region, see G. Le Strange, *The Lands of the Eastern Caliphate: Mesopotamia, Persia, and Central Asia from the Moslem Conquest to the Time of Timur* (London: Frank Cass, 1966).

Daniel Guiet and Timothy Smith, *Scholars of Mayhem* (New York: Penguin Books, 2019). Although primarily about Jean Claude Guiet and his OSS and SOE exploits, it also chronicles the wartime activities of English warrior Violette Szabo, who fought with Guiet's team and the Maquis in the Limoges region against the German Das Reich SS Division. She would earn the St. George Cross for her bravery during the fight against the Germans. She was subsequently captured and tortured by them before being executed at the Ravensbrück concentration camp.

Niel Gunson, "Sacred Women Chiefs and Female 'Headman' in Polynesian History," *Journal of Pacific History,* Vol. 22, #3 (1987), pp. 139–172. The author believes that the role of women, both in terms of politics and standing as well as in terms of warriorhood, was submerged by missionaries and early anthropologists and needs to be revised significantly. For example, in Polynesia, "the *mana* of a great warrior was inherited through his daughter, not a son." (p. 139) Female headmen were common in Polynesia and "Very often they were known for their prowess in warfare" (p. 142) whether on Tonga, Samoa, Tahiti, the Society or Cook Islands, or the Marquesas.

Alisha Haridasani Gupta, "Rani of Jhansi," *New York Times*, August 19, 2019, pp. D8. Quite a nice write-up of the woman warrior about whom the British general who defeated her during the Indian Rebellion of 1857 said, "The Indian Mutiny had produced but one man and that man was a woman."
   Note: See Gregory Fremont-Barnes, *The Indian Mutiny 1857–58* (Oxford: Osprey Publishing, 2007) for a short introduction to the entire campaign from uprising to final suppression, pp. 91–106.

Archana Garodia Gupta, *The Women Who Ruled India: Leaders. Warriors. Icons* (Gurugram: Hachette India, 2019). Stimulating, albeit breezy, portraits of Rani of Jhansi, Chand Bibi, Rani Karnavati, and Begum Samru, among others.

Stephanie Gutmann, *The Kinder, Gentler Military: Can America's Gender-Neutral Fighting Force Still Win Wars?* (New York: Scribner, 2000). The author takes singular exception to the way the U.S. military has tried to integrate and feminize the armed forces, declaring the process has greatly weakened America's fighting capabilities and concluding, "Living in the real world is so much more interesting and fun than attempting to live in a politically correct state enforced by threats, fear, constant vigilance, and policing" (p. 285).

Barton C. Hacker, "Women and Military Institutions in Early Modern Europe: A Reconnaissance," *Signs,* Vol. 17 (1981), pp. 643–671. The author argues that in Europe from the 14th to the 18th century, large numbers of women participated in military campaigns, sometimes the ratio of noncombatants to combatants was two to three and, in fact, the armies could not function without these women, who provided supply, nursing, morale, and other services. He also points out that women took part as combatants in a number of situations such as the Dutch wars of independence against Spain, the English Civil War, the American and French Revolutions, and the Spanish war of independence against France.

Barton Hacker and Margaret Vining (eds.), *A Companion to Women's Military History* (Leiden: Brill, 2012). Contains a wide variety of pieces covering women and their participation in warfare across a broad set of topics. Most useful for readers of this volume is chapter 3, "Essential Women: Necessary Wives, and Exemplary Soldiers: The Military Reality and Cultural Representation of Women's Military Participation (1600–1815)" by John Lynn, pp. 93–136.

Janet Hart, *New Voices in the Nation: Women and the Greek Resistance, 1941–1964* (Ithaca: Cornell University Press, 2009). A substantial look at the myriad of important roles women played in the Greek resistance against the Nazis, the Greek Civil War, and beyond. Shows how the heroines of the resistance became enemies of the state. Poignant.

Andrew and Nicola Hallam, *Lady Under Fire: The Wartime Letters of Lady Dorothie Fielding MM 1914–1917* (South Yorkshire: Pen and Sword, 2010). Dorothie Fielding was the first English women to be awarded the Military Medal for bravery in the field. Working as an intrepid ambulance driver and "dodging shells and misogynist officers," she showed great compassion and courage under fire and wrote with dry wit: "It's topping being up near things and so jolly and interesting." Quite an adventurous role model.

E. Hancock, "Women as Killers and Killing Women: The Implications of 'Gender Neutral' Armed Forces," in M. Evans and A. Ryan (eds.), *The Human Face of Warfare* (St. Leonards: Allen and Unwin, 2002). Puts in sharp focus a number of the conundrums and differing moral and ethical aspects of "gender neutrality" when it comes to warfare.

Catherine Hanley, *Matilda: Empress Queen Warrior* (New Haven: Yale University Press, 2019). An outstanding work, not simply because it is the best biography of Empress Matilda (1102–1167) but because it casts into sharp relief the prejudice against female warriorhood, especially where it does not involve putting on armor and fighting at the front. In arguing for Matilda's inclusion in the warrior company, Hanley argues persuasively that:

> Military generalship involved more than merely riding into battle; the political and strategic decision taken around the command table were as important a maneuvers in the field, and Matilda knew this. It was, after all, her crown. (pp. 122–123)

And what a life story it is. Sent off to be married by the King of England Henry I when she was eight years old and later married to the son of The Holy Roman Emperor Henry V, whose holdings included much of what is now German, Switzerland, Luxembourg, the Netherlands, the Czech Republic, Belgium, and the northern third of Italy. Queen of Germany, Empress of the Holy Roman Emperor, widowed at the age of 23 when Henry V died in 1125 and remarried to Geoffrey of Anjou, a 13-year-old old boy, she is in line for the English throne when her brother, the heir apparent, dies and Henry I gets his nobles to agree. But when Henry I dies in 1135, Stephen of Blois, his nephew, gets to England first and proclaims himself king, she returns to England, lands in Arundel, and actively seeks to win in battle, as a contemporary chronicle, *History of the Dukes of Normandy and the Kings of England*, declares:

> The Empress rode with the army every day and gave the best and most valuable advice; in all the army there was no baron as astute or as experienced in war as she. (p. 123)

She was in control of the logistical operations during the civil war, made the deals that marked her successes and failures, and was directly involved in several military campaigns (Le Sap 1136, Winchester in 1141, Oxford in 1142, and Arundel in 1139) and was eventually outmaneuvered by another woman, Queen Matilda of Boulogne, wife of King Stephen. But she was master over the decision-making process and at the command table as the tide of battle swung back and forth during the long and bloody time of troubles known as "The Anarchy." Although she would never become queen in England (having to settle for "The Lady of the English"), her son Henry II would be the next king after Stephen and would begin the Plantagenet line on the English throne. For our part, we think the most telling argument for her warriorhood comes from the *Deeds of Stephen*, written by her opponents:

> After strengthening and encouraging her garrison to resist the kin, she sent a great many troops of cavalry to plunder in every direction, earnestly besought, by letter and message, those who were bound to her by faith and homage to lend the best support to her enterprise, and fortified castles in various places, wher-

ever she most conveniently could, some to keep the king's men more effectively in check, some to give her own more careful protection. (p. 184)

Note: For a useful overview of the military tactics and weapons used during "the Anarchy," see Chris Peers, *King Stephen and The Anarchy: Civil War and Military Tactics in Twelfth-Century Britain* (Barnsley: Pen and Sword Books, 2018). Contains a very useful "Who Was Who in 'The Anarchy,'" pp. 157–172. Very little on Matilda as a female warrior, however, and takes a very male-centric view of the period, although the author gives some credit to Matilda of Boulogne for her part in the war and diplomacy of the period.

Note: Matilda's martial reputation is thought by some to have been the inspiration for Alfred Lord Tennison's poem "Maud" (1855).

Abdelmajid Hannoum, "Historiography, Mythology, and Memory in Modern North Africa: The Story of the Kahina," *Studia Islamica*, #85 (1997), pp. 85–130. Using extensive sources from all the backstories of Kahina, the Berber woman warrior who resisted the Arab invaders, the author concludes that there is an Algerian heroine, a Tunisian heroine, *and* an antiheroine, an Egyptian figure, an anti-colonialist Kahina, an enemy of the Muslims, a Jewish heroine, an enemy of the Arabs, and perhaps most of all, a female heroine regardless of origin. Quite an intriguing mix of perceptions, right?

Note: For a fuller examination of all these issues, see Hannoum's extensive and useful work *Colonial Histories, Post-Colonial Memories: The Legend of the Kahina North African Heroine* (Portsmouth: Heinemann, 2001).

Peter Harrington, "Women in War," *MHQ: The Quarterly Journal of Military History,* Vol. 22, #1 (Autumn 2009), pp. 88–93. An engaging look at women at war through the eyes of various artists. There is Eugene Delacroix's "Liberty Leading the People," David Wilkie's "The Defense of Saragossa," and Francisco de Goya "And they are like wild beasts" among others.

Kathryn Harrison, *Joan of Arc: A Life Transfigured* (New York: Doubleday, 2014). An extraordinary work examining in great detail many sources including the thousands of pages from her two trials (one held long after her death to exonerate her), Harrison goes into excellent and telling detail about her military activities and weaves into the narrative a parallel construction of the life of Jesus. Anyone doing a project on Joan of Arc should avail themselves of this source.

Zaur Hasanov, "The Cult of Female Warriors and Rulers in the Scythian and Sarmatian Cultures," *Annales Universitatis Apulensis, Series Historia*, Vol. 1, #22 (June 2018), pp. 131–150. Extensive examination of graves in the Northern Black Sea region has produced many of women with weapons, queens, and "ordinary" women leading to wondering if queens ever used weapons. So far, the evidence is inconclusive, although the author does not deal conclusively with the 2nd century BCE Sarmatian queen Amage, who attacked the Scythians.

Ewa Hauser, "Traditions of Patriotism, Questions of Gender: The Case of Poland," in Ellen Barry (ed.), *Genders 22: Postcommunism and the Body Politic* (New York: New York University Press, 1995), pp. 78–104. With special emphasis on Adam Mickiewicz (1798–1855) and his paean to the "hero-martyr," Emilia Plater. Mickiewicz's "Death of a Colonel" concludes with:

> On a shepherd's cot he is laid out—
> In his hand a cross, by his head a saddle and belt,
> By his side, a sword and a rifle.
> But this warrior though in a soldier's attire,
> What a beautiful, maiden's face had he?
> What breasts?—Ah, this was a maiden,
> Lithuanian born, a maiden-hero,
> The leader of the uprising—Emilia Plater.

Thomas R. H. Havens, *Valley of Darkness: The Japanese People and World War Two* (New York: W.W. Norton and Company, 1978). While focusing on the Japanese home islands, this account offers a tantalizingly brief account of the "Lilly Brigade" (*Himeyuri Butai*), a unit of young women that was wiped out in the battle for Okinawa (p. 189). More detail is provided, however, on how Japanese housewives were trained to be civilian Kamikazes, attacking American troops while armed only with bamboo spears for the final "Decisive Battle," the Ketsu Go, when the United States finally invaded the Home Islands.

———, "Women and War in Japan, 1937–45," *American Historical Review*, Vol. 80, #4 (1975), pp. 913–934. Unfortunately, most of this article deals with the impacts of World War II on women in civilian and economic life but does point out that five million women were involved in the Japanese labor market during the period 1937–1945.

Anne Haverty, *Constance Markievicz: An Independent Life* (London: Pandora, 1988). See especially chapter 10, "The Easter Revolution, 1916," pp. 144–158. Points out that the revolutionaries could have seized the Castle early in the Rising, but probably could not have held it although it would have been a much better symbol of the Rising than the Post Office. Says that 15 out of 120 revolutionaries at St. Stephens Green were women and mentions a "sister sniper" of Constance's, Margaret Skinnider.

David Hay, *The Military Leadership of Matilda of Canossa 1046–1115* (Manchester: Manchester University Press, 2008). "The most powerful woman of her time," Matilda of Canossa led in war and battle for 40 years, putting popes on the throne and keeping them there and defeating the Holy Roman Emperor Henry IV in battle at Sorbara (1084) and for six years afterward. Well-documented scholarship enables the author to declare her "one of the most successful military commanders of the age."

Jennifer Heath, *The Scimitar and the Veil* (Mahwah: Hidden Spring, 2004). A paean to the women of Islam in all walks of life and in all incarnations. The chapter "Women Warriors and Amazons" contains portraits of women combatants such as Umm Omara, Umm Salim, Nisiba bint Ka'ah, and Safiyya.

Mary Jennings Hegar, *Shoot Like a Girl: One Woman's Dramatic Fight in Afghanistan and on the Home Front* (New York: The New American Library, 2017). A bittersweet account of one woman's fight to fly and fight and the obstacles she faced before, during and after she was wounded in combat during a dramatic rescue mission in Afghanistan. Very telling on the reentry process and the ongoing pull of the allure of combat as she states categorically, "Nothing I tried could get me that high I'd become addicted to."

Peter Hegseth, *Modern Warriors; Real Stories From Real Heroes* (New York: Fox News Books, 2020). Good focus on a female Navy weapons officer on a Super Hornet, Caroline Johnson, one of the first woman fighting against ISIS in Syria, Iraq, and Afghanistan, doing 42 missions in combat. See pp. 191–209.

Jaymie Patricia Heilman, "Family Ties: The Political Genealogy of Shining Path's Comrade Norah," *Journal of the Society for Latin American Studies,* Vol. 29, #2 (2010), pp. 155–169. Heilman claims, with clear justification, that "Family was central to the political life of Augusta La Torre (or Comrade Norah), the second-in-command of the Peruvian Communist Party-Shining Path (PCP-SL). La Torre was the daughter of a Communist Party militant and the granddaughter of a prominent provincial political figure. She was also the wife of Shining Path founder Abimael Guzmán." (p. 155). Trifecta.
    Note: For additional context and depth dealing with contemporary events in Peru, consult Miguel La Serna, *With Masses and Arms: Peru's Tupac*

Amaru Revolutionary Movement (Chapel Hill: The University of North Carolina Press, 2019).

Dagmar Hellmann-Rajanayagam, "Female Warriors, Martyrs and Suicide Attackers: Women in The LTTE," *International Review of Modern Sociology*, Vol. 34, #1 (Spring 2008), pp. 1–25. The author argues that although there were some suicide bombers among the LTTE, the real motivation of the Tigers was not to die but to fight and that their attitude was often to feel superior to other women (who in turn often feel uncomfortable), and their life in warfare seems to give them an added sense of autonomy.

James Henderson and Linda Roddy Henderson, *Ten Notable Women of Latin America* (Chicago: Nelson Hall, 1978). Among these tales of poets, spies, and grand, caring ladies are some women warriors from the Nun Ensign to Tania. Somewhat romantic in conception and presentation, but still providing context for women who inspired and led. Some almost ethereal pen wash drawings of the women in question.

Benjamin Hendrickx, "Al-Kahina: The Last Ally of the Roman-Byzantines in the Maghreb Against the Muslim Arab Conquest?," *Journal of Early Christian History,* Vol. #3, #2, pp. 47–61. A superb unwinding of the myths and legends surrounding Al-Kahina, squarely putting her in reality of Roman-Byzantine ideology and military tradition, the *symmachoi*. Arab incursions from Egypt into Roman-Byzantine Africa from 663 onward, while they ultimately achieved success, had numerous failures and setbacks, the Muslims being defeated by a coalition of Berbers and King Kusyla and Byzantine forces in 683. After Kusyla's death, however, the Berbers regrouped around Al Kahina, advancing behind the use of Christ icon, which the author identifies as the *Hodigitria*, the Mother of God with Christ, as a baby, pointing the way to victory. Eventually, despite her early successes, the Arabs eventually conquered them, and the Berbers gave up their Christian faith and adopted Islam.

Heather Hennes, "Bringing the Bicentennials into the Language and Culture Classroom," *Hispania*, Vol. 94, #2 (June 2011), pp. 348–359. Illustrates the way heroic women warriors from the past are now being woven into the fabric of national life as part of the history of revolution in Venezuela and Mexico and utilizing the stories of Manuela Saenz and Gertudis Bocanegra.

———. "Viking Warrior Women? Reassessing Birka Chamber Grave Bj.581," *Antiquity*, Vol. 93, #367 (2011), pp. 181–198. Makes a strong case that the Birka grave not only proves she was a Viking warrior, but urges a more careful reexamination of Viking Age warrior graves to test DNA for additional female counterparts.

Note: The reexamination of the Birka chamber grave using advanced DNA techniques has spurred their use in other explorations. Among the news findings are a 9,000-year-old woman with hunting weapons found in the Andes. The transition from female hunter to female warrior seems relatively easy to imagine as the 5th-century South American grave of a Moche woman buried with war weapons in what is now Peru adds to our growing knowledge of ancient women warriors.

Note: Increasingly the term "burials with weapons" has been adopted to replace the early, more subjective "warrior burial." See Matthew Lloyd, "Death of a Swordsman, Death of a Sword: The Killing of Swords in the Early Iron Age Aegean (ca. 1050–ca. 690 B.C.E.)," in Geoff Lee, Helene Whittaker, and Graham Wrightson (eds.), *Ancient Warfare: Introducing Current Research* (Newcastle upon Tyne: Cambridge Scholars Publishing, 2015), pp. 14–31.

Tamara Herath, *Women in Terrorism: Case of the LTTE* (Los Angeles: Sage, 2002). The Liberation Tigers of Tamil Eelam (LTTE) are examined in the context of the 30 years of warfare in Sri Lanka. The author argues that the liberation movement has provided an alternative bonding experience for the women involved.

Melissa Herbert, *Camouflage Is Not Only for Combat* (New York: New York University Press, 1998). The author argues that the military is a "gendered institution" and as such women are often judged to be either "too masculine" or "too feminine" by that culture and the military's masculine ideology will continue to limit women's participation in the military for the military service as long as the military remains a male domain for the achievement of manhood.

Margaux Herman, *Sabla Wangêl, the Queen of the Kingdom of Heaven* (Master's Thesis, Addis Ababa University, 2009). Well documented and carefully researched. Herman makes a strong case for the political importance of Wangel in the 16th century and shows her interaction with the Portuguese. Does not make a claim for any military leadership actions on her part.

Herodotus, *The Landmark Histories*, in Robert Strassler (ed.) (New York: Anchor Books, 2007). Quoting Admiral Artemisia from Halicarnassus extensively, Herodotus has her speaking truth to power and telling King Xerxes not to engage the Greek fleet at Salamis, saying "But if you rush into a sea battle immediately, I fear that your fleet will be badly mauled, which would cause the ruin of your land army as well" (8.68). Other admirals think she would be killed for speaking so frankly. But Herodotus reports:

> When these opinions were reported to Xerxes, however, he was quite pleased with Artemisia's answer. Even prior to this, he had considered her worthy of his serious attention, but now he held her in even higher regard. Nevertheless, his orders were to obey the majority; he strongly suspected that off Euboea they had behaved like cowards because he was not present, but now he was fully prepared to watch them fight at sea. (8.69)

Indeed, after the Persian and allied fleet was destroyed by the Greeks, Xerxes would entrust his son to Artemisia for the trip back to Asia Minor.

Note: The roots of the Persian invasion began when the Greek Ionian states (in what is now Turkey) revolted and the Persians eventually retaliated against Athens, which supported their revolt. See Marc DeSantis, "Revolt of the Ionians," *MHQ: The Quarterly Journal of Military History,* Vol. 22, #2 (Winter 2121), pp. 70–78.

Charlton Heston (narrator), "Women Spies and Warriors," *Secrets of War* (Mill Creek Entertainment DVD), Unit #5 (1998). Looks at actual women working at warcraft during World War II in the American OSS (Organization of Strategic Services), the British SOE (Special Operations Executive), and the SIS (Secret Intelligence Service) as well as the French Resistance. A wide range of important activity by women is chronicled.

Linda Heywood, *Njinga of Angola: Africa's Warrior Queen* (Cambridge: Harvard University Press, 2017). An amazingly rich biography of a strong warrior woman who dominated south central Africa (present-day Angola) from 1624 to 1663. Her military prowess, including a decade-long stretch of successful battles both guerrilla and set-piece (1624–1663), is matched only by her strategic and diplomatic efforts as she played the Portuguese, Dutch and African tribes off against each other, even communicating with the Pope Alexander VII. Also noteworthy is her successful flouting of gender norms (she took both men and women as lovers and sometimes dressed as a man but then made her male lovers dress as women) and her most skillful blending of Mbundu, Impangala (Jaga), and Christian traditions to support her legitimacy.

Margaret Randolph Higonnet, Jane Jenson, Sonya Michel, and Margaret Collins Weitz (eds.), *Behind the Lines: Gender in the Two World Wars* (New Haven: Yale University Press, 1987). A wide-ranging set of essays looking at various war-related impacts on both women and men. The editors declare it is a myth "that men are naturally fierce and warlike while women are mothers and have an affinity for peace." Central to the work is the trope of Higonnets, "the double helix" (see below) which underscores the "illusory nature of wartime change in World War I and II" and declares "a feminist revision of the *time* in war can make the history of war more sensitive to the full range of experience of both men and women."

Margaret Randolph Higonnet and Patrice L. R. Higonnet, "The Double Helix," in *Behind the Lines: Gender in the Two World Wars* (New Haven: Yale University Press, 1987), pp. 31–47. The authors assert that men and women are two strands of a linked "double helix" in which, regardless of the level of either, the female strand is made subordinate. Therefore, it asks and answers the question, "When is change not change? The social and economic roles of many women undergo rapid and radical transformation both at the onset of war, and, in a symmetrically opposed direction at its conclusion."

   Note: A most interesting variation on this theme is found in Bridget María Chesterton, "Composing Gender and Class: Paraguayan Letter Writers during the Chaco War, 1932–1935," *Journal of Women's History*, Vol. 26, #3 (Fall 2014), pp. 59–80, which shows how during the Chaco War, many upper-class women became *madrinas de guerra* (godmothers of war) and wrote to lower-class *ahijads de guerra* (godsons of war) in order to boost their morale, but "As soon as the men left the battlefield, strict notions about the proper distance between rural men and elite women returned to the pre-war norm" (p. 75). This work also provides a surprisingly succinct account of the 1923–1935 Chaco War's origins and outcomes: the 1939 peace treaty gave Paraguay most of its claims to the Chaco frontier, and Bolivia got port rights on the Paraguay River.

Vera Hildebrand, *Women at War: Subhas Chandra Bose and the Rani of Jhansi Regiment* (New York: Harper Collins, 2016). A fascinating history of the women who joined that regiment of the Indian National Army during World War II. Recruited in 1943 from Indian families in Malaya, Singapore, and Burma, these women and the INA fought with the Japanese for the independence of India from British rule. Regarded as traitors by the British, the INA, and the Rani of Jhansi, Regiment members became heroes and heroines to many Indians, especially after 1947. Named for the 1857 Rani of Jhansi, and led by Lakshmi Bai Swaminathan Sehgal (1914–2012), the unit was sent to Burma during the Battle of Imphal (1944–1945) and eventually retreated all the way from Rangoon to Bangkok. Although the Ranis never saw direct action as a coherent unit, they were under severe attack by Allied planes, and several were also killed by sniper fire and disease.

Kristina Hilliard and Kate Wurtzel, "Power and Gender in Ancient Egypt: The Case of Harshepsut," *Art Education*, Vol. 62, #3 (2009), pp. 25–31. Shows how this female pharaoh depicted herself to the largely illiterate Egyptian population as both a male and a female, descendent from the gods, in order to enhance her legitimacy.

   Note: For a useful introduction to the armed forces of ancient Egypt, see Nic Fields, *Soldier of the Pharaoh* (Oxford: Osprey Publications, 2007) and Terence Wise, *Ancient Armies of the Middle East* (Oxford: Osprey Publications, 1981).

Richard Hingley and Christina Unwin, *Boudica: Iron Age Warrior Queen* (London: Hambledon and London, 2005). Calling Boudica "a woman of many faces," the authors point out how she is at once an actual ruler, an imperial icon and an impediment to Rome's declared "civilizing" mission. They urge us to look to archaeology for the foundation of her facts.

———, "Warrior Queen," in *National Geographic History* (September–October 2019), pp. 53–59. A breezier version of the above account of the Rani with some nice illustrations, especially the battle formations thought to have occurred during her final battle near the Anker River.

———, "Big Bad Boudica: Britain Rebels Against Rome," *National Geographic History* (September/October 2019), pp. 46–58. A brief summary of the work above but with excellent maps showing the routes of her conquest and a diagram of her last battle.

Marko Attila Hoare, *Genocide and Resistance in Hitler's Bosnia: The Partisans and the Chetniks* (London: Oxford University Press, 2006). Clearly establishes that the Partisans achieved what they did precisely because of their inclusion of large numbers of women whereas the Chetniks did not. See especially "Women in the Partisans," pp. 285–289.

Jean Holm, *Women in the Military: An Unfinished Revolution* (Novato: Presidio, 1982). This Air Force major general provides an extensive history of women and the military from World War I through the first Gulf War, arguing that women should be allowed to take their rightful place in combat. Dedicated to Major Marie Rossi, who lost her life in the first Iraq war, this should be required reading for all those who wish to know how hard it has been for women in the United States to fight for their country and receive the opportunity to do so. A very necessary examination of the obstacles they have faced. More power to those who have persevered.

Kirsten Holmstedt, *Band of Sisters: American Women at War in Iraq* (Mechanicsburg: Stackpole, 2007). The author looks carefully at the experience of women Marines and finds that most felt they were just doing their job, but with more than 500 women killed or wounded in the Iraq wars, more of them were clearly in combat than many in American society understood at the time or even now.

————, *The Girls Come Marching Home: Stories of Women Warriors Returning from War in Iraq* (Mechanicsburg: Stackpole, 2009). Pointing out that the 2003 war in Iraq sufficiently blurred the lines between combat and noncombat roles for women, the author captures both their rising to the occasion and the often heart-wrenching nature of their return. In fact, her interviews of these Marine, Navy, Army, and Air Force veterans as well as the writing of the book produced a post-traumatic stress disorder–like syndrome in Holmstedt for which she had to seek medical treatment. Powerful. To put the return of these specific women and this specific war into the broader context of all returning warriors since the time of Homer, see C. P. Potholm, "The Return of the Warriors" in his *Understanding War* (Lanham: University Press of America, 2016), chapter 38, pp. 575–582.

Maureen Honey, *Creating Rosie the Riveter: Class, Gender and Propaganda during World War II* (Amherst: University of Massachusetts Press, 1984). Shows how World War II got women into the workforce and ended much prejudice about women performing certain jobs through propaganda. But it also shows how after the war, the return to the nuclear family overrode some of the gains, albeit not all.

Doo-Seung Hong, "Women in the South Korean Military," *Current Sociology*, Vol. 50, #5 (September 2002), pp. 729–743. Finds the American military much more open to female talent than its South Korean counterpart despite the greater militarization of that society.

Fan Hong, "'Iron Bodies': Women, War and Sport in the Early Communist Movement in Modern China," *Journal of Sport History*, Vol. 24, #1 (Spring 1997), pp. 1–23. With "grander" goals than sheer feminism, Mao and the early Communists produced athletic, hardened women warriors with "iron bodies" to further the revolution.

For a useful introduction to the political importance of women during the period in question, see Jung Chang, *Big Sister, Little Sister, Red Sister: Three Women at the Heart of Twentieth-Century China* (New York: Alfred A. Knopf, 2019). The incredible story of the American-educated Soon sisters: Red Sister (Ching-ling), the wife of Sun Yat-sen and later Mao's vice-chairman; Little Sister (Mi-ling) who married Chiang Kai-shek, and Big Sister (Ei-ling) who made a huge fortune on her own and advised Chiang as well.

Note: For an illustrated and brief introduction to the Chinese Civil War, see Michael Lynch, *The Chinese Civil War 1945–49* (Oxford: Osprey Publishing, 2010). For a broader perspective on Chinese women seeking equality, see also Li Yu-ning (ed.), *Chinese Women Through Chinese Eyes* (London: M. E. Sharpe, 1992), "Chinese Women's Fight for Freedom," pp. 87–101.

Note: While many works focus on Mao's theoretical and political skills, Geoffrey Perret in "Warrior Mao," *MHQ: The Quarterly Journal of Military History*, Vol. 19 (Spring 2007), pp. 6–15, looks at his actual war-fighting experience.

James W. Hoover, "Holkar, Anilyabhai," in Pennington, *op. cit.*, pp. 205–209. The author makes a convincing case that Holkar (1715–1795), the Rani of Indore, played a key role in preventing the Mughals from taking over the Maratha Confederacy from her position in Malwa, which abutted Mughal forces at Delhi. He shows that on the death of her husband and then her father-in-law, she assumed military and political control and led her troops in battle, often on an elephant. She was indeed in charge of the Maratha artillery in the Battle of Panipat (1761), one of the largest battles of that era. Although the Mughals won, she subsequently maintained her hold on Malwa and defeated several uprisings and attempts to defeat her.

Note: For an Indian perspective on the role of women during the period of Mughal dominance, see Rkha Misra, *Women in Mughal India 1526–1749* (Delhi: Munshiram Manoharlal, 1967).

John Horne, "1848 and the Language of Politics," *Saothar*, Vol. 25 (2000), pp. 67–76. Not much about women warriors per se but provides good background on the intellectual and conceptual aspects of the Revolutions of 1848 and the women's varying outlooks on the importance of specific goals as they fought against the male hegemony of the era.

Myra Ann Houser, "Avenging Carlota in Africa: Angola and the Memory of Cuban Slavery," *Atlantic Studies*, Vol. 12, #1 (2015), pp. 50–66. The author finds that "Carlota the Afro-Cuban and the woman had become an appropriate symbol for Cuban troops in Africa during the century preceding her use. Afro-Cubans served in their country's military in large numbers, and women enlisted during both the liberation struggle and the revolution" (p. 57).

Note: For an in-depth look at the mid-18th-century slave revolts in Cuba, see Aisha Finch, *Rethinking Slave Rebellion in Cuba: La Escalera and the Insurgencies of 1841–1844* (Chapel Hill: University of North Carolina Press, 2015). The author traces the interconnections between urban and rural resistance and the rise and violent suppression of those who challenged the plantation system with skill and dispatch and feeling. She has also written a somewhat broader-gauge investigation of race, gender, and masculinity in this era. See her "The Repeating Rebellion: Slave Resistance and Political Consciousness in Nineteenth Century Cuba 1812–1844," in Aisha Finch and Fannie Rushing, *Breaking the Chains Forging a Nation: The Afro-Cuban Fight for Freedom and Equality 1812–1912* (Baton Rouge: Louisiana State University Press, 2019), pp. 138–157. Michele Reid-Vazquez, "Formidable Rebels: Enslaved and Free Women of Color in Cuba's Conspiracy of Las Escalera, 1843–1844," in the same volume provides additional depth to the analysis of La Escalera, pp. 158–177. Finch is also the author of "'What Looks Like a Revolution": Enslaved Women and the Gendered Terrain of Slave Insurgencies in Cuba, 1843–1844," *Journal of Women's History,* Vol. 26, #1 (Spring 2014), pp. 112–134 in which she highlights "the variegated ways that a wide spectrum of women came to the movement, defining its ideologies, scripting its notions of masculinity, and leading and executing its most difficult labors" (p. 133). In the process, she highlights the participation of Fermina and Carlota, two African-born women of the Lucumi nation.

Georgina Howell, *Gertrude Bell: Queen of the Desert, Shaper of Nations* (New York: Farrar, Straus and Giroux, 2007). Billed as "the driving force behind the creation of Iraq," this remarkable woman was the first female officer in the history of modern British intelligence and served with distinction during World War I. King Faisal said she had "a genius for war," and she did. See especially the chapters, "War Work" and "Cairo, Delhi, Basra." Gives a good glimpse into the sacrifices made by the peoples of the British Empire to the World War I effort—192,000 were killed, captured, or "went missing," and 300,000 were recruited from India alone.

Swanee Hunt, *Rwandan Women Rising* (Durham: Duke University Press, 2017). While the segment on women military warriors in the Rwandan Patriotic Front (RPF) is small, it does capture the sense of empowerment so many women the world over feel when they have a gun and are treated the same as men: "The women who were soldiers were on the front line, carrying guns like anybody else. No one said, 'This is a man, this is a woman, so therefore you do these things'" (p. 57).

Stephen Hunter, *Sniper's Honor* (New York: Simon & Schuster, 1914). (F) Women warriors continue to fascinate. Witness this novel centered around a Soviet sniper from World War II, nicknamed "the White Witch," Ludmilla "Mili" Petrova.

Duong Thu Huong, *Novel without a Name* (New York: William Morrow, 1995). (F) An absorbing and deeply depressing Vietnamese novel about war in the jungle, lost youth, and the immense problem of keeping one's humanity in the middle of a struggle without end: "In times of war, the future belongs to the combatants." She concludes with "Chants of the months, of the years spent in the Truong Son Mountains. Soldier, the dawn is icy. You fall under the bullets. On the white of the parachute cloth, I see your blood spreading." Powerful and evocative, a fitting counter to "the glories of war," whether in a revolutionary context or not.

Nancy Huston, *The Matrix of War: Mothers and Heroes in Susan Rubin Suleiman, The Female Body in Western Culture* (Cambridge: Harvard University Press, 1986). The author cautions that "Eliminating women from reproduction and integrating them into destruction tends to obfuscate the psycho-historical matrix of war and may prevent us from ever understanding it sufficiently to bring it to an end."

Alexander Ingle, "Arsinoe III Philopator," in Pennington, *op. cit.*, p. 25. Arsinoe III was Queen of Egypt and one of the commanders at the Battle of Raphia. The author argues that the Battle of Raphia was one of the most significant turning points in the history of the Mediterranean world following the death of Alexander and ended up protecting Ptolemaic Egypt until the conquest by Octavian.

Note: For a useful introduction to the Ptolemaic armies, see Arnold Blumberg, "*The Armies of the Ptolomies, 305–30 BC*," *Strategy and Tactics,* #328 (May–June 2021), pp. 34–42.

Sherrie Inness, *Tough Girls: Women Warriors and Wonder Women in Popular Culture* (Philadelphia: University of Pennsylvania Press, 1998). Our society seems to expect a great deal from women. And it is not always easy to fulfill those expectations, even in the military.

Douglas Jackson, *Hero of Rome* (New York: Corgi Books, 2011). (F) Boudica's rebellion seen through the somewhat sympathetic eyes of the Roman legionnaire Valerius. Grudging respect for Celtic warcraft.

Tami Amanda Jacoby, *Women in Zones of Conflict: Power and Resistance in Israel* (Montreal: McGill-Queen's University Press, 2005). The section "The Campaign for Women in Combat in Israel" effectively documents the way the entry of women into combat positions overturned much bias against them, in "the last bastion of male privilege in the modern world."

Sharon Jansen, *The Monstrous Regiment of Women: Female Rulers in Early Modern Europe* (New York: Palgrave Macmillan, 2002). Reacting to John Knox's conviction that women in power is "repugnant to nature" and "the subversion of good orders of all equality and justice," the author dives deeply into the female rulers and regents who helped shape European politics. Quite light on military accomplishments, however.

Jane S. Jaquette, "Women in Revolutionary Movements in Latin America," *Journal of Marriage and Family*, Vol. 35, #2 (May 1973), pp. 344–354. Although perhaps overly ambitious in trying to carry too many themes to a successful conclusion, the author does prove her first assertion that "there is a female revolutionary tradition in Latin America." (p. 344). In the process, she exposes the reader to glimpses of Cecilia Tupac Amaru, Juana Azurduy, Juana Robles, Loreto Sanchez, Margarita Neri, Haydee Santamaria, Celia Sanches, Vilma Espin, Policarpa Salavarrieta, Antonia Sanchez, and others from Cuba, Colombia, Venezuela, Guatemala, Brazil, Bolivia, Argentina, and Uruguay.

George Jennings, "Mexican Female Warrior: The Case of Marisela Ugalde, the Founder of Xilam," *Uploaded MS* (New York: Palgrave Macmillan, 2015), pp. 119–134. The author traces the development Xilam back to the warrior traditions of three previous cultures, the Mexica of central Mexica, the Maya of southern Mexico and Central America, and the Zapotec of the coastal state of Oaxaca.

Caroline Johnson, *Jet Girl: My Life in War, Peace and the Cockpit of the World's Most Lethal Aircraft, the F/A-18 Super Hornet* (New York: St. Martin's Press, 2019). This is one of the few books in this list that is absolutely must reading to understand today's warfare, and the complex crosscurrents to be navigated by women warriors. Johnson, the first woman to drop weapons (as Weapons Officer flying from the U.S. George Bush) in combat against ISIS and flying other missions in Iraq, Afghanistan, and Syria, tells a heartwarming story of her success in training and combat. But she also tells the heart-crushing tale of sexual discrimination and the debilitating aspects of the Navy's culture of male dominance.

Linda Cook Johnson, *Women of the Conquest Dynasties: Gender and Identity in Liao and Jin China* (Honolulu: University of Hawaii Press, 2011). In the turbulent northeast China in what is now Manchuria during the Liao (907–1125) and Jin (1115–1234) dynasties, women of the steppe people were noted warriors. The author looks at the lives of Empress Dowager Chengrian (954–1009) and the bandit leader Yan Miaozhen (d. 1234) as case studies. The women fought with and against both the Song and the Mongols. Yan Miaozhen was made governor by the Mongols after they finally defeated her.

Richard Johnson, "The Role of Women in the Russian Civil War (1917–1921)," *Conflict*, Vol. 2, #2 (1980), pp. 201–217. Over 70,000 women fought in the Russian Civil War and "the contribution women made to the military victory of the Red Army was considerable" (see pp. 207–208).

Steven Johnson, "The Longest War: Vietnam's War of Independence from 111 BC–938 AD," in his *Unknown Wars of Asia, Africa and the Americas That Changed History* (New York: Atlas, 2013). This work contains an exciting story of the Trung sisters and their fight against the Han Chinese. They led an uprising which was one-third women and their initial successes in 39 AD were spectacular, although the Hans eventually returned and crushed the revolt.

Note: For an engaging set of works dealing with Chinese armies from the ancient and early imperial periods, see C. J. Peers, *Ancient Chinese Armies 1500–200 BC* (Oxford: Osprey Publications, 1990) and his *Imperial Chinese Armies 200 BC–AD 589* (Oxford: Osprey Publications, 1995).

David Jones, *Women Warriors: A History* (Washington: Brassey's, 1997). Female warrior heritage is celebrated and judged to be deeper and richer than previously thought, the author concluding, "women can share equally with men the title of warrior." Looking at "the Female Martial Heritage" across time and space, the author concludes "Women's martial history is much richer and deeper by far than is commonly understood in the West." For many women, "the sword is my child." Good section on the World War I and Russia's all-female "Battalions of Death" that fought for the Czar and later, the Provisional Government.

Note: See Anne Eliot Griesse and Richard Stites, "Russia: Revolution and War," in Nancy Loring Goldman (ed.), *Female Soldiers—Combatants or Non Combatants* (reviewed above) which provides a most interesting vignette. On October 25, 1917, a detachment of a Petrograd women's battalion helped the Provisional government turn back a Bolshevik (including women in the Red Guards) attempt to storm the Winter Palace.

J. Graham Jones, *The History of Wales* (Cardiff: University of Wales Press, 2014). A wide-ranging source for the background and context of the Great Revolt of 1136, featuring Gwenllian ferch Gruffydd, albeit little information on her role, whatever it might have been. The same short shrift is given her in John Davies, *A History of Wales* (New York: Penguin Books, 1995).

Gwyn Jones (translator), *The Norse Atlantic Saga* (Oxford: Oxford University Press, 1986). Note especially the account of Freydis Eiriksdottir, the Viking woman warrior who drove off the Skraelings by sharpening a sword on her bare breasts while pregnant, berating the Viking men who were being bested by the Skraelings. The Skraelings fled and the Viking men were presumably embarrassed and ashamed. As well they should have been.

   Note: For further background on Freydis and the other Vikings in North America, see also Gwyn Jones, *A History of the Vikings* (Oxford: Oxford University Press, 1984), Erik Wahlgren, *The Vikings and America* (London: Thames & Hudson, 1986), Eleanor Rosamund Barraclough, *Beyond the Northlands: Viking Voyages and the Old Norse Sagas* (London: oxford University Press, 2014), Lars Brownworth, *The Sea Wolves: A History of the Vikings* (London: Crux Publishing, 1988), and especially Ian Heath, *The Vikings* (Oxford: Osprey Publishing, 1985).

Emily Jordan and Johnathan Jordan, "Women of War," *Military History*, Vol. 37, #4 (November 2020), pp. 22ff. Rounds up the usual suspects from Queen Elizabeth and Njinga to Cleopatra. Does introduce some interesting background on Cleopatra's military activities before the arrival of Julius Caesar. According to the authors, she got her military experience in her struggles with her brother Ptolemy when she took her army of 20,000 into the desert and survived his efforts to destroy them.

————, *The War Queens: Extraordinary Women Who Ruled the Battlefield* (New York: Diversion Books, 2020). This very enjoyable and useful book provides an excellent example of the blending of research on important women at war in readable fashion, but also does by also providing military context and fine maps to help the reader understand the total situation in which their campaigns were conducted. Among those examined are Nzinga, Boudica, Queen Tamar, Golda Meir, Indira Gandhi, Catherine the Great, and Caterina Sforza. A very fine piece of work indeed.

Chen Jo-shui, "Empress Wu and Proto-Feminist Sentiments in T'ang China," in Frederick Brandauer and Chun-Chieh Huang (eds.), *Imperial Rulership and Cultural Change in Traditional China* (Seattle: University of Washington Press, 1994), pp. 77–116. The only woman ever to declare herself Emperor in the history of China succeeded briefly in upsetting gender norms, but soon the normal patterns of cultural sexual dominance emerged in T'ang China upon her death.

Teressa Kaminski, *Angels of the Underground: The American Women Who Resisted the Japanese in the Philippines in World War II* (London: Oxford University Press, 2016). By tracing the actions of four women—Gladys Svary, Claire Phillips, Yay Panlilio, and Peggy Utinsky—the author paints a complex picture of resistance to the Japanese occupation of the Philippines and assistance to the American and Filipino prisoners of war.

Note: For a brief but pithy introduction to Filipino and American guerrilla military activities during World War II, see John Whitman, "They Remained: Filipino Guerrillas in World War II," *MHQ: The Quarterly Journal of Military History,* Vol. 14, #2 (Winter 2002), pp. 36–65.

Karen Kampwirth, *Women and Guerrilla Movements* (University Park: The Pennsylvania State University Press, 2002). The author looks at the reasons why women joined guerrilla movements in Nicaragua, El Salvador, Chiapas, and Cuba, shows the diverse reasons for their mobilization, and documents their role in all four of these struggles. Makes the salient point that there were many classes and ethnicities involved and regardless of the outcome of their struggles, mobilized many women and men for their causes.

Dean Karalekas, "Women in the Military," in *Civil-Military Relations in Taiwan: Identity and Transformation* (Bingley: Emerald Publishing Limited, 2018), pp. 11–127. While suggesting that Taiwan's inclusion of women in the military, especially in combat positions, may smack of tokenism, the author points out that by 2013, 11% of the country's military were female. This is substantially ahead of the rates of 3 to 4% that obtain in Japan and South Korea, countries with similar Confucian backgrounds.

Marjoleine Kars, "Dodging Rebellion: Politics and Gender in the Berbice Slave Uprising of 1763," *American Historical Review* (February 2016), pp. 39–69. A much-needed and refreshing look at a well-documented rebellion in Berbice in Guyana, which was a Dutch colony from 1627 to 1815. The author rightly assets that most slave revolts were short lived and also shows how so many women (and men) simply tried to avoid being drawn into slave rebellions on either side. Yet others, such as Amelia, Barbara, and Pallas, were executed for their participation.

Note: One important slave revolt, that of 1811 in New Orleans and the German Coast, does seem to have been lacking female participation. See Daniel Rasmussen, *American Uprising: The Untold Story of America's Largest Slave Revolt* (New York: Harper, 2011). The author believes it was the largest slave revolt in the history of the United States, involving between 200 and 500 slaves.

Joyce Kaufman and Kristen William, *Women at War, Women Building Peace: Challenging Gender Norms* (Boulder: Kumarian Press, 2013). Argues that women now expect to play major roles in war as well as peace. Looks at women as agents of resistance and political violence as well as peacemaking. Case studies from Northern Ireland, the Israeli-Palestinian conflict, and Sri Lanka are provided.

Judith Keene, "Mika Etchebehere," in Pennington (ed.), *op. cit.*, pp. 160–162. Interesting case of Mika Etchebehere (1902–1990), the Argentine woman *Miliciana* who fought in the Spanish Civil War. Mika was apparently a rare woman leader with men under her command in the Spanish Civil War. After her husband Hypo was killed, Mika remained with his Partido Obrero de Unification Marxista (POUM) and commanded a combat unit during 1936. Active in the battle for the Siguenza Cathedral and on the Moncloa front. Had women under her command and also men until the unit was disbanded after 1936.

Susan Kellogg, *Weaving the Past: A History of Latin America's Indigenous Women from the Prehispanic Period to the Present* (London: Oxford University Press, 2005). While women warriors were not widespread among the Mayan, Inca, and Mexica peoples, stelae from Coba, Calakmul, Usumacinta, and Yaxchilan depict women in warrior gear and headdresses. See especially chapter 2, "Of Warriors and Working Women: Gender in Later Prehispanic Mesoamerica and the Andes," pp. 18–52. The author also underscores the activities of women in some revolutionary organizations as well, highlighting the role of such women as Comandante Ramona of the Zapatista Army of National Liberation (EZIN), and pointing out that as many as 40% of EZIN soldiers were female (p. 122).

Linda Kelly, *Women of the French Revolution* (London: Hamish Hamilton, 1987). Looking at the roles of various women of the salon class such as Madame Roland, Madame de Staël, and Theroigne de Maricourt, the author also mentions Olympe de Gouges, who stormed the Tuileries, but her emphasis is not really on the martial side of the women involved.

Thomas Keneally, *Daughters of Mars* (New York: Atria Books, 2013). (F) Two sister nurses go to Gallipoli and the Western Front and confront a deluge of casualties, the horrors of war, and self-exploration. This novel captures the ongoing impact of war across time and space.

William Kessel and Robert Wooster (eds.), *Encyclopedia of Native American Wars and Warfare* (New York: Facts on File, 2005). Provides some interesting examples of women warriors in Native American cultures, including The Other Magpie (Crow), Pine Leaf (Crow), Running Eagle (Blackfoot), Old Woman Grieves the Enemy (Pawnee), Strikes Two (Absaroke), Comes Together (Cheyanne), The Other Magpie (Cheyenne), Buffalo Calf Road Woman (Cheyenne), Wild Hemp (Cherokee), Beloved Woman or War Woman (Cherokee), One Who Goes About (Cherokee), Women Chief (Crow), Yellow Haired Woman (Cheyenne, Hanging Cloud Woman (Ojibway), Kuillx (Pend d'Oreille), and Chief Earth Woman (Ojibway).

Le Minh Khue, "The Distant Stars," in *The Stars, the Earth, the River* (Willimantic: Curbstone Press, 1997), pp. 1–20. Khue tells the powerful story of three young North Vietnamese volunteers who go south to keep the Ho Chi Minh trail open. For Khue, "The war years were both the worst time and the best time for me." She captures the sense of comradeship echoing down throughout history, "I loved everyone . . . that was the love of the people in smoke and fire, the people of war." Other chapters in the book depict both the pride and disillusionment following the end of the war and the seemingly inexorable march of the double helix in yet another time and place.

Kathleen Khuhnast, Chantal de Jorge Oudraat, and Helga Hernes, *Woman and War* (Washington: United States Institute of Peace Press, 2011). This wide-ranging volume helps us to understand how gender structures conflict, causing women to suffer a great deal more than normal through increased rapes, sexual violence, lost economic opportunities and the like.

Yun-Jung Kim, "International Comparison of Women's Participation in the Military Service in the U.S. and Korea," *Journal of International Trade & Commerce*, Vol. 13, #1 (February 2017), pp. 111–125. A very forward-looking piece which concludes that the armed forces of the future will be much more receptive to female participation due to the importance of computers and cyber-warfare, in which women will not be at a disadvantage physically, nor as likely to be dominated by a macho male warrior ethos. The conclusion: "The arguments against the full integration of women in the military, which have revolved around the suitability, fitness, and appropriateness of females for war, may be, in the contemporary age, behind the times."

John M. Kistler, *War Elephants* (Lincoln: University of Nebraska Press, 2007). In addition to providing a substantial history of the use of elephants in warfare, the author provides evidence of the Thai queen consort Suriyothai, who in 1548 fought against Burmese invaders while riding a war elephant.

John Klassen, "Women and Religious Reform in Late Medieval Bohemia," *Renaissance and Reformation*, Vol. 5, #4 (1981), pp. 203–221. Although there were long-standing prohibitions in medieval Central Europe against women dressing as men or participating in battle, during the Hussite revolt in Bohemia during the 1420s there were numerous examples of women dressed as men as well as women participating in a variety of battles. In fact, the author suggests that many contemporaries blame these women for the high levels of violence, claiming the radicals showed no quarter because of their attitudes.

Note: Of course the protagonists in the Hussite revolt (1419–1435) did not need a charge of being a transvestite in order to show no quarter. As Stephen Lahey points in his revisionist book, *The Hussites* (Leeds: ARC Humanities Press, 2019), theology of the most vicious sort was in and of itself a well-spring of violence during the Hussite reform/revolt and its subsequent repression. For a good overview of the entire revolt as seen through the career of Jan Zizka, see Victor Verney, *Warrior of God: Jan Zizka and the Hussite Revolution* (London: Frontline Books, 2009). Verney also illuminates the women warriors who played a pivotal role in the defeat of the Empire forces during the initial siege of Prague, especially in the battle for Vitkov Hill: "Without guns, they were reduced to hurling stones and lances. One woman showed special courage and let a counter-charge, reportedly shouting "No true Christian must ever retreat from Antichrist!" She was killed and has passed into the realm of legend (p. 79). Also later with the development of the Hussite war wagon innovations and its offensive actions, women and children often traveled with the wagons and were thus sometimes in the middle of the fighting when it occurred.

John Klassen, *Warring Maidens, Captive Wives, and Hussite Queens: Women and Men at War and at Peace in Fifteenth-Century Bohemia* (New York: East European Monographs distributed by Columbia University Press, 1999). See especially chapter 8, "Women, Revolution and Political Order," pp. 183–210, in which he quotes extensively from Lawrence of Brezova, who, he concludes, "integrated the action of women into his chronological account of the revolutionary events and provided a relatively calm and credible outline of women's combat roles in the revolution and participation in the defense of their country" (p. 185). At the same time, the revolutionaries later quickly moved to reduce the role of women in terms of maintaining positions of military and political authority.

John Klassen and Cynthia Paces, "Women in Hussite Wars," in Reina Pennington (ed.), *Amazons to Fighter Pilots Vol. I* (Westport: Greenwood Press, 2003), pp. 216–219. The authors make a strong case that between 1420 and 1428, significant numbers of Czech women joined in fighting the Catholic crusade against the reform-minded Hussite movement. Citing Laurence of Brezova and his *Hussite Chronicles*, large numbers of women joined General Jan Zizka, and "equipped with lances and maces, female soldiers from the Bohemian towns of Tabor, Louny, Slany, and Zatec participated in the march to Prague" (p. 27). Women from Tabor acted on their own at various times during the struggle. Other examples of women in this combat are cited by Brezova include Johanna of Ruzmita.

Note: The Hussite movement is often considered to be a forerunner of the eventual Protestant Reformation of the 16th century. The best description of Hussite warfare in action can be found in H. W. Koch, *Medieval Warfare* (New York: Barnes & Noble, 1978) with its excellent contemporary accounts, illustrations, and analysis of not only Hussite innovations (including its war wagons) and tactics but also useful sections on the condottieri, castle building, and the growing professionalism of the state armies in the twilight of the medieval period.

Heinrich Kleist, *Penthesilea* (New York: Harper/Collins, 1998). (F) A new translation of the 1808 play. An army of one-breasted women (the better to shoot their bows) arrives in the middle of the Trojan War. Penthesilea, daughter of Ares and Queen of the Amazons, shows carnal lust for Achilles ("her beloved enemy") and convinces him she wishes to marry him. While one seldom feels sorry for Achilles in real life, not least for his cruel treatment of Hector after killing him, his final words in this play as she hunts him down and, together with her dogs, tears him apart and then devours portions of him, catch our attention. Surely Achilles deserves our consideration and sympathy when he cries, "Penthesilea! My Bride! What are you doing? Is this the rosy feast you promised me?" Penthesilea then kills herself. This play is not for the faint of heart, but it underscores the ongoing fascination with a true daughter of Mars and how she seems to upset the balance of the "natural" order in the minds of many.

Note: For a less-fanciful examination of war in the Bronze Age, see Nicholas Grguric, *The Mycenaeans c. 1650–1100 BC* (Oxford: Osprey Publications, 2005).

Franklin W. Knight and Henry Louis Gates, Jr. (eds.), *Dictionary of Caribbean and Afro-Latin American Biography* (Oxford: Oxford University Press, 2016). See especially "Dandara of Palmares," https://www.oxfordreference.com/view/10.1093/acref/9780199935796.001.0001/acref-9780199935796–e-595 for a description of an Afro-Brazilian warrior woman who fought in many battles for the free Black community of Palmares and who, when arrested, committed suicide (1694) rather than be enslaved. Although we are left with scanty details about her life overall, Dandara and her husband Zumbi are considered important symbols of racial and social equality in Brazil.

Note: A good introductory history of the overall Caribbean with an emphasis on plantation agriculture and its ramifications for its various peoples is Frank Pons, *History of the Caribbean: Plantations, Trade, and War in the Atlantic World* (Princeton: Markus Wiener Publishers, 2007).

Halik Kochanski, "Women at War: Poland," in Celia Lee and Paul Strong (eds.), *Women in War: From Home Front to the Front Line* (Barnsley: Pen and Sword, 2012), pp. 194–203. Covers the many situations in which women found themselves at war in Poland, with the German and Soviet invasions, the German drive on the Soviet Union and the subsequent Russian push back through Poland. Women fought in all dimensions of the conflict.

Philip Koslow, *Hausaland: The Fortress Kingdoms* (New York: Chelsea House Press, 1995). Provides insights into the military efforts and fortresses of Amina of Zaria, who expanded the boundaries of her kingdom to the confluence of the Niger and the Benue. Zaria is now home to Ahmadi Bello University in present-day Nigeria.

Note: The military history of the Sahel is quite understudied. See, for example, Norman Kotler, "The Golden Mirage of Songhai," *MHQ: The Quarterly Journal of Military History,* Vol. 4, #3 (Spring 1992), pp. 92–99, which documents the early (1590) conquering expedition of the sultan of Morocco against the empire of Songhai.

John Koster, "The Other Magpie and the Woman Chief Were Crow Warriors of the 'Weaker Sex,'" *Wild West,* Vol. 26, #1 (June 1913), pp. 24–25. Also highlights another Crow woman warrior as well, the companion of The Other

Magpie, named Finds Them and Kills Them. Finds Them and Kills Them, who is described a "neither a man nor a woman," helps The Other Magpie rescue Bull Snake. Hard to find a better warrior name, male or female.

Dr. Heidi Kraft, *Rule Number Two: Lessons I Learned in a Combat Hospital* (New York: Little, Brown, 2007). This an extraordinarily powerful work. The author takes her cue from the Korean War TV show and film *M*A*S*H*, which stated "There are two rules of war. Rule number one is that young men die. Rule number two is that doctors can't change rule number one." Without melodrama or forced pathos, Kraft describes young Marines dying in her arms and warriors, men and women, young and old, breaking down under the strain of combat and the loss of comrades, feeling ashamed for feeling fear or for surviving while buddies did not. And how she, a devoted mother of two small children, copes halfway around the world from them. A warrior's warrior she seems to me. And a cogent voice against war.

Remke Kruk, *The Warrior Women of Islam: Female Empowerment in Arabic Popular Literature* (London: I.B. Tauris, 2014). Using popular literature and legendary epics, the author explores the world of female warriors such as Princess Dhat al-Himma, Ghamra, and Jayda. After intriguing the reader with many glimpses, the author concludes that we must remember that this "agreed upon fiction" actually reflects male composition and presentation.

Krishna Kumar (ed.), *Women and Civil War* (Boulder: Lynne Rienner Publishing, 2000). A potpourri of essays covering "a vast territory" including Rwanda, Cambodia, Georgia, Guatemala, El Salvador, and Bosnia. They fight and in many cases seem to play a significant role. Why are these women not more widely celebrated in the polyphony of women's histories, the author asks.

Ismail KushKush, "In the Land of Kush," *Smithsonian* (Sept. 2020), pp. 52ff. The appropriately named author provides a breezy but informative introduction to the historical legacy of the Kushite Empire, especially during its Meroite period. Particularly relevant are his explorations of several of the various historical "Candices," including Kandake (Queen) Amanirenas (40 BCE–10 BCE) the "Candice" of Kush during the Meroitic period (543 BCE–4th century CE) and Black African female war leader and queen. The kingdom of Kush with its capital of Meroe epitomizes the long tradition of Black African kingdoms in the area, from Kema (3000 BCE) through other kingdoms known as Nubia or Kush. She led an army to defeat Romans at the battles of Syene and Philae. The Romans drove the Kushites south the next year, but the frontier stabilized. Also provides information on Kandake (Queen) Amkanitore (1 BCE 25 AD), the Black African co-regent with King Natakamani of Kush. Note: many scholars believe that Amanitore's successor, Amanitere, is the "Candace queen of the Ethiopians," mentioned in the New Testament as one who went to Jerusalem on a spiritual quest.

L–O

Keith Laidler, *Female Caligula: Ranavalona the Mad Queen of Madagascar* (New York: Wiley, 2005). The title says it all. This woman, Ranavalona (1778–1861), seized the throne of the Merina and ruled with an iron fist for 33 years, fighting off the French and English and suppressing her own subjects. Often missing from anthologies of women warriors (or rulers for that matter), Ranavalona deserves a new look in terms of how much of the military commands she directed.

Note: Interestingly enough, Queen Ranavalona became quite a foil in the minds of the British government and populace to the "benign" reign of Queen Victoria. See Arianne Chernock, "Queen Victoria and the 'Bloody Mary of Madagascar,'" *Victorian Studies*, Vol. 55, #3 (Spring 2013), pp. 425–449. Queen Ranavalona became "an emblem of savage femininity and a terrifying manifestation of what could happen to polities that allowed women to govern in more than a purely ceremonial capacity" (p. 427).

Denise K. Lajimodiere, "American Indian Females and Stereotypes: Warriors, Leaders, Healers, Feminists; Not Drudges, Princesses, Prostitutes, Multicultural Perspectives," *Multicultural Perspectives*, Vol. 15, #2 (2013), pp. 104–109. A heart-wrenching account of a Native American woman who encounters great prejudice and shows great resilience and some liberation through Critical Indigenous Feminist Theory. Along the way, she exposes the reader to the many dimensions of Native American womanhood, including that of warriors such as the Other Magpie, Running Eagle, Yellow-head Woman among the Cherokee, Blackfoot, Crow, Lakota, Cheyenne, Shawnee,

149

Winnebago, Natchez, and others and shows how stereotypes (princess versus squaw, etc.) are doubly hurtful and perpetuate a gender hierarchy that is corrosive for all concerned.

Ruby Lal, *Empress: The Astonishing Reign of Nur Jahan* (New York: W. W. Norton, 2018). The 20th wife of the Mughal emperor Jahangir, Nur led troops in several key battles to rescue her husband after he was captured on the way to Kashmir. While this work is mostly about the rest of her life, the battle stories are well worth a look purely from the point of her as a warrior.

Asma Lamrabet, *Women in the Qur'an: An Emancipatory Reading* (Leicestershire: Square View Press, 2016). This Moroccan woman pathologist provides a rereading of the Muslim Holy Scriptures from a female perspective. For example, she quotes the Prophet describing a woman warrior, "Who else could endure all that you are suffering here Umm 'Umarah?" (p. 19). Says Umm was wounded 13 times in various battles including Uhud, Hudaybiyyah, Hunayn, and Al-Yamama, where she lost a hand.

Vina Lanzona, *Amazons of the Huk Rebellion* (Madison: The University of Wisconsin Press, 2009). An in-depth look at the rise and success and ultimate failure of the Huk rebellion (1941–1954) first against the Japanese and then against the Filipino government and the United States. Many women commanders in both periods. A great deal of detail about the role of women in all aspects of the Huk rebellion.

Vina Lanzona and Frederik Rettig (eds.), *Women Warriors in South East Asia* (London: Routledge, 2020). A wide-ranging look at women warriors from China, India, Malaya, Cambodia, Vietnam, the Philippines, Aceh, and Timor, with numerous interviews with female participants from the more recent conflicts. In addition to providing insights into the motivations of these women and the scope of their activities, the various authors put their lives in gender and revolutionary perspectives.

Richard Lapchick and Stephanie Urdang, *Oppression and Resistance: The Struggle of Women in Southern Africa* (Westport: Greenwood Press, 1982). A look at women in the struggle to liberate Southern Africa with introductory observations of their efforts in South Africa, Zimbabwe, and Namibia. Strangely silent on their role in Umkhonto we Sizwe, the "Spear of the Nation," however.

Antal Leisen, "Lebstuck, Maria," in Pennington, *op. cit.*, pp. 254–255. Fighting in the Revolution of 1848, she joined the Death's Head Legion of General Giron and was promoted to lieutenant for shooting three Austrian officers in Hungary (p. 245). Subsequently, she fought in many battles during the uprising and survived it.

Note: Even a much earlier work on the revolutions, Priscilla Robertson, *Revolutions of 1848: A Social History* (Princeton: Princeton University Press, 1952) with its emphasis on the role of women advocating for education, political rights, and economic justice notes how in Hungary, "Women were almost more ready to serve than men. . . . Many stories went around of women in the ranks, while two at least reached the rank of captain before they were discovered" (p. 289).

Gayle Tzemach Lemmon, *Ashley's War: The Untold Story of a Team of Women Soldiers on the Special Ops Battlefield* (New York: Harper, 2015). Poignant account of Ashley White, a member of an early Cultural Support Team (CST) in Afghanistan, who was killed in battle. Her training, integration into a traditionally male-only Special Forces unit, and her untimely death are all sketched here. One interesting insight: American female soldiers were able to talk to Iraqi women whereas many Afghani and Iraqi women were not permitted to speak to males (including U.S. soldiers) unless they were blood relatives. Ashley earned the Bronze Star for her bravery.

———, *The Daughters of Kobani* (New York: Penguin, 2021). Presents the story of the Kurdish women who, in the Syrian Civil War and the fight against ISIS, liberated Kobani and Raqqa and distinguished themselves with great courage and valor. The author believes they also serve as a vanguard of liberated women in the Middle East. The Kurdish Women's Protection Units (YPJ) fought with Americans and Kurdish men, playing an instrumental role during the successful prosecution of that war. One female commander, Azeema, who was wounded multiple times and led women and men in battle, gave the author considerable access to events, much to our advantage.

Elizabeth Leonard, *All the Daring of the Soldier: Women of the Civil War Armies* (New York: W.W. Norton, 1999). A wide-ranging account of "Spies," "Half-Soldier Heros," and "A Host of Women Soldiers." Forerunner of *They Fought Like Demons*, this work contains interesting accounts of how women got around recruitment examinations, many of which were cursory or nonexistent.

Ulises Estrada Lescaille, *Tania: Undercover with Che Guevara in Bolivia* (New York: Ocean Press, 2005). A Cuban revolutionary with extraordinary credentials chronicles the life and career of Tania and her ultimate death in action fighting with Che Guevara in Bolivia.

Desi Fitri Ayu Lestari, Dejono, and Musa Pelu, "Between Femininity and Masculinity: The Leadership of Admiral Malahayati in Historical Perspective," *International Journal of Education and Social Science Research,* Vol. 2, #4 (2019), pp. 43–51. Looks at the strikingly important career of Admiral Malahayati in both historical and leadership perspective and illuminates other important female leaders in the Aceh tradition: Fatmawati Soekarno, Opubaeny Risaju, AgungHj, AndiDepu, Ratu Saffiatudin, Ratu Naqiatuddin, Ratu Zakiatuddin, Cut Nyakdien, and Cut Nyakmeutia, among others.

Elizabeth Lev, *The Tigress of Forli: Renaissance Italy's Most Courageous and Notorious Countess, Caterina Riario Sforza de 'Medici* (Boston: Houghton Mifflin Harcourt, 2011). A long, fascinating biography by an art historian of Caterina Riario Sforza de' Medici. See especially chapter 17, "Italy's Idol," pp. 216–234, for a fascinating account of Caterina's heroic stand in 1499 against Cesare Borgia and his army of mercenaries and French Royal Troops. For hours she fought in battle with her troops, finally betrayed by someone on her own side, for "she had no intention of leaving the battlefield alive" (p. 226).

Isaac Levine, *My Life as Peasant, Officer and Exile: The Life of Maria Bochkareva* (New York: Frederick Stokes, 1919). A truly amazing tale of a young woman who survived extreme poverty, abusive men, and incarceration to find liberation of a kind in the Russian armed forces during World War I after petitioning the Czar to let her join the army. Wounded a number of times, she eventually was selected to lead the all-female "Battalion of Death" during 1917. After the revolution broke out, she tried to fight the Bolsheviks, meeting Kerensky, Kornilov, Lenin, and Trotsky along the way. Although she eventually made it to America via Vladivostok, she ultimately returned to Russia, only to be captured and killed by the Bolsheviks. See also the reissued copy of this work, which includes a new preface and conclusion (which claims an eyewitness knew her to be alive after her supposed execution): Maria Bochkareva, *Maria's War: A Soldier's Autobiography* (Montpelier: Russian Life Books, 2016).
   Note: Another Russian woman who fought in World War I is Anna Alekseevna Krasilnikova, a daughter of a miner from the Ural Mountains who was

accepted as a volunteer in the 205th Infantry Regiment as Anatoly Krasil-nikov, participating in 19 battles and winning the St. George's Cross.

Note: For context on the Russian Revolution and its military aspects and recruitment of soldiers both men and women, see David Bullock, *The Russian Civil War 1918–22* (Oxford; Osprey Publishing, 2008), Mikhail Khvostov, *The Russian Civil War (1) The Red Army* (Oxford: Osprey Publishing, 1996) and *The Russian Civil War (2) White Armies* (Oxford: Osprey Publishing, 1997), Richard Luckett, *The White Generals* (New York: Viking, 1971).

Darline Levy and Harriet Applewhite, "Women and Military Citizenship in Revolutionary Paris," in Sara Melzer and Leslie Rabine (eds.), *Rebel Daughters: Women and the French Revolution* (Oxford: Oxford University Press, 1991), pp. 79–101. Makes a strong case, including images, of women in action during the French Revolution as well as contributing to the intellectual and social upwelling.

Paul H. Lewis, *Guerrillas and Generals: The "Dirty War" in Argentina* (Westport: Praeger, 2002). A good book for a detailed account of the Dirty War and what worked in bringing down the government that prosecuted it. For a useful background presenting the rise of leftist Montoneros and their relationship to Juan Perón and his successor Evita, see Richard Gillespie, *Soldiers of Perón: Argentina's Montoneros* (Oxford: Clarendon Press, 1982).

————, "A Short History of United Nations Peacekeeping," *MHQ: The Quarterly Journal of Military History,* Vol. 5, #1 (Autumn 1992), pp. 33–47. Sets the stage for the uses of female soldiers in peacekeeping units both as a matter of national priority and/or as a way of reintegrating former rebels into the army in question, such as in the cases of Sierra Leone and Rwanda. By 2020, 5% of UN "Blue Helmets" were female.

Joyce Libra-Chapman, *The Rani of Jhansi: A Study in Female Heroism in India* (Honolulu: University of Hawaii Press, 1986). The author casts a wide net looking at the Rani as both a historical figure but also, as in the case of Joan of Arc, a mythic model and feminist/nationalist prototype. An easy read and yet one which provides a lot of information and insights, this work draws on many unpublished sources, such as ballads, poetry, and folklore.

Note: See Gregory Fremont-Barnes, *The Indian Mutiny 1857–58* (Oxford: Osprey Publishing, 2007) for a short introduction to the entire campaign from uprising to final suppression. For an account in greater depth, See Christopher Hibbert, *The Great Mutiny: India 1857* (New York: Viking Press, 1978). Another, more recent telling of that cataclysmic set of events is William Dalrymple, *The Last Mughal: The Fall of a Dynasty: Delhi, 1857* (New York: Alfred Knopf, 2006). Dalrymple's telling includes previously unutilized Persian and Urdu sources and provides much-needed perspective from the Indian point of view.

Drew Lindsay, "Why Not Send Women to War?," *MHQ: The Quarterly Journal of Military History,* Vol. 25, #3 (Summer 2013), pp. 50–61. A wide-ranging study from ancient times through World War II and the wars of decolonization, concluding "some people will never accept women in battle—at least, that is, until women are needed."

Kathryn M. Linduff and Karen Rubinson (eds.), *Are All Warriors Male?* (Lanham, MD: Altamira Press, 2008). Scholarly anthropological studies of the Eurasian steppe Iron Age graves from the Black Sea to Afghanistan, Northern Kazakhstan, Western Siberia, and Xiongnu says, emphatically, "No." This work uses archaeological evidence from prehistory to look at the woman warrior in fact and fiction, coming up with plenty of evidence that Xena the Warrior Princess was not sui generis and had many real antecedents. Grave sites and grave goods are "living" proof. There is a reason contemporary cultures still carry the image of strong, powerful women righting wrong and fighting evil.

Lisa Lines, "Female Combatants in the Spanish Civil War: Milicianas on the Front Lines and in the Rearguard," *Journal of International Women's Studies,* Vol. 10, #4 (Jun. 2013), pp. 168–187. This article is one of the best on the role of the Milicianas in action during the first eight months of the Spanish Civil War. First, it gives ample evidence that the Milicianas fought in frontline situations with men and fought on equal terms with them. Second, it points out that the many women who were organized to defend their cities and formed the "rear guard" ended up actually fighting when the front moved to their locations. Third, it introduces the reader to a number of specific women fighters including Mika Etchebehere, Lina Odena, Fidela Fernandez de Velasco Perez, Rosario Sanchez de la Mora, Margarita Ribalta, Trinidad Revolto Cervello, Aurora Arnaiz, Casilda Mendez, Sukzanne Birbe, August Marx, Juliette Baudard, Eugenie Casteu and Georgette Kokoczinski, Maria Elisa Garcia, Jacinta Perez Alvarez, and Francisca Solano. A must read on this subject.

   Note: Although many contemporary and even current accounts accent the centrality of the communist contribution to the Republican side, a recent work by Giles Tremlett, *The International Brigades: Fascism, Freedom and the Spanish Civil War* (London: Bloomsbury, 2020) argues that in reality anti-fascism, not procommunism, explains the motivation behind the actions of most who joined the International Brigades.

Lisa Lines, *Milicianas: Women in Combat in the Spanish Civil War* (Lanham: Lexington Books, 2005). The Nationalist insurrection in Spain began in July 1936 and from the beginning there were hundreds and then thousands of women who joined the Republican cause. While initially they fought at the front in integrated units with men, by 1937, they had gone from being welcomed "warriors" to discarded "whores" as "Men to the Front, Women to the Home Front" became the cry of even the most leftist of groups. The author skillfully explains the hows and the whys of that change. Of course, things would get much worse for these women once the Nationalists won.

Tabea Alexa Linhard, *Fearless Women in the Mexican Revolution and the Spanish Civil War* (Columbia: University of Missouri Press, 2005). Looking the articles, plays, books, and cinema on the Mexican Revolution (1910–1919) and the Spanish Civil War (1936–1939), the author tries to sort out who was included, who was excluded, and why. "Do not allow my name to vanish in history," says one women warrior executed by the Nationalists after the Spanish Civil War, and that hope inspires this work from beginning to end.

Larry Loftis, *Code Name: Lise: The True Story of the Woman Who Became WWII's Most Highly Decorated Spy* (New York: Gallery Books, 2019). The seemingly incredible story of Odette Sansom, the Special Operations Executive (SOE) operative who risked all—many times—to assist in the French Resistance. She was born in France but married an Englishman and could have sat out the war in rural Somerset with her three children. Instead she went off to France as an SOE operative and worked with the resistance. Sold out, she was captured by the Germans, tortured unmercifully by the Gestapo, and put in the Ravensbrück concentration camp, where she was miraculously liberated by American troops. She would later receive the St. George's Cross, only the second SOE operative and first woman to receive it. When anyone talks about the SOE, remember that of the 42 sent to France, 42% of them were killed. Only the British Bomber Command among Allied services, with 45%, had a higher death rate during World War II (p. 61).

Angelika Lohwasser, "Queenship in Kush: Status, Role, and Ideology of Royal Women," *Journal of the American Research Center in Egypt*, Vol. 38 (2001), pp. 61–76. Looks at the varied roles and interpretations of the royal mothers, wives, sisters, and daughters from the Kushite 25 Dynasty to Napatan Period and concludes that their ties were often religious and power related in addition to being matrilineal in import.

Pasi Loman, "No Woman, No War: Women's Participation in Ancient Greek Warfare," *Greece and Rome*, Vol. 51, #1 (Apr. 2004), pp. 34–54. The author argues that, far from being victims or mere spectators, women in Ancient Greece were not pacifist by nature and often showed strong support for a variety of wars.

Lois Ann Lorentzen and Jennifer Turpin (eds.), *The Women and War Reader* (New York: New York University Press, 1998). A variety of essays concerning war's impact on women (and in some, men as well) taken from Bosnia, Korea, Israel, Nicaragua, El Salvador, Mozambique, Afghanistan, India, and Pakistan as well as the United States. Unfortunately, there is neither an introduction nor a conclusion, so the various essays float unattached and episodic.

William F. Lye, "The Difaqane: The Mfecane in the Southern Sotho Area, 1822–24," *Journal of African History*, Vol. 8, #1 (1967), pp. 107–131. By the time of this publication, studies of the Mfecane had already become something of a cottage industry with revision piled upon revision. Lye's work managed to focus on the specifics of the "Difaqane" that took place among the Southern Sotho peoples during the much larger Mfecane over much of southern Africa. Lye focuses on MmaNthatisi, whose band because a symbol for the greater disorder, and argues that although she did not necessarily lead in battle often, she planned and led the strategy of her people during this time of trouble.

John Lynn, "Women in War," *Military History* (October 2001), pp. 60–66. A short, stimulating look at female camp followers in the 16th century, describing how the armies of the day often had a nearly 1–1 ratio of men to women and children and "great crowds of women and children were not unusual; they were the rule." They carried food and clothing, treated the sick and wounded, participated in the looting, and protected its rewards, for "pillage was also the business of the army."

———, *Women, Armies and Warfare in Early Modern Europe* (Cambridge: Cambridge University Press, 2008). See especially chapter 4 "Warrior Women, Cultural Phenomena, Intrepid Soldiers, and Stalwart Defenders," pp. 164–214. Many specific cases are illustrated, including Alberte Barbe d'Ernecourt, Catherine Meurdrate de la Guetter, Anne-Marie-Clouise d'Orleans, Hendrik Van den Berg, Maria van Antwerpen, Christian Davies, Hannah Snell, Anna Maria Chritmannin, Chatarina Linck, Jeanne Bensar, Marie Magdelaine Mouron, and Catalina de Erauso. This is a very worthwhile source. The author also argues that the period from 1500 to 1815 saw hundreds of women who became soldiers and sailors. He also points out that the "modern armies" which followed offered far fewer opportunities for women to participate in warfare as combatants.

Note: Lynn's work *The French Wars 1667–1714* (Oxford: Osprey Publishing, 2002) proves much-needed context for the warfare of Louis XIV, showing as it does how women could be so central to the process as huge armies and accompanying civilians wandered around Europe. Also most helpful is his contrasting of Louis's "War as process" style with Napoleon's later "War as event." In the former, war has a slow tempo, battles and sieges were often indecisive, and there was always considerable negotiation even as the fighting progressed, stalemated, and/or regressed. In the latter, the aim was always to seek a single decisive knockout blow.

Note: For additional background on the style of warfare during the era of Louis XIV, see Lynn's "The Sun King's 'Star Wars,'" *MHQ: The Quarterly Journal of Military History*, Vol. 7, #4 (Summer 1995), pp. 88–99. For a broader, in-depth look at the life, time, and military campaigns of Louis XIV, see Philip Mansel, *King of the World: The Life of Louis XIV* (New York: Alan Lane, 2019).

———, "The Strange Case of the Maiden Soldier of Picardy," *MHQ: The Quarterly Journal of Military History*, Vol. 2, #3 (Spring 1990), pp. 54–56. Three examples of women who fought during the wars of Louis XIV. Also an interesting reference to the Irish author of *The Vicar of Wakefield* and playwright Oliver Goldsmith, who asserted that so many women masqueraded as men in the British army they ought to have formed their own regiments.

———, "Saint-Baslemont, Alberte-Barbe," Pennington, *Amazons to Fighter Pilots, op. cit.,* Vol. 2, pp. 381–382. The amazing story of Madame Alberte-Barbe D'Ernecourt Saint-Baslemont (1607–1660), a French military leader who defended her lands during the Thirty Years' War. She armed and led her own band of retainers to fight off brigands and other hostiles in the shifting horror of that war. Wearing hunting garb, she led from the front and won numerous clashes. She was also very pious and became known as the "Christian Amazon." The Pennington volume also has a section on Madame de Laguette, Catherine de Meudrac, who also fought in the Thirty Years' War.

Tanya Lyons, *Guns and Guerilla Girls: Women in the Zimbabwean National Liberation Struggle* (Trenton: Africa World Press, 2004). Illuminating "the Problems with Women in War," the author argues that although as many as 20,000 women were involved in the armed struggle, fewer than 10% were actually involved any type of combat. She does a good job in outlining the complexities of the multiple roles of women in the struggle in this African revolution.

Anna Macias, "Women and the Mexican Revolution, 1919–1920," *The Americas*, Vol. 74, #1 (2017), pp. 53–82. A thoughtful and inclusive look at the various roles played by women in a series of Mexican wars and upheavals, including the independence movement of 1810–1820, the American invasion of 1846–1848, and the French intervention from 1857 to 1867, as well as the Mexican Revolution itself. Of the actual combatants in the Revolution itself, there are the examples such as Coronel Maria de la Luz Espinosa Barrera and La Negra Angustias, who became a lieutenant colonel under Emiliano Zapata. Wish there had also been more material about Margarita Neri, the Dutch-Mayan from Quintana Roo who became a Zapatista commander.

 Note: For insights into the climactic battle of the Revolution, Ceyala, see Ronald Gilliam, "Turning Point of the Mexican Revolution," *MHQ: The Quarterly Journal of Military History,* Vol. 15, #3 (Spring 2003), pp. 41–51. For background on the first Mexican Revolution (1810–1820), see Vincent O'Hara, "The Unintended Revolution," *MHQ: The Quarterly Journal of Military History,* Vol. 21, #2 (Winter 2009), pp. 63–71. O'Hara argues that even after the second Mexican Revolution of 1910, "even today the issues of caste, justice, and privilege in Mexican society continue to simmer" (p. 71).

Ben Macintyre, *Agent Sonya: Moscow's Most Daring Wartime Spy* (New York: Crown, 2020). The author of the James Bond series, Ian Fleming, once called her "the best spy of all time." This is not hyperbole. The Jewish German communist woman Ursula Kuczkynski had the most amazing career as a spy, effective saboteur, and resistance warrior, eventually becoming a colonel (the first and only woman known to attain that rank at that time) in the Soviet GRU and received the Order of the Red Banner, the highest Soviet military medal, an award for courage and heroism on the battlefield (Stalin and Trotsky were also recipients) *twice.* "Red Sonya" successfully spied on the Chinese Nationalists, led resistance forces against the Japanese in their puppet state of Manchukuo, and went undercover in Poland, Germany, and eventually Great Britain for the USSR. Reading this account, it is hard to imagine what kept her going and thriving except for her true devotion to Communism and the Soviet Union. She was however an amazing warrior with ice water in her veins. Her career is also a testament to the poor efforts of the Chinese Nationalist, Japanese, German, Polish, British, and American counterintelligence services and treachery on the part of MI6 and Kim Philby. The American OSS even hired her to create a network of Germans to parachute into Germany. Ursula and her GRU superiors were delighted to assist.

Under suspicion, she still managed to move her whole family to East Germany, where she gave up spying (and wasn't punished by Moscow Center). Quite unbelievable really.

Megan Mackenzie, *Beyond the Band of Brothers: The U.S. Military and the Myth That Women Can't Fight* (Cambridge: Cambridge University Press, 2015). A wide-ranging look at why women have been excluded from combat and why they should not be. The author sees this exclusion as a continuing effort to reaffirm male supremacy in any and all aspects of communal life.

Marianne Mackinnon, *The Naked Years: Growing up in Nazi Germany* (London: Chatto and Windus, 1987). An engaging tale of a young woman drawn into war, serving in the Hitler Youth, drafted into the Organisation Todt doing farm and construction work, and narrowly escaping death in the Dresden firebombing raid. She fortunately ended up in the British sector after the war, ultimately arriving in Oxford.

Margaret MacMillan, *War: How Conflict Shaped Us* (New York: Random House, 2020). Explores war's many impacts and sees a very complex relationship between society and warfare. Feels that for too long military history has been the province of "toys for boys"—with guns, battles, strategy, and tactics getting the lion's share of attention. For her part, she is more interested in the ways societies have shaped war and war has shaped various societies. An interesting and pleasantly provocative read on the subject.

Grace Harriet Macurdy, *Hellenistic Queens: A Study of Woman-Power in Macedonia, Seleucid Syria, and Ptolemaic Egypt* (Chicago: Ares Publishers, 1932). See especially her examination in chapter 3, "Ptolemaic Queens," pp. 102–228, for background on the court and dynastic lives of that era.

Christoph Maier, "The Roles of Women in the Crusade Movement: A Survey," *Journal of Medieval History,* #30 (2004), pp. 61–82. Presents instances of women fighting as man and concludes: "Despite the fact that gender divisions did exist and gender roles were promoted to cement these division, the crusades were fought by men *and* women, not only because some women did participate in the military campaigns but because women's involvement on the home front played a large part in making men's crusades happen" (p. 81). Also looks at the activities of Margaret Beverly in the 1180s and Catherine of Siena in the 1370s to show the impact of both piety and exuberance.

John Man, *Searching for the Amazons* (New York: Penguin Books, 2018). A breezy once-over-lightly account of the legends and realities of the Amazons from the ancient Greeks to the present-day Peshmerga women warriors, with many literary stops along the way.

Emily St. John Mandel, *Station Eleven* (New York: Alfred Knopf, 2014). (F) A marvelous, inventive dystopian novel with women leaders ("The Symphony") and women warriors of note (Kirsten). Note: women do not always have to be "macho" to be true warriors.

Herman Mann, *The Female Review: Life of Deborah Sampson the Female Soldier in the War of the Revolution* (Boston: J. IK. Wiggin, 1866 reprint of the 1796 edition). "The American Rebellion Was a Great Event" says this work, and she was in it. At 22 she, pretending to be her dead brother, joined a regiment, the Light Infantry Company of the Fourth Massachusetts Regiment, fought in a number of battles (including Tarrytown), was wounded (not discovered), but then became ill (discovered) and mustered out with an honorary discharge. Ended up very poor thereafter, but proud of her service.

Edward Margetts, "The Masculine Character of Hatshepsut, Queen of Egypt," *Bulletin of the History of Medicine*, Vol. 25, #6 (1951), pp. 559–562. Assumed masculine "beard" and attire, depicting herself as descendent from the gods Amen-Ra and Aahmes.
   Note: For an introduction to war in ancient Egypt and surrounding areas, see Brian Carey, Joshua Allfree, and John Cairns, *Warfare in the Ancient World* (Barnsley: Pen and Sword, 2009).

Thomas Marks, "A Preliminary Reconnaissance: Female Combatant Participation in Nepal's Maoist People's War," *Mantraya Occasional Paper,* #4 (June 2017). An insurgency against a democratic state employing Maoist ideology and tactics is explored though interviews with 45 female combatants whose participation increased dramatically as the movement suffered manpower losses during the overt phase of the conflict, 1996 through 2006.

Dolores Mayano Martin, "A Sanguinary Obsession," *MHQ: The Quarterly Journal of Military History,* Vol. 4, #4 (Summer 1992), pp. 90–103. The Paraguayan war, which pitted Paraguay against Brazil, Uruguay, and Argentina, is much understudied in Anglo-American military circles. This article is an excellent introduction to the second-bloodiest war in the history of North and South America after the American Civil War. In it was Jovita Feitosa (1848–1867), a Brazilian woman who joined to fight in the Paraguayan War

(1864–1870), Paraguay against Brazil, Argentina, and Uruguay. Including civilians, 440,000 people were killed with 300,000 of total deaths occurring among Paraguayans, and only a truncated version of Paraguay emerged from the conflict. Jovita was honored for her bravery in action and died, either murdered in 1867 or killed in the Battle of Acosta in 1869.

Note: A fine exception to the above criticism of Anglo-American omission is Gabriele Esposito, *Armies of the War of the Triple Alliance 1864–1870* (Oxford: Osprey Publications, 2015). The interested reader will find a good succinct account of the war and excellent illustrations of the combatants in action. The author points out that Paraguay might have been totally dismembered but that Brazil wanted a buffer state between itself and Argentina and thus insisted on its existence.

Gina Martino, *Women at War in the Borderlands of the Early American Northeast* (Chapel Hill: The University of North Carolina Press, 2018). A real gem. Highlights in very incisive ways the many war roles—war-making, participation in martial activities—played by women of various cultures in this theater from 1630 to 1700. The author concludes: "Returning French, English, and Native women to the tumultuous borderlands of the early American northeast reveals surprising similarities between the contesting parties' political and military strategies and goals." Drawn from the wealth of contemporary diaries and accounts, the author puts everything in a much-needed reconceptualization. A good companion piece to the works on the Squa Sachem Weetamoo cited above. One fine example of a woman fighter in the borderlands is Marie-Madeleine Jarret De Vercheres (1678–1747), who fought the Iroquois.

Note: The intense struggle for the fur trade within the context of British-French worldwide rivalry is well covered in Stephen Brown, *The Company: The Rise and Fall of the Hudson's Bay Empire* (New York: Doubleday, 2020).

Note: While not focusing on Weetamoo or Ninigret, Ann Little does provide a fascinating look at the struggle between Native American and European notions of masculinity and warfare. See her *Abraham in Arms: War and Gender in Colonial New England* (Philadelphia: University of Pennsylvania Press, 2007).

Arthur Marwick, *Women at War 1914–1918* (London: Fontana, 1977). Using "the Great Spotlight of War" to show the myriad contributions made by British women during World War I, the author shows the wide range of activities from munitions work to the Women's Forage Department, to the Voluntary Aid Detachments (VAD) and the Women's Army Auxiliary Corps (WAAC) and their huge overall contribution to the war effort, and he argues that these contributions greatly enhanced the progress of the suffragette movement. Finely illustrated.

Roger Marwick and Eridice Cardona, *Soviet Women in the Frontlines of the Second World War* (New York: Palgrave McMillian, 2012). It richly covers the one million women the authors claim fought for the Soviet Union during World War II, including partisans (28,000), the Night Witches and Falcons, and the 1st Volunteer Rifle Brigade (first all-women's brigade since the revolution). These *frontovichki* fought long and bravely. You will be very sad upon finding out the fate of the returning warriors of the USSR, but especially those who were tragically paralyzed.

Mujib Mashal, Najim Rahlm, and Fatina Faize, "A Storied Female Warlord Surrenders, Taliban Say, Exposing Afghan Weakness," *New York Times*, October 18, 2020, p. 17. This storied woman warlord, 70 years old and with bad knees, Bibi Ayesha, known as "Kaftar" or Pigeon, fought the Soviets and the Taliban for 20 years only to eventually have to surrender to them as the surrounding districts all went over to the Taliban beforehand.

Robert Massie, *Catherine the Great* (New York: Random House, 2012). A fascinating woman who richly deserves this fascinating account of her life, especially a close look at her actions promoting the Russian empire. The expansion of Russia into Poland and to the Black Sea set the stage for further expansion in the 19th century, all the way to the Pacific. Interesting dynamic of the backward portions of Russia and their flow into new lands. Also good on the political machinations of Frederick the Great, France, England, and Austria in the Seven Years' War and beyond. This was a woman who reigned, ruled, and drove her country onward. See especially Catherine as military strategist and leader in "The First Partition of Poland and the First Turkish War" and "The Second Turkish War and the Death of Potemkin."

Gustave Masson, *The Story of Medieval France* (London: T. Fisher Unwin, 1893). See especially chapter 13, "Charles VII—End of the Hundred Year's War," for a 19th-century take on La Pucelle and Charles VII.

Jerry Matney and D. A. Gordon, *Woman War Chief: The Story of a Crow Warrior* (Bloomington: First Books, 2002). A long, thinly disguised praise poem about Woman Chief, the Gros Ventres woman who was captured by the Crows at age 10 and grew to womanhood with them. She worked hard to master the arts of soldiering and became a first-class warrior especially against the Blackfeet. She was invited to join the Big Dog Society, normally an honor reserved only for males, and became a rare woman chief and taking that name. Ironically, she was eventually ambushed and killed by a Gros Ventres raiding party.

Adrienne Mayor, *The Amazons: Lives and Legends of Warrior Women Across the Ancient World* (Princeton: Princeton University Press, 2014). Holistic, scholarly, well-illustrated, overarching, and multidisciplinary, this is the work on Amazons that must be consulted by those doing any research on this fascinating subject. Both the realities and the myths are breathtaking. Most illuminating is her close examination of the 1,000 years of history across 4,000 miles of geography from the Don Basin to China, concluding, "Between Greece and China stretched the vast homeland of nomadic horsewomen archers, the equals of men, whose heroic lives and deeds inspired awe, fear, respect, and desire in all who knew them."

Note: For a dissenting view, see Eleni Boliak's review of Mayor, *The Amazons* in the *Bryn Mawr Classical Review* (2015), p. 17.

James McCaffrey, *Army of Manifest Destiny* (New York: New York University Press, 1992). While skeptical that there were *many* women involved in the War of 1812, the author points to several instances when female soldiers were discovered although only after being wounded (pp. 25–26).

Stephanie McCurry, *Women's War: Fighting and Surviving the American Civil War* (Cambridge: Harvard University Press, 2019). Sees women—Confederate bushwhackers, formerly enslaved people, and Union fighters—playing more important roles than historians normally give them credit for.

Note: It is unfortunate that the author of the highly praised *Armies of Deliverance: A New History of the Civil War* (London: Oxford University Press, 2020), Elizabeth Varon, spends considerable time on the various roles of women (North and South) during the Civil War, including spying, authors, relief and hospital workers, etc., but surprisingly provides virtually nothing on women fighters on both sides as she airbrushed out of any consideration the hundreds and hundreds of women (North and South) who fought in that war. Most surprisingly, she does not seem to take the very valuable information contained in Deanne Blanton and Lauren Cook, *They Fought Like Demons: Women Soldiers in the Civil War* (see review above) into account. Sadly, we still have a long way to go to redress the historical imbalance of undervaluing women warriors in our collective remembrances.

Megan McLaughlin, "The Woman Warrior: Gender, Warfare and Society in Medieval Europe," *Women's Studies*, Vol. 17, #3–4 (1990), pp. 192–209. This is a seminal work. First, it provides a very useful dichotomy of women at war as generals versus women as foot soldiers. Second, the author rightly looks at much of medieval warfare involving the defense of castles as "domestic warfare" and points out the advantages this type of war provides for women. Drawing on examples such as the Lombard princess Sichelgaita, Countess Blanche of Champaign, and Therasia of Portugal, she gives evidence of this pattern, although one may be surprised to see her making no reference to Jeanne La Flamme. Concludes by asserting (correctly) that that rise of professional armies reduced the opportunities for women to operate in the domestic warfare space. Taken in its totality, this article proves that warrior women were fairly widely distributed in 12th-century Mediterranean Europe. A very worthwhile piece.

Note: To see just how worthwhile, consult Philip Warner, *The Medieval Castle: Life in a Fortress in Peace and War* (London: New Noble, 1971); Maurice Keen (ed.), *Medieval Warfare* (London: Oxford University Press, 1999); Brian Carey, Joshua Allfree, and John Cairns, *Warfare in the Medieval World* (Barnsley: Pen and Sword, 2006); and A. V. B. Norman, *The Medieval Soldier* (New York: Barnes & Noble, 1999), as well as David Nicolles's two worthwhile works, *European Medieval Tactics (1): The Fall and Rise of Cavalry 450–1250* (Oxford: Osprey Publishing, 2011) and *European Medieval Tactics New Infantry, New Weapons 1260–1500* (2) (Oxford: Osprey Publishing, 2011). Ivy Corfis and Michael Wolfe (eds.) broaden the lens to include the city (often with a citadel) under siege in their *The Medieval City under Siege* (Suffolk: Boydell Press, 1999).

Note: There were quite a few instances during the medieval period and beyond when women acting as castellans defended their castles during the absence of their husbands or their previous deaths. These include Agnes of Dunbar (1300–1369) in Scotland, Lady Mary Banks (d. 1661) during the English Civil War, Jeanne d'Albert (1528–1572) during the Wars of Religion, and Aluzehen (1115–1234) during the Chinese Jin dynasty. There was also Stamira of Ancona (?–1172) who defended the city of Ancona when she fought against the archbishop of Mainz during the Byzantine-Venetian conflict (1170–1177) as did Alruda Frangipani who liberated the town of Ancona from imperial siege during the same war and Marzia Degli Ubaldini (1330–ca 1374) who defended the castle of Cesena (near Forli) against papal attacks in 1335 and 1357. Emma de Gauder (1059–1096), Countess of Norfolk, also defended her husband's castle against the king, as did Nicolaa de la Hay (1160–1230) of Lincoln, who commanded during two sieges, one in 1191 and the other in 1216–1217 and Marguerite de Valois (1553–1615), who fought in the Wars of Religion in France.

Maaza Mengiste, *The Shadow King* (New York: W.W. Norton, 2019). (F) A finely woven, mystical, almost magical tale that puts a warrior woman, Hirut, at the center of the Italian conquest of Ethiopia in 1936 and the resistance to it. "I'm a soldier, a blessed daughter of Ethiopia, proud bodyguard of the King of Kings." Killing Italian soldiers, she is captured, escapes, and fights again. "And here is Hirut: wondrous soldier in the great Ethiopian army, daughter of Getey and Fasil, born in a blessed year of harvest, racing toward the enemy unafraid."

For a short but meaningful account of the Italian conquest of Ethiopia, see David Large, "Mussolini's 'Civilizing Mission,'" *MHQ: The Quarterly Journal of Military History,* Vol. 5, #2 (Winter 1993), pp. 44–53 and one of the efforts to reclaim Ethiopia for the Ethiopians during World War II, see Christian Potholm, *Liberation and Exploitation: The Struggle for Ethiopia* (Washington, DC: University Press of America, 1976).

Lois K. Merry, *Women Military Pilots of World War II: A History with Biographies of American, British, Russian and German Aviators* (Jefferson: McFarland and Company, 2011). Students find this work especially helpful. Some were astonished that no African American women pilots were mentioned despite so many African American men serving in the armed forces. Provides a good overview of what happened with a useful evaluation of many female pilots' memoirs. Some good biographical material at the end. See especially chapter 4, "Becoming Military Pilots."

Molly Merryman, *Clipped Wings: The Rise and Fall of the Women Airforce Service Pilots (WASPS) of World War II* (New York: New York University Press, 1998). These women brought thousands of planes from factory to ports but were denied military status at the end of the war.

Myriam Miedzian, *Boys Will Be Boys: Breaking the Link between Masculinity and Violence* (New York: Doubleday, 1991). Argues that war and its history and celebration help to perpetuate not only gender stereotypes but also male domination. See especially chapter 15, "When the Toy Store Looks Like a Military Arsenal," pp. 261–279.

Joseph Miller, "Nzinga of Matamba in a New Perspective," *Journal of African History,* Vol. 16, #2 (1975), pp. 201–216. Makes a strong case that Nzinga's rise and staying power were most unusual given the strong Mbundu strictures against female political leadership and suggests that her "skillful manipulation of the aliens present on the Mbundu border" was one of the reasons she succeeded. One hopes Nzinga would indeed have lumped the Portuguese and Dutch and the Jaga in the same category.

Madeline Miller, *The Song of Achilles* (New York; HarperCollins, 2012). (F) Putting Achilles in a homoerotic frame due to his love of Patroclus, the author accounts for his success with speed (shades of John Boyd, great American strategist of the 20th century and his OODA loop), and "the best warrior of his generation" who goes on to immortality in story and song. Achilles is not frightened of war, for "It was what I was born for." This account of Achilles can certainly help us understand how important the legend of Penthesilea was (and remains) from a feminist perspective because Achilles alone among the Greek warriors could kill her in mortal combat. Many exegetes have missed the symbolic vitality of her killer, and it is worth pondering why.

Stephanie Mitchell and Patience Schell (eds.), *The Women's Revolution in Mexico, 1910–1953* (Lanham, MD: Rowman & Littlefield, 2007). A strange piece of business, as all the essays seem determined to stay away from any women warriors who actually engaged in combat. Martha Rocha's "The Faces of Rebellion," in fact, goes out of its way to avoid talking about "soldiers leading troops," but instead concentrates on the lives of seven women officially recognized as "Veterans of the Mexican Revolution" but who did not fight in this traditional way. Pity, as there were many important *soldaderas* to examine.

Bernard Moitt, *Women and Slavery in the French Antilles, 1635–1848* (Bloomington: Indiana University Press, 2001). See especially "Women and Resistance," pp. 125–150. Some interesting observations that women were as likely as men to resist and "Women's enthusiasm for the struggle never waned even when defeat seemed inevitable" (p. 129). Provides a number of insights into the insurrections in Guadeloupe and Saint-Dominque with cameo appearances by Solitude and Martha-Rose.

Molly Moore, *A Woman at War* (New York: Scribner's, 1993). The author, a reporter for the *Washington Post*, had access to General Walter Boomer, commander of the Marine expeditionary force, and thus was on the inside of many of the key field decisions of the First Gulf War. Written at a time when it was still unusual for American women to be at war and writing about it up close and personal. Clearly shows women in harm's way and worthy of equal opportunity to remain so *if* they so choose.

Caroline Moorehead, *A House in the Mountains: The Women Who Liberated Italy from Fascism* (New York: Harper, 2020). While the title is a bit of an exaggeration, this work does capture the widespread courage and effects of the women (called *staffette*) in northern Italy in the Piedmont who resisted the Germans, the Fascists of Mussolini, and a variety of other forces through strikes, passive resistance, and widespread insurgent warfare. By using four specific women, the author gives us a poignant glimpse of their actions over time.

Scott Lauria Morgensen, "Settler Homonationalism: Theorizing Settler Colonialism within Queer Modernities," *GLQ: A Journal of Lesbian and Gay Studies,* Vol. 16, #1–2 (2010), pp. 105–131. Looks at the life and times of Osh-Tisch, known as Finds Them and Kills Them. She (taking the pronoun she and others among the Crows chose to describe her) was born in 1854 and lived as both a warrior and a *botes* or two-spirit and, for the author, represents a fine example of the repression of human sexuality by both Christian church elders and pastors as well as agents of the U.S. government. He argues further that "Queer scholarship on race and sexuality has been effective at marking colonial relations and discourses and inviting the study of settlement" (p. 118).

Note: The long shadow of the "two-spirit" phenomenon and the stunning example of Osh-Tisch are present in contemporary LGBTQ? Native Americans and their search for cultural, historical and sociological identity. See Brian Gilley, *Becoming Two-Spirit: Gay Identity and Social Acceptance in Indian Country* (Lincoln: University of Nebraska Press, 2006). Based on his research primarily with the Green Country Two-Spirit Society and the Two-Spirit Society of Denver, the author seeks to explore these and other issues.

Mildred Mortimer, *Women Fight, Women Write: Texts on the Algerian War* (Charlottesville: University of Virginia Press, 2018). Delves into the many ways women contributed to the Algerian Revolution and were subsequently disappointed in it. Very detailed and containing significant levels of literary criticism. For discussions of women's roles as presented in fiction, see especially chapter 2, "Herstory is the War Story," pp. 49–76.

Note: Nicole Ladewig, "Between Worlds: Algerian Women in Conflict," DeGroot and Peniston-Bird, *op. cit,* pp. 240–255, puts the combat and resistance roles in Algeria in a wider gender perspective, arguing that "women will remain the hallmark of national dialogue and stratagems with or without their consent" (p. 255).

Howard Moses, *Nzinga, African Warrior Queen* (Seattle: Jugum Press, 2016). Very useful on her early life and the African context of her times. Shows the many pressures operating on all African polities in the area.

Nazneen Moshina, "Growing Trends of Female 'Jihadism' in Bangladesh," *Counter Terrorist Trends and Analyses,* Vol. 9, #8 (August 2017), pp. 7–11. Points out that increasing number of female *jihadis* in Bangladesh are caused by heavy counterterrorism efforts by the military and the resulting need for new cadres.

Sherry Mou, "Xian," in Pennington (ed.), *op. cit.*, pp. 495–497, provides a provocative portrait of this Chinese woman who died in 601 CE. She was a military commander who engaged in many battles and wars during her lifetime as Grand Mistress of Gaoliang, Commander Mistress of Songkang, and Mistress of Qiaoguo.

Robert Mrazek, *The Indomitable Florence Finch: The Untold Story of a War Widow Turned Resistance Fighter and Savior of American POWs* (New York: Hachette, 2020). Incredible heroism shown by a true woman warrior. She saved the lives of many U.S. POWs during their horrible imprisonment after the fall of Bataan and despite being captured by the Japanese and tortured severely, she never revealed those she had helped. After the war she was awarded the highest civilian award, the Medal of Freedom.

Patrick Kagbeni Muana, "Masarico," in Pennington (ed.), *op. cit.,* pp. 285–286. Masarico (1470–1545) was a Mende queen who hived off from north central Africa and led her followers (subsequently known as the Manes) into what is now Liberia and Sierra Leone. Portuguese sources describe her military innovations, including complex three-pronged attacking units and other strategic imperatives, as well as their own fierce fighting with the Manes at their fortress at Mina. For a history of the Manes invasions, see Joe Alie, *A New History of Sierra Leone* (New York: St. Martin's Press, 1990), pp. 37–42.

Robert Mugabe, *Women's Liberation in the Zimbabwean Revolution* (San Francisco: John Brown Book Club, 1979). See especially "The Armed Struggle Stage," pp. 14–16, for the role of the Special Women's Detachment of the Zimbabwe National Liberation Army. For a snapshot overview of the Rhodesian war, see Dana Benner, "The Wages of War," *Military History,* Vol. 36, #2 (July 2019), pp. 32–41.

Kate Muir, *Arms and Women* (London: Sinclair-Stevenson Publishing, 1992). An overview of the usual suspects but with some useful historical background.

Clare Mulley, *The Spy Who Loved: The Secrets and Lives of Christine Granville* (New York; St. Martin's Press, 2013). The absorbing story of a Polish woman (born Christine Skarbek) who served various spy organizations before, during, and after World War II and undertook some extremely dangerous missions into Nazi-occupied Europe, including Poland, Hungary, Bulgaria, Yugoslavia, and France. Makes a strong case for the importance of the resistance in Poland and the fact that Poland provided more support for Great Britain than previously credited. Christine was ultimately killed by a man who "loved" her but felt that killing her was the ultimate way of controlling this woman who lived her life to the fullest: without boundaries and without remorse. In this sense, her tale is a sad reminder of the problems many men have with independent women and why control issues lie at the heart of so many domestic violence issues.

————. *The Women Who Flew for Hitler* (New York: St. Martin's, 2017). The truly incredible story of Melita von Stauffenberg and Hana Reitsch, who flew very important test missions in a variety of high-performance (and dangerous) aircraft including the famous JU-87 Stuka, ME 262, and Me 163 Komet Rocket planes. Melita, who was part Jewish, got her "Reichssipenant," i.e., officially recognizing her status as "equal to Aryan" (p. 137), flew 15 tests of dive-bombing in one day and 2,000 overall, "a performance unmatched by any pilot in history" (p. 167). Both received several Iron Crosses. Hana, a devoted follower of Hitler, even flew *into* Berlin in April, 1945 to try to rescue him from his bunker and wanted to commit suicide with him when he would not go with her. But instead, he sent her out of the bunker. She would die in 1979, either of heart attack or by taking the suicide pill Hitler had given her. Melita was shot down and killed by American fighters three weeks before the end of the war. Amazing women, amazing times, amazing footnotes for the history of women warriors.

Alicia Muñoz, "To Kill A General: The Fragmentation of Women's Political Violence in Fiction and Journalism," *Chasqui*, Vol. 43, #1 (2014), pp. 158–171. Looks at the images and roles of women revolutionaries in fiction, especially those in Brazil and Nicaragua, and finds considerable ambiguity in the acceptance of women of violence.

Mahani Musa, "Women in the Malayan Communist Party," *Journal of Southeast Asian Studies*, Vol. 44, #2 (June 2013), pp. 226–249. Argues that women were involved in the founding, sustaining, and revolutionary activities of the Malayan Communist Party (1941–1989), including serving with guerrilla bands acting against the Japanese during World War II and later against the British Colonial Authorities (1949–1960) during "The Emergency." Based on interviews with survivors, the author demonstrated the variety of roles, including combat, played by women such as Lee Ming and Ah Chow and others in the 10th Regiment. Musa believes they should have their own space in war history.

Meagan Muschara, "Kurdish Women Guerrilla Fighters," *History in the Making*, Vol. 8, #1 (2015), pp. 202–225. Looks at actual Kurdish women fighters and concludes that they have joined in order to defend their homeland *and* to emancipate themselves from the male hierarchies in the villages and locales where they live. The PKK (Kurdish Communist Party) has had need for fighters and they have fulfilled that need and in return have gained some important autonomy (40% of fighters are women and there are some all-female units). At the same time, the author seems overly optimistic that this newfound autonomy would endure should the PKK be successful when ISIS resistance is over. The author also provides a good short history of the Kurdish people and their long-term struggle for independence.

Pamela Murray, *For Glory and Bolívar: The Remarkable Life of Manuela Saenz* (Austin: University of Texas Press, 2008). A long paean to a remarkable woman and Latina (and other) icon. Manuela Saenz of Peru (1797–1856) was the *"Libertadora del libertador"* as designated by *For Glory and Bolívar* after she saved him from an assassination attempt. Married to an English businessman in Peru, she met and worked with *Bolívar* for eight years and was "one of the most prominent women of the revolution" eventually given the "Dame of the Sun" award. Does not seem to have actually participated in battles but did important intelligence gathering and intervened to prevent his assignations. A huge feminist icon for her revolutionary activities (and her subsequently being airbrushed out of history for so long). This work reestablishes her place in the history of Latin American liberation and provides considerable background and detail on her entire life and afterlife.

   Note: A further exploration of the life and legacy of Manuela Saenz through the various lenses of sexism, male chauvinism, the cult of Bolívar, nationalism, and Latin American feminism, see Pamela S. Murray, "'Loca' or 'Libertadora': Manuela Sáenz in the Eyes of History and Historians,

1900–c. 1900," *Journal of Latin American Studies*, Vol. 33, #2 (May 2001), pp. 291–310.

Theresa Denise Murray, "Gráinne Mhaol, Pirate Queen of Connacht: Behind the Legend," *History Ireland*, Vol. 13, #2 (2005), pp. 16–20. Provides a great deal of necessary historical information in which to place this Irish pirate warrior, concluding:

> Behind the myths of Grace O'Malley, pirate queen, and Grainne Mhaol, icon of Ireland, stands Grainne Ni Maille, a proud and courageous woman, determined to ensure that she and her family received their rights. She earned and lost fortunes, each time rebuilding, "by land and sea." (p. 20)

Bruce Myles, *Night Witches: The Untold Story of Soviet Women in Combat* (Chicago: Academy Press, 1997). A fascinating story of the Soviet women who flew against the Germans during World War II. Features women who dropped bombs and provided close air support and assistance to partisans and ground forces and especially those in the "free hunter" units who targeted German aircraft. Many personal stories of women in action are presented. Anyone interested in the subject of women in combat should read this work, for it is a soaring tribute to women as wartime heroes.

Byran Nakamura, "Palmyra and the Roman East," *Greek, Roman and Byzantine Studies*, Vol. 34, #2 (1993), pp. 133–150. Looks at Zenobia's rise to power and short reign (270–272 CE) while she expanded and tried to hold territory in the Levant, Arabia, and Egypt and her rapid downfall. Interesting description of her military force, a mixture of heavy cavalry, light bowmen and auxiliaries; and how she was hampered by her lack of a large standing army.

Akanksha Narain, "Roles and Participation of Women in Indian Left-Wing Extremism: From 'Victims' to 'Victimizers' of Violence," *Counter Terrorist Trends and Analyses*, Vol. 9, #8 (August 2017), pp. 12–16. During the 50 years of the Naxal Maoist insurgency in India, women have become combatants and somewhat more empowered although pejorative male hierarchical structures exist within the movement, and "rapes and sexual slavery are often legitimized in the name of boosting the 'morale of the troops'" (p. 15).

Mary Nash, "'Milicianas' and Homefront Heroines: Images of Women in Revolutionary Spain," *History of European Ideas*, Vol. 11 (1989), pp. 235–244. Finds that the outbreak of the Spanish Civil War brought many women and their roles into sharp relief and forced a multiplicity of images and assumptions into the general population.

Amy Nathan, *Yankee Doodle Gals: The Women Pilots of World War II* (Washington: National Geographic Society, 2001). Lavishly illustrated and breezily written, this paean to the WASPs (Women Airforce Service Pilots), reports that 25,000 applied, 1,102 served, and 38 died. They towed targets for male pilots to shoot at and also delivered 12,000 aircraft of 77 kinds (including the "tough-to-fly biggies" the B-25, B-17, and especially the B-29) to the major theaters of war. These "gals" delivered the goods and are worthy of high praise. They deserved much better than they received at the end of the war.

National Geographic Profiles, "Christine de Pizan: France's First Lady of Letters," *National Geographic History* (Mar./Apr. 2020), pp. 8–11. Highlights her extraordinary life and career and points out that her portrait of Joan of Arc is the only contemporary account we have of "La Purcell."

Lindie Naughton, *Markievicz: A Most Outrageous Rebel* (Dublin: Merrion Press, 2016). A very lively and supportive account of Markievicz as a national heroine. Useful chapters on her role(s) in "Easter Week 1916—Year One of Irish History," pp. 155–174 and "Condemned to Live," pp. 175–198.

Mary Lou Colbert Neale, "Women of War," *Military History* (Dec. 1993), pp. 35ff. Astonishingly enough to most Americans, 800,000 Soviet women served at the front during World War II. This short article gives a good overview of what they did, including most of the roles normally reserved for males in the American military of the period. Contains a very interesting interview with "Tamar Pamyatnikh, Soviet Heroine." There is perhaps not much to honor about the Soviet system, but their need for warriors gives us a powerful example of how successful women can be when given a chance women are denied in other societies.

Tim Newark, *Women Warriors* (London: Blandford, 1989). From Amazons of legend and fact to Jeanne Countess of Montfort and Christine de Pizan, female military leaders are examined. A useful introduction for those not used to seeing women in battle. See especially the chapters, "The True Amazons," "Amazons of the Jungle," "Braver than Her Husband," "Celtic Queens," "Women of Christ," and "Hundred Years War Women."

Sharon Newman, *Defending the City of God* (New York: Palgrave, 2014). A useful look at Melisende, "A True Ruler," the first hereditary queen of Jerusalem (who was *Melisende Regina Sola* from 1143–1149). Offers insights into what it took to be a Christian female ruler in a sea of Muslims and predatory male Christians.

Josephine Nhongo-Simbanegavi, *For Better or Worse? Women and ZANLA in Zimbabwe's Liberation Struggle* (Harare: Weaver Press, 2000). Challenging "the myth of gender equality" during the war, the author distinguishes between the use of women freedom fighters in liberated zones versus contested zones and argues that in general, the ZANLA leadership did not make much use of women in the latter. See especially chapter 4, "ZANLA Women at the Front," pp. 79–98.

John Nichol, *Spitfire: A Very British Love Story* (New York: Simon & Schuster, 2018). See especially "Spitfire Women," pp. 121–135, for a look at the female pilots of the Air Transport Auxiliary (ATA). Interestingly enough, these did not consist of UK women alone but also some Poles and others such as Stefania Wojtulanis and Anna Leska.

Helen Nicholson, "Women on the Third Crusade," *Journal of Medieval History*, Vol. 23, #4 (December 1997), pp. 335–349. Author concludes that women played an active role in the Third Crusade (1189–1192) after looking at Muslim sources including Amad al-Din and Baha al-Din. Argues that their role was promoted by Muslims to show their moral superiority and downplayed by Christians to show that the crusades were "moral."

David Nicolle, *Yarmuk AD 636: The Muslim Conquest of Syria* (Oxford: Osprey Publishing, 1994), pp. 70–71. Contains an engaging but tantalizingly brief portrait of Hind Bint 'Utba, mother of the future Caliph Mu'awiyah, who, at the battle of Yarmuk, leads other women in rallying the Muslims when the Byzantines reach the Muslim camp. Contains a great admonishment from the camp followers:

> We are the daughters of the Night;
> We move among the cushions.
> With the grace of gentle kittens
> Our bracelets on our elbows.
> If you attack we shall embrace you;
> And if you retreat we will forsake you
> With a loveless separation. (p. 72)

Carolyn Niethammer, *Daughters of the Earth: The Lives and Legends of American Indian Women* (New York: Macmillan, 1977). Contains an engaging section, "Warrior Women," pp. 165–185, with quick looks at a great variety of Native American groups from the Acoma Pueblo to the Cocopah, Comanche, Mandan, Ojibwe, Osage, Tingit, Yavapai, and others rarely covered in companion works.

Marco Nilsson, "Muslim Mothers in Ground Combat Against the Islamic State: Women's Identities and Social Change in Iraqi Kurdistan," *Armed Forces & Societies*, Vol. 44, #2 (2017), pp. 261–279.
  Shades of Umm 'Umara (a.k.a. Umm 'Uhud) and Hind Bint 'Utbah. This stimulating argument looks at the roles of Kurdish women warriors in the fight against ISSIS as part of the Peshmerga Army. Based on interviews with 10 women fighters (the majority of whom are married) in the all-woman battalion of the Patriotic Union of Kurdistan (PUK), the author concludes that they do not wish to fight as "honorary men" but as women, and not as equals (in terms of strength) but as equivalents, able to participate fully in combat. While many of them argue that they did not join the fight in order to advance society, being in the military has indeed altered society for the better, they claim.

Anne Noggle, *A Dance with Death: Soviet Airwomen in World War II* (College Station: Texas A&M University Press, 1995). A big, bold and exciting story of the Soviet pilots who were female. A gripping tale, especially the sections on the female night fighters. They were true warriors by any measure.

Natalie Marie-Louise Nolte, *Why Arab-Muslim Women in War Matters: A Case Study Analysis in the United Arab Emirates* (Lund University: Master's Thesis, 2015). The author argues that the inclusion of women in the United Arab Emirates' armed forces had been enabled by a top-down approach by state authorities to suggest that women are now playing more significant roles in a "modern" United Arab Emirate nation.

Holly Norton, *Estate by Estate: The Landscape of the 1733 St. Jan Slave Rebellion* (Syracuse: Maxwell School of Citizenship and Public Affairs Dissertation, 2013). Most interestingly, the author notes in an appendix that there were 135 slave revolts in the New World, and the author warns that "this list is not exhaustive" (p. 318). Quite detailed and gives good information of specifics on the slave revolt leader Breffu (?–1734).

Barbara Oberg (ed.), *Women in the American Revolution: Gender, Politics, and the Domestic World* (Charlottesville: University of Virginia Press, 2019). Astonishingly, this wide-ranging set of essays dealing with women and the American Revolution does not include any portraits of the women—white, Black, and Native American—who actually fought in the American Revolution. This work certainly could have used a chapter on the likes of Nonhelema Hokolesqua, Deborah Sampson, Nancy Hart, Rebecca Motte, Sybil Ludington, Margaret Cochran Corbin, Kate Barry, Anna Maria Lane, Prudence Cumings Wright, Nancy Ward, the two Ann Bailys (Ann Baily and Anne Hennis Trotter Bailey), Tyonajanegen (Two Kettles Together), the various "Molly Pitchers" such as Mary Ludwig Hays, and many others. It would appear that we have yet a ways to travel in fully appreciating the many roles of women in our Founding Revolution.

Lana Obradovic, "Comparative Analysis of Women's Military Participation in East Asia," *Res Militaris: Ergomas*, #1 (September 2015), pp. 1–16. A very illuminating piece. Shows that because of a Confucian set of cultural values, Japan, China, North Korea, and the South Korea of today have not utilized their female resources in the military context to full value. All three East Asian countries check in at almost the same rate of women in terms of their military ratios for female participation: 4.7% for China, 4.1% for Japan, 4.6% for North Korea, and 3.35% for South Korea. For the latter two countries, among the most militarized in the world, these numbers are truly astonishing. The author points out that the paucity of women warriors in the history of Japan and Korea adds to the negativity of societal interest in higher levels of female participation.

Wale Ogunyemi, *Queen Amina of Zazzau* (Ibadan: University Press PLC, 1999). Another male author obsessed with the legend of Amina's taking a young man to bed whenever her army captured a city and then killing him in the morning. This play does celebrate her warcraft as well, however, calling Amina "a strategist for all times." It would be interesting if her tale were told in high school to boys and girls, and their teachers, men and women.

Stephen O'Harrow, "From Co-loa to the Trung Sisters' Revolt: Vietnam as the Chinese Found It," *Asian Perspectives*, Vol. 22, #1 (1979), pp. 140–164. A most useful mining of poetry and archaeology as well as history to set the stage for the Trung Sisters.

Lynne Olson, *Madame Fourcade's Secret War* (New York: Random House, 2019). Engaging and fulsome portrait of Marie-Madeleine Fourcade, whose

Alliance (Code named "Noah's Ark" by the Germans for its use of animal names for its operatives) unit was the largest and most effective of the French Resistance intelligence networks. The only woman to serve as a French *chef de resistance*, her network operated as she moved from Vichy to Pau to Marseille to Toulouse to Lyon to Cahors and finally to Paris. Her network worked with MI6 to provide invaluable information necessary on many subjects including the D-Day invasion, the advent of the V-1 and V-2 rockets (which led to the bombing of Peenemunde on August 17, 1943) and German U-boats operating out of Lorient. Twice captured by the Gestapo, she escaped to survive the war. Reading this work, however, one is struck with how truly effective the Gestapo in was rolling up portions of her network and other networks time and time again. See her own account of the war, *Noah's Ark*, reviewed above.

Note: The effectiveness of the French Resistance or the lack thereof is explored in robust fashion by Douglas Porch in his "The Myth of the French Resistance," *MHQ: The Quarterly Journal of Military History,* Vol. 1, #2 (Winter 1998), pp. 98–107.

For a balanced overview of all the resistance movements in Europe during World War II, see Olivier Wieviorka, *Resistance in Western Europe 1940–1945* (New York: Columbia University Press, 2012).

Organization of Angolan Women, *Angolan Women Building the Future: From National Liberation to Women's Emancipation* (London: Zed Books, 1984). This somewhat polemical work suggests the validity of "the double helix" dynamics of women's suppression offered by Margaret and Patrice Higonnet (see above) operating in southern Africa.

Note: For a more scholarly and holistic treatment of the decolonization struggle and liberation of Angola, see John Marcum, *The Angolan Revolution Volume I The Anatomy of an Explosions (1950–1962)* (Cambridge: MIT Press, 1969) and especially *The Angolan Revolution Volume II: Exile Politics and Guerilla Warfare (1962–1976)* (Cambridge: MIT Press, 1978).

Iris Origo, *War in Val D'Orcia 1943–1944* (Boston: David R. Godine, 1947). A touching, illuminating, and very satisfying diary account of an English woman married to an Italian and living on a Tuscan property with dozens of farms and a castle. Amazing chaos in Italy after the king changes sides (July 1943), but she does not join the Allies until the Germans have taken a measure of control, especially over the Italian armed forces. An almost unbelievable situation with refugees, escaped Allied prisoners, partisans, Fascists, Fascist militias, monarchists, communists, and deserters (both German/Austrian and Italian as well as false German/Italian ones) roaming around and all coming to her household for food, clothing, shelter, and often directions (a Moroccan escaped POW is headed north instead of south). Lots of ineffectual Allied bombing is recorded as well. This is a fine read describing a most turbulent time.

Dorinda Outram, "Revolution, Domesticity, and Feminism: Women in France after 1789," *The Historical Journal,* Vol. 32, #4 (1998), pp. 971–979. Puts the French Revolution in perspective with regard to the advances women made and did not make and why.

P–S

Julia Papp, "Female Body–Male Body: The Valiant Hungarian Women of Eger and Szigetvár from the 16th Century in Historiography, Literature, and Art," *Cogent Arts & Humanities,* Vol. 3, #1 (2016), pp. 1–17. Analyzes the way these women warriors were granted transformation from the normal gender roles of the era by their heroics in standing against the Other in the form of the Ottoman Turks and their sieges of the Hungarian homeland.

Geoffrey Parker, "The Spanish Road to the Netherlands," *MHQ: The Quarterly Journal of Military History*, Vol. 17, #2 (Winter 2005), pp. 35–44. Gives the reader an excellent background on the Duke of Alba's campaign to subdue the Netherlands. This piece also sets the stage for the 1473 battle for Haarlem, where Kenau Simonsdochter Hasselaer and other Dutch women fought toe-to-toe with the Spanish regulars.

Note: Some of these changes were already happening on the ground during the Netherlands campaign. See Ignacio and Ivan Notario Lopez, *The Spanish Tercios 1536–1704* (Oxford: Osprey Publishing, 2013).

Note: Parker's seminal work on warfare in this period should also be consulted for an overview of the revolution in military affairs which was occurring at this time: Geoffrey Parker, *The Military Revolution: Military Innovation and the Rise of the West, 1500–1800* (Cambridge: Cambridge University Press, 1996). Parker is also a very good guide for the background covering the Thirty Years' War period. See his *Global Crisis: War, Climate Change and Catastrophe in the Seventeenth Century* (New Haven: Yale University Press, 2008).

Simon Parkin, *A Game of Birds and Wolves: The Secret Game That Won the War* (London: Sceptre, 2020). The World War II story of how in 1942 an intrepid band of WRENs (Women's Royal Naval Service) worked with an imaginative captain to perfect, through gaming, the strategy and tactics that would defeat the German U-Boat campaign against Great Britain. These brilliant young women (one was 17) brought fresh eyes, natural curiosity, and an ability to sift through sea battles as they were happening. An amazing, overlooked story.

David J. Parkinson, "Listening for *Blak Annes* at Dunbar Castle," *Preprint* (May 2019), pp. 1–12. Looks at the various narratives concerning one Agnes Randolph's defiance at Dunbar in 1338.

Sonia Parnell, *A Woman of No Importance: The Untold Story of the American Spy Who Helped Win World War II* (New York: Viking, 2019). Talk about women warriors, this American woman, with a wooden leg, led a highly successful French Resistance movement for the British OSS, killed many German soldiers, and ended up with highly prestigious Croix de Guerre with Palm Clusters "for her heroism in combat," the OSS Distinguished Service Cross. What a tale of courage and fortitude!

Rod Paschall, "Folly in the Philippines," *MHQ: The Quarterly Journal of Military History,* Vol. 23, #1 (Autumn 2010), pp. 83–87. Shows the American intervention after the Spanish-American War would come back to haunt the United States, as in the cases of various insurgencies including the post–World War II Huk rebellion against the Filipino government in 1946–1954 featuring Commander Leonora Hipas.

Juliette Pattinson, *Behind Enemy Lines: Gender, Passing and the Special Operations Executive in the Second World War* (Manchester: Manchester University Press, 2007). A scholarly examination of the gender aspects within the SOE and the impact they had on training and operations, especially among female recruits. See especially chapter 6, "The Best Disguise," pp. 136–154.

C. R. Pennell (ed.), *Bandits of the Sea* (New York: New York University Press, 2001). This collection highlights the notion that for the marginalized, piracy was something of an equal opportunity employer. See especially Marcus Rediker, "Liberty Beneath the Jolly Roger: The Lives of Anne Bonny and Mary Read, Pirates," pp. 299–320.

Reina Pennington, *Wings, Women and War* (Topeka: University Press of Kansas, 2007). Women aviators deserve more publicity than they have received. This book is a start. There are quite a few superlative, if relatively unknown, Russian and German female pilots.

————, "Reaching for the Sky: Hanna Reitsch and Melitta Schiller," *MHQ: The Quarterly Journal of Military History*, Vol. 22, #1 (Autumn 2009), pp. 33–43. Two of Hitler's favorite pilots, one of whom was Jewish, were female. An amazing story of virtue rewarded and unrewarded, a cautionary tale on many levels.

———— (ed.), *Amazons to Fighter Pilots*, two vols. (Westport: Greenwood Press, 2003). Probably the best overall collection of short essays on women at war. Students find excellent short essays by a variety of specialty authors, pieces that stimulate interest and debate. A must resource for those looking for unusual subjects and a great feast for those hungry for forgotten women warriors in action and "hiding in plain sight." Writing this annotated bibliography was greatly enhanced by all the useful information and follow-up sources it contains (see the many Pennington [ed.], *op. cit.* references). Any student looking for the unusual as well as the controversial in terms of the wide-net inclusion criteria will not be disappointed. Outstandingly comprehensive and very well organized.

————, "'Do Not Speak of the Services You Rendered': Women Veterans of Aviation in the Soviet Union," DeGroot and Peniston-Bird, *op. cit*, pp. 152–171. Arguing, persuasively, that "Women were never received as a part of the Soviet military elite" (p. 171), the author describes precisely why they should have been. They were regarded as temporary, yet these women were very brave, very dedicated, and gave their lives in service to their country. Their place was in the home, the authorities insisted, even though they had passed every test in combat and should have been regarded as true warriors.

Theda Perdue (ed.), *Shifters: Native American Women's Lives* (London: Oxford University Press, 2001). Although there are numerous examples in chapters dealing with all manner of Native American women's lives, the one of principal interest to those perusing this annotated bibliography will be Laura Moore, "Lozen: An Apache Woman Warrior," pp. 92–107. This chapter contains important information of note. First, it provides essential decoding of the only photograph of Lozen taken when the train was taking the defeated Apaches to their exile (and early deaths) in Florida. Moore positions Naiche, the chief, in the center of the photograph, with Geronimo in the place of honor to his left and Lozen sitting next to Geronimo as evidence of her occupying the Apache position of second-in-command. Second, Moore sums up vital dimensions of Lozen's life, concluding, "Lozen forswore Chiricahua gender norms. But although she did not marry, did not have children, did not perform women's typical tasks and instead excelled at masculine pursuits, her community perceived her as neither a threat nor a deviant" (p. 106).

Barbara Bennett Peterson (ed.), *Notable Women of China: Shang Dynasty to the Early Twentieth Century* (London: M.E. Sharpe, 2000). In a work filled with many poets, courtesans, queens, and writers come some important women warriors, including Fu Hao, the Shang dynasty general; Madam Lu, leader of a peasant uprising during the Western Han dynasty; Madam Xian, general and military strategist from the Northern and Southern dynasties; Princess Pingyang, general and daughter of the first Tang emperor; Quin Liangyu, general of the Ming dynasty; and Wang Cong'er, leader of the White Lotus Rebellion during the Qing dynasty.

Note: See also Paul Lococo, Jr., "The Qing Empire" in Graff and Higham, *op. cit.*, pp. 11–134.

Angeliki Petridou, *Female Fighters in the Greek Civil War. Personal Narratives of Survivors* (Thessaloniki: International Hellenic University, 2018). This work, based on a number of personal accounts, can help the interested reader plumb the depths of the participants of the women who fought for their cause and why.

Captain Katie Petronio, "Get Over It! We're Not All Created Equal," in *Marine Corps Gazette* (July 2012), pp. 29–32. A 2010 Bowdoin graduate, after serving tours of duty in Iraq and Afghanistan, concludes that women should *not* be placed in *all* combat situations. Her personal experience is cogent.

William Philbrick, *The Last Stand: Custer, Sitting Bull, and the Battle of the Little Bighorn* (New York: Viking, 2010). Describes the roles of a number of Native American women at the Battle of the Little Bighorn, including the Hunkpapa Sioux Moving Robe Woman who went into battle to avenge the death of her 10-year-old brother Deeds. She jumped on her horse and went into the battle, being described as "pretty as a bird" by Rain in the Face, who said "Always when there is a woman in the charge . . . it causes the warriors to vie with one another in displaying their valor" (p. 179). Later she would kill the African American interpreter Isaiah Dorman in revenge.

Note: Paul Hutton provides a counterfactual account of the battle as presented by Philbrick, "Could Custer Have Won?," *MHQ: The Quarterly*

Journal of Military History, Vol. 25, #2 (Winter 2013), pp. 28–39, including the classic painting *Last Stand*. Hutton argues that this defensive posture was his only one and that at various points during the long-running battle Custer might have been able to capture many noncombatants and hold them for a standoff. Perhaps the most useful map of Custer's attack at the Little Bighorn (pp. 34–35).

Maj Tracy A. Phillips, *Nidia Díaz: Guerrilla Commander*, Research Paper (Montgomery: Air Command and Staff College, 1997). The author provides a once-over-lightly account of Nidia Díaz's various roles within the Farabundo Martí (FMLN) and in the peace process and believes she was a significant factor in that success, which eventually allowed FMLN participation in the political life of El Salvador.

Ursula Phillips, "Apocalyptic Feminism: Adam Mickiewicz and Margaret Fuller," *The Slavonic and East European Review*, Vol. 87, #1 (Jan. 2009), pp. 15ff. Interesting analysis of the portrayal by Mickiewicz of Emilia Plater, "soldier-heroine of the 1830–1831 insurrection in Lithuania."
    Note: For an illuminating look at the military aspects of the Polish November Uprising (and its suppression) of 1830, see Maciej Jonasz, "Poland 1830–1831: The November Insurrection," *Strategy and Tactics*, #326 (Jan.–Feb. 2021), pp. 44–53.

Manulea Lavinas Picq, *Vernacular Sovereignties: Indigenous Women Challenging World Politics* (Tucson: The University of Arizona Press, 2018). See especially Lorenza Avemanay's chapter, "The Inheritance of Resistance," pp. 63–78, for information on Bartolina Sisa, Gregoria Apaza, and other women warriors, who, the author claims, resisted the Spanish from the beginning. Today's politically active women draw directly on their "inheritance of resistance" from colonial times.

Plato (trans. Benjamin Jowett), *The Republic* (Luton: Andrews UK Limited, 2012). Socrates weighs in, perhaps ironically, on women warriors:

> The guardians of our state are to be watch-dogs, as we have already said. Now dogs are not divided into he's and she's—we do not take the masculine gender out to hunt and leave the females at home at look after the puppies. The have the same employments—the only difference between them is that the one sex is stronger and the other weaker. But if women are to have the same employments as men, they must have the same education—they must be taught music and gymnastics, and the art of war. I know that a great joke will be made of their riding on horseback and carrying weapons; the sight of the naked old, wrinkled

women showing their agility in the palestra will certainly not be a vision of beauty and may be expected to become a famous jest. (pp. 48–49)

Note: James Blythe provides the interested reader the views of scholastic writers Ptolemy of Lucca (1236–1327) and Giles of Rome (1243–1316) who labor long and hard to rebut the argument in Aristotle's *Politics* that women should receive the same military training as men and take an equal part in fighting. See James M. Blythe, "Women in the Military: Scholastic Arguments and Medieval Images of Female Warriors," *History of Political Thought,* Vol. 22, #2 (Summer 2001), pp. 242–269.

Gerhard Pollauer, *The Lost History of the Amazons* (New York: Didactic Press, 2014). This work ransacks antiquity and the Middle Ages to find stories of and evidence for Amazonian warfare in fittingly didactic fashion.

Sahar Pomeroy, *Spartan Women* (London: Oxford University Press, 2002). A very detailed, in-depth look at all facets of the lives of Spartan women, with reliance on the observations of Xenophon and Plutarch and many other sources. The definitive account of them available in English.

Elena Poniatowski, *Las Soldaderas: Women of the Mexican Revolution* (El Paso: Cinco Pirto Press, 2006). Lavishly illustrated, this work illuminates Petra Herrera, Angela Jimenez, Amelio Robles, Maria de La Luz Espinosa, and other *soldaderas.*

J. M. B. Porter, "Ermengarde of Narbonne," Pennington (ed.), *op. cit.*, p. 158. Indicates how Ermengarde of Narbonne (c. 1120–c. 1194) led troops in battle from 1172 to 1173, when the Aquitaine nobles revolted against King Henry II of England.

Esther Portillo-Gonzales, *FMLN Reflections, 20 Years Later: An Interview With Nidia Díaz*, NACLA Report on the Americas (New York: North American Congress in Latin America, 2012). Maria Marta Valladares, known as Nidia Díaz, became an important commander of the guerrilla forces of the Farabundo Martí National Liberation Front (FMLN). She looks back on her wartime sacrifices and believes they were worth it.

Johannes Postma, *Slave Revolts* (Greenwood Press, 2008). This very useful work puts in perspective the 100,000 Africans who died in slave revolts or their following executions coming to the New World during the centuries of the transatlantic slave trade and the prominent role played by unnamed women because of their more frequent access to different parts of the ships in question and usually not being shackled. Also contains biographies of such women leaders as Zeferina of Brazil and Queen Nanny of Nanny Town in Jamaica.

Christian P. Potholm, *Winning at War* (Lanham, MD: Rowman & Littlefield, 2010). Analyzes the seven ingredients necessary for success in warfare regardless of time or place. These include superior discipline, superior technology, sustained but controlled ruthlessness, protection of capital from people and rulers, superior will, receptivity to innovation, and the belief there will always be another war. Students should consult this work when doing their research to help explain the success or failure of particular women warriors and warrior queens by putting them in broader contexts. Some aspects of the nature of warfare change throughout history even though the ingredients for success do not.

Margaret Poulos, *Arms and the Woman: Just Warriors and the Greek Feminist Identity* (New York: Columbia University Press, 2008). The best source encountered on the role of the Greek women in the resistance against the Nazis and in the subsequent Greek Civil War, especially in the cases of the National Liberation Front (EAM) and the Democratic Army of Greece (DSE). The author, for example, asserts that women made up 30% of the combat forces of the DSE and 70% of its logistical support (p. 111). A nice blend of feminist history and military dimensions.

James Powell, "The Role of Women in Fifth Crusade," in B. Kedar (ed.) *The Horns of Hattin* (Jerusalem: Israel Exploration Society, 1992), pp. 294–301. In an article taken from his book *Anatomy of a Crusade* (Philadelphia: University of Pennsylvania Press, 1986), the author shows how women served in many capacities, including that of guards, and fought Muslims at the siege of Darnietta in the Fifth Crusade. Some amusing anecdotes are highlighted as when the devout prelate Jacques de Vitry encountered some Genoese who were attacking another city-state and "The burghers took my horses and I made their wives crusaders" (p. 301).

Grace Pratt, "Female War Chiefs of the Blackfeet," *Frontier Times* (1971), pp. 22–23, 46. Despite the claims of others, the Blackfeet did have women warriors, including Running Eagle who, born Brown Eagle, worked her way up into the Braves' Society by counting coup and fighting the Crows.

Richard Pressfield, *The Last of the Amazons* (New York: Doubleday, 2002). (F) This tale portrays the Amazons as beset by "bad" Greeks such as Heracles and Theseus, who envy and fear their freewheeling lifestyles and the prominence (and promiscuity) of their women leaders. Most useful in providing the Greek perspective on Amazons; their exploits end badly versus the much more positive perspectives of the Central Asian peoples who portray Amazons, who often triumph in warfare no matter how much myth and cosmology the Greeks bring to bear.

Neil Price, *Children of Ash and Elm: A History of the Vikings* (New York: Basic Books, 2020). This fascinating look at the Vikings from their own perspective (including their creation myth that Odin and the other gods carved men from ash and women from elm driftwood) provides the reader with an excellent overview of their political, economic, and warring accomplishments. In the process the author is careful to examine the scholarship surrounding women at war, including the famous shield-maidens, and points out that the sagas are not totally reliable, that grave evidence is up for interpretation, and that stories about Viking warrior women are not dispositive, concluding:

> Taking a clear-eyed look at the archaeological data,
> It seems that there really were female warriors in the
> Viking Age, including a least one of command rank.
> They were never numerous, and few have been even
> tentatively identified, though this may change as we
> re-examine our sources and our consciences. There
> were rare exceptions—unusual people to be sure—
> but they were there. (p. 330)

Note: Price is also important in helping us understand some understudied elements essential to Viking Age life. For example, Viking society involved extensive slaveholding and especially slave-trading elements, while polygamy and concubinage contributed importantly to Viking raiding because young men without women of their own could reduce the gender imbalance in this way. The Viking age of raiding and plundering extensively did *not* originate in the British Isles but along the Baltic coast. Also Viking warriors were well trained, often from a young age, and this gave them an additional advantage in dealing with the levies of other groups of the era.

Note: For earlier works examining the Viking period and the warfare that accompanied it with more emphasis on the modalities of fighting, see Philip Parker, *The Northmen's Fury: A History of the Viking World* (London: Jonathan Cape, 2014) and Robert Ferguson, *The Vikings: A History* (New York: Viking, 2014).

Richard Price (ed.), *Maroon Societies: Rebel Slave Communities in the Americas* (Baltimore: The Johns Hopkins University Press, 1979). A holistic look at Maroon societies in Jamaica, Spanish America, the French Caribbean, the Guianas, and Brazil.

Christina Proenza-Coles, *American Founders: How People of African Descent Established Freedom in the New World* (Montgomery: NewSouth Books, 2019). This broad-gauge study pays a compliment to Queen Nanny of Jamaica:

> Queen Nanny, the adroit maroon leader, is featured on a five hundred dollar bill. Born in Ghana, she governed a Jamaican maroon community designated as Nanny Town in the early 1700. Considered a gifted military leader by friend and foe, she repeatedly defended her community against colonial militias and organized raids that liberated approximately one thousand Afro-Jamaicans. (p. 173)

Alexander Prusin, *Serbia Under the Swastika: A World War II Occupation* (Urbana: University of Illinois Press, 2017). A most useful introduction to the many-sided struggle during World War II among various partisan groups and German forces. Puts paid to the national myth of extremely widespread participation however, suggesting that of the 3 million Serbs under German control, no more than 4% actually participated in the Resistance (p. 161).

Natalia Pushkareva, *Women in Russian History: From the Tenth to the Twentieth Century* (London: M.E. Sharpe, 19970). In addition to a sprinkling of women warriors such as Nadezhda Durova, the author highlights the "Russian Joan of Arc." Alena Arzamasskaia was a peasant girl who ran away from a convent, cut her hair, dressed as a man, and posing as a Cossack leader, rallied thousands of men to rebel, taking over the fortified city of Temnikov. Regarded as an excellent shot and fine leader, she was eventually captured by Tzarist forces and, like Joan of Arc, tortured and burned at the stake.

Sayyid Ahmad-Ullah Qadri, *Memoir of Chand Bibi: The Princess of Ahmednagar* (Hyderabad: The Osmania University Press, 1939). A long praise poem to the Sultana, who lived from 1550 to 1599, fought off the Mughals, and put down various rebellions, ultimately taking her own life by filling a well with acid and then jumping into it as the Mughals closed in. Other accounts have her killed by her own troops for negotiating with the same Mughals. See also the life and times of Tarabai Bhonsale (1675–1761), a Maratha Maharani who also resisted Mughal incursions and led her armies with a cavalry regiment.

Quintus of Smyrna, *The Trojan Epic Posthomerica*, trans. Alan James (Baltimore: Johns Hopkins University Press, 2004). Written 1,000 years after the *Iliad*, but based on a long oral tradition, it was compiled by Quintus of Smyrna (on the west coast of Asia Minor) and covers what happens after the death of Hector and the *Odyssey*. Book 1 accents the warrior and daughter of Mars, Penthesileia, and her death at the hands of Achilles.

Raquel Ramsay and Tricia Aurand, *Taking Flight: The Nadine Ramsey Story* (Topeka: University Press of Kansas, 2020). The heartwarming story of Nadine Ramsey, the WASP pilot who showed courage and distinction ferrying top aircraft all across the United States in wartime America.

Margaret Randell, *Sandino's Daughters* (Rutgers: Rutgers University Press, 1995). Firsthand accounts of women warriors who fought for the Sandinista National Liberation Front (FSLN). See especially pp. 40–79.

Countess Ranfurly, *To War with Whitaker: The Wartime Diaries of the Countess of Ranfurly 1939–1945* (London: William Heinemann, 1994). Bound and determined to follow her husband to war, the Countess keeps a most engaging diary as she helps to make war in the Mediterranean theater, meeting Wingate, Wavell, Eden, Churchill, Auchinleck, Patton, the kings of Greece, England, and Egypt, and many others while her poor husband languishes in Italy as a prisoner of war, having been captured in the Western Desert early in the war. He later escapes and joins her. Some of her revelations are quite arresting and even amusing, as when she reports that General Maitland "Jumbo" Wilson goes duck hunting in the Nile Delta, during which he and his party shoot 2,300 ducks in a single day! Jumbo later becomes Supreme Allied Commander of the Mediterranean Theatre and subsequently, ambassador to the United States.

Mike Rapport, *1848: The Age of Revolutions* (New York: Basic Books, 2008). Shows how the various revolutions failed to emancipate women or even get them the vote but shows on pp. 176–178 the variety of roles they played in the street fighting of February and March as well as June in Paris and Prague and in the Rhineland in 1849, especially in the Dresden insurrection in May. Numerous women were killed in the struggle, although they go unnamed in this account. No mention either of Maria Lebstuck, "First Lieutenant Maria," who was promoted to lieutenant for shooting three Austrian officers in Hungarian uprising, or Julia Banyai, an equestrian in a circus who also joined that revolution under her dead husband's name, Gyula Sarossy.

Note: In Gabriella Hauch, "Did Women Have a Revolution? Gender Battles in the European Revolution of 1848/49," in Axel Korner (ed.), *A European Revolution? International Ideas and National Memories of 1848* (New York: Palgrave Macmillan, 2000), pp. 64–84. Mentions two specific women, Pauline Wunderlich and Jeanee Deroine, as having participated in the German uprisings. For an eyewitness contemporary account, see Hanna Ballin Lewis (ed.), *A Year of Revolutions: Fanny Lewald's Recollections of 1848* (Province: Berghahn Books, 1997).

Donald Rayfield, *Edge of Empires: A History of Georgia* (London: Reaktion Books, 2017). See especially the chapter on the "King of Queens," Queen Tamar of Georgia, a warrior queen of the first order, "Queen Tamar" pp. 107–117.

Owen Rees, "Charlemagne," *Medieval Warfare* Vol. 5, #2, pp. 6–9. The would-be—and actual—military heir to Rome in the West is presented in this short introduction, but no mention is of Charlemagne's wife Fastrada, who is supposed to have impressed him by fighting against him. There is no mention of this Internet claim in Elina Screen and Charles West (eds.), *Writing the Early Medieval West* (Cambridge: Cambridge University Press, 2018) nor does Alessandro Barbero, *Charlemagne: Father of a Continent* (Berkeley: University of California Press, 2000) mention anything about her supposed military prowess. See also Rachel Stone, *Morality and Masculinity in the Carolingian Empire* (Cambridge: Cambridge University Press, 2012).
    Note: The warfare of the age of Charlemagne is told in a sprightly manner by David Nicolle in his *The Age of Charlemagne* (Oxford: Osprey Publications, 1984).

Roger Reese, "Soviet Women at War," *Military History* (May 2011), pp. 44–53. Soviet women, motivated by patriotism and revenge, proved themselves in battle, not just as medics and battlefield surgeons, but as machine-gunners, snipers, and pilots was well. Women in combat were all volunteers, and training was often more rigorous than for men.

Linda L. Reif, "Women in Latin American Guerrilla Movements: A Comparative Perspective," *Comparative Politics,* Vol. 18, #2 (1986), pp. 147–169. Contrasts the underutilization of women warriors in the Cuban and Colombian revolutionary movements with their much wider usage in those of Nicaragua, Uruguay, El Salvador, and Guatemala.

Tanya Reimer, *Amazons and Viragos: Warrior Women Rulers of the European Renaissance*, Master's Thesis (San Diego State University, 2011). Looks at the two terms and argues that in the Renaissance period, both were thought of as praise, not derision, as "virago" translated into "masculine woman." Citing Gentile Malatesta, Caterina Sforza, Isabella D'Este, Eleanora d'Aragona, Catherine de' Medici, Queen Elizabeth I, she terms them "warrior women rulers" (p. 16).

João José Reis, "Slave Resistance in Brazil: Bahia, 1807–1835," *Luso-Brazilian Review,* Vol. 25, #1 (1988), pp. 111–144. Looks at the various factors that seem to have inhibited or promoted quite a number of slave revolts in Bahia during the period under review including the ethnic dimensions, i.e., Hausa, Ewe, or Yoruba backgrounds.

Lucy Riall, *Sicily and the Unification of Italy* (Oxford: Clarendon Press, 1998) provides many insights into the unification of Italy and its impact on Sicily and provides a different perspective on Garibaldi and his women warriors. See also Peter Harrington, "Garibaldi's Panoramic Exploits," *MHQ: The Quarterly Journal of Military History*, Vol. 20, #4 (Summer 2008), pp. 82–87.

Stephen W. Richey, *Joan of Arc: The Warrior Saint* (Westport: Praeger, 2003). See especially his extensive study of her military accomplishments (both strategic and tactical) in chapter 6, "Joan's Achievements as a Military Leader," pp. 45–88. He sees her as "an essential factor" in the rise of the Valois dynasty and the ultimate French triumph in the Hundred Years War. Believes her breaking of the siege of Orleans in 1429 was the best proof positive of her military leadership.

Omar Manual Roberto-Cáez, *Women in Insurgent Groups in Latin America*, Master's Thesis (Monterey: Naval Postgraduate School, 2014). See pp. 52–55 for some useful information on the role of Haydée Tamara Bunke Bider ("Tania the Guerrilla"), Tanja Nijmeijer, Elda Neyis Mosquera Carcia, Nidia Díaz, Maria Marta Valladares, August La Torre, and Lori Berenson. This wide-ranging thesis looks at the motivation behind female participation in revolutionary movements primarily in Colombia, Peru, and Chiapas, examines the careers and impact of a number of female warriors. The author concludes that the implementation of the counterrevolutionary COIN strategy needs to pay far more attention to the role of women in both revolutionary and counterrevolutionary operations. The author also makes a strong case for the wide-ranging patterns of motivation from ideological commitment to domestic abuse, poverty, a love of adventure, and liberation theology and states that the level of female participation has ranged from 5% in the Cuban Revolution to 30% in the Colombian FARC effort.

Nancy Robinson, "Women's Political Participation in the Dominican Republic: The Case of the Mirabel Sisters," *Caribbean Quarterly*, Vol. 52, #2/3 (2006), pp. 172–183. Looks at the lives and deaths of three courageous sisters who were assassinated by President Trujillo after participating and in some cases leading revolutionary cells (in Minera's case the pro-Castro 14 June Movement). Patria, Minera, and Maria Teresa Mirabal were strangled and bludgeoned to death after visiting their husbands in jail. Their lives and deaths opened up opportunities to create a "female space in the political landscape" (p. 174). Their deaths also sparked growing opposition to Trujillo's dictatorship (1930–1961).

   Note: For a more extensive examination of all these issues, see Lisa Krause, *The Metamorphosis of Las Mariposas: A Memory of the Mirabel Sisters in the Dominican Republic and Its Diaspora in the United States*, Master's Thesis (Gainesville: University of Florida, 2018). Krause argues that in the Dominican Republic the seemingly countless honors and recognitions have led to a transition in commemoration, including those memories among Dominicans in the diaspora. Julia Alvarez has also fictionalized the lives of the Mirabel sisters in her novel *In the Time of the Butterflies* (New York: Algonquin, 2010).

Sherry Robinson, "Lozen," in *Apache Voices* (Albuquerque: University of New Mexico Press, 2000), pp. 3–15. This work shows how "the myth" is real and that "Woman Warrior" Lozen who "could ride, shoot and fight like a man" did so effectively with both the Chiricahua Apaches and the Warm Springs Apaches. Even among legendary Apache warriors such as Cochise, Germonimo, Tuh, and Victorio, she stood out.

Lucia St. Clair Robson, *Ghost Warrior* (F) (New York: Forge Books, 2012). Celebrating the life and times of Lozen, a warrior's warrior, this novel presents her 30-year struggle on behalf of the Dineh. After campaigns in the New Mexican and Arizona territories and the Mexican states of Sonora and Chihuahua, she and her tiny band of 17 are pursued and finally cornered by 9,000 American and Mexican troops and others. "The odds made Lozen proud." A true and brave warrior well worthy of even further study.

Catharine Roehrig, *Hatshepsut: From Queen to Pharaoh* (New Haven: Yale University Press, 2005). Although there is precious little here about her internal military campaigns or those to Syria-Palestine and Nubia in this gorgeous coffee-table book, there is much about the art and court during the Early Period of the New Kingdom when she was a joint (dominant) ruler with her nephew Thutmose III (1473–1458) during which she went from being queen to being pharaoh.

Duane Roller, *Empire of the Black Sea: The Rise and Fall of the Mithridatic World* (London: Oxford University Press, 2020). Brings to our attention that the Amazons were originally reported to have lived on the shores of the Black Sea, but that successive generations have always pushed them "beyond civilization." "Like most mythical people, they tended to be just beyond the limits of civilization, and at the time of the death of Mithridates VI they were in the Caucasus, but they were originally in or around Pontos" (p. 20). The author also connects Alexander the Great with Queen Thalestris and her Amazons although the actual event behind the legend is thought to be the offer of a Scythian king to have Alexander marry one of his daughters.

Will Roscoe, *Changing Ones: Third and Fourth Genders in Native North America* (New York: St. Martin's Press, 1998). A truly decorticating look at women warriors in Native American life, including examples of many female *berdache* in action among the Cheyenne, Kalispel (Pend D'Oreille), Salish (Flathead), Crow, Siksikas (Blackfoot), Kaska, Nootka, Tingit, Kutenai, Yuki, Mohave, Maricopa, Quechan, Cocopa, Tipai, Yavapai, Navajo, Apache, and Papago. The author urges us to see societal tolerance in the sanctioning of fluid gender norms and suggests that the history of Native Americans needs to be rewritten to include this dimension. His case is convincing.

Sarah Rose, *D-Day Girls: The Spies Who Armed the Resistance, Sabotaged the Nazis, and Helped Win World War II* (New York: Crown, 2019). An engaging read about the exploits of Andree Borrel, Lise de Baissac, Odette Sansom, Yvonne Rudellat, Mary Herbert, and all their compatriots who gave their talents and often their lives to assist the Resistance forces during World War II, concluding that the Resistance fighters probably shortened the war by six months or more.

Lilach Rosenberg-Friedman, "Religious Women Fighters in Israel's War of Independence: A New Gender Perception or a Passing Episode?," *Nashim: A Journal of Jewish Women's Studies & Gender Issues,* #6 (2003), pp. 119–147. Looks at the participation of religious women starting with the Second Aliyah (1904–1914), and later the military organization of the Haganah in 1920 and War for Independence and concludes that despite many objections from the religious parties, women, especially those on kibbutzes, participated despite that opposition. They saw "the front line and the home front as one." Nevertheless, the study concludes that their actions "did not lead the religious Zionist Knesset members to recognize their participation in the army as a worthy and desirable goal" (p. 139).

Margaret Rossiter, *Women in the Resistance* (New York: Praeger, 1986). Lots of good information about the many roles played by women in the French Resistance, especially good on Georgette Gerand, the only woman to become a regional chief of the Maquis and on the June 1944 firefight in the woods of Taille de Ruine, where "Pauline" and 150 Maquisards held off the Germans for 14 hours after the unit had blown up the Touraine to Paris rail lines 400 times in the run-up to and following the Allied landings in Normandy.

Norman Roth, "The Kahina: Legendary Material in the Accounts of the Jewish Berber Queen," *The Maghrib Review*, Vol. 7, #5–6 (1982), pp. 122–125. A very important article debunking the myths that Kahina was a Jewish Deborah or a Christian Joan of Arc and arguing that this fascinating woman warrior, be she pagan or not, is worth of our study irrespective of the "propagandistic interpretation" others have mounted.

Guy Rothery, *The Amazons* (Charleston: Bibliobazaar, 2014). Seeks to buttress the legends of the Amazons with examination of artworks, especially sculpture. Sees Amazons in Central Asia, the Caucasus, and Kurdish country as well as Africa and America.

Edward Rugemer, *Slave Law and the Politics of Resistance in the Early Atlantic World* (Cambridge: Harvard University Press, 2018). A multi-society (Barbados, Jamaica, and South Carolina) look at a variety of dimensions included in the organized violence of rebellion. Would have liked to see more on the Bajan Bussa's rebellion of 1816 and the role of Nanny Grigg.

Brett Rushforth, "The Gauolet Uprising of 1710: Maroons, Rebels, and the Informal Exchange Economy of a Caribbean Sugar Island," *William and Mary Quarterly,* Vol. 76, #1 (Jan. 2019), pp. 75–110. The tale of Lawrence and her flight to a small Maroon settlement in Martinique shows how the high prices for sugar demanded more and more slaves which increased white owner angst and Black slave unrest.

Michael Rustad, *Women in Khaki: The American Enlisted Woman* (New York: Praeger, 1992). Looking at the plight of women in U.S. Army stationed in West Germany, the author quickly and then overwhelmingly documents the difficulties, obstacles, and lack of integrative support faced by women at that time in that army. Amusing portraits of male typologies are also presented, including "Heads," "Lifers," "Barracks Rats," "Goon Squads," "Brothers," and the like. The concluding chapter suggests some ways to reform "His and Her Army." Using the microcosm of a single American base in West Germany, the author looks at the emergence of the role of enlisted women in the U.S. Army. Notes the rise of women in the military from 1% in 1972 to 8% in 1979. See especially, "Her Army," pp. 138–180.

Lakshmi Sahgal, *A Revolutionary Life: Memoirs of A Political Activist* (New Delhi: Kali for Women Publications, 1997). A sprightly autobiography of the woman who led the Rani Regiment, which fought with the Japanese against the British in Burma. Of particular interest is chapter 6, "In Burma," which details the chaos at the end of World War II, when she is first captured by her Japanese allies (who think she is a Karen guerrilla) and then by the Karen guerrillas and the British. When she returns to India after the war, she is hailed as a hero.

Elizabeth Salas, *Soldaderas in the Mexican Military* (Austin: University of Texas Press, 1990). A wide-ranging and fascinating look at the role of women camp followers and soldiers in all of the Mexican wars, tracing their antecedents back to Mesoamerica and the Toltec Queen Xochitl, who led a woman's battalion and was killed in battle.

Jessica Amanda Salmonson, *The Encyclopedia of Amazons: Women Warriors from Antiquity to the Modern Era* (New York: Paragon House, 1991). A most thought-provoking collection of historical and mythological references from Aba, the 1st century BCE warrior daughter of Xenophanes to Zoulvisia of Armenian legend, they are all here. A treasure trove to stimulate your exploration of women warriors throughout the ages.

P. B. Sanders, "Sekonyela and Moshweshwe: Failure and Success in the Aftermath of the Difaqane," *Journal of African History,* Vol. 10, #3 (1969), pp. 439–455. Sanders argues that despite other explanations, Moshweshwe's ultimate success over Sekonyela was due to his success in warfare during the Mfecane, where he gained in cattle wealth while Sekonyela lost wealth and therefore could not expand his power base beyond that left to him by his mother MmaNthatisi.

Flora Sandes, *An English Woman-Sergeant in the Serbian Army* (London: Hodder and Stoughton, 1917). Going to Serbia during World War I as an ambulance driver, this intrepid English woman eventually joined the Serbian army, fought on the front lines, and was wounded. Eventually promoted to lieutenant and given the Serbian Cross (The Order of Karadorde's Star—also won by Milunka Savic) for bravery. This is her account, crisply, positively, and often humorously outlining her military career around Serbia, into Albania, and eventually evacuated to Corfu before returning to Serbia. She apparently loved "becoming an ordinary soldier" and missed it after retirement.

Francisco Sanin and Francy Franco, "Organizing Women for Combat: The Experience of the FARC in the Colombian War," *Journal of Agrarian Change* (Aug. 2017), pp. 770–777. Despite initial opposition from male FARC leaders, women became a very important element in the later FARC campaigns, numbering between 20% and 40% of combatants, one of the highest degrees of feminization recorded in the literature.

Thomas Sankara, *Women's Liberation and the African Freedom Struggle* (New York: Pathfinder, 2007). The former leader of Burkina Faso (1983–1987), who was assassinated while in power in 1987, using the "Marxist understanding of human society" declares how women are an important part of the struggle for liberation. This work also contains an interesting photo of women antiaircraft gunners from Angola.

Note: This pattern of military men seizing power and claiming to be inspired by Marxist-Leninism was a widespread phenomenon in Africa during the 1970s and 1980s as they sought to provide instant albeit often superficial legitimacy to their regimes. For a more in-depth look at this pattern, see C. P. Potholm, "The Marxist Modernizers," in *The Theory and Practice of African Politics* (Englewood: Prentice Hall, 1979), pp. 212–246.

Rosnida Sari, "Acehnese Women," *Gender Equality: International Journal of Child and Gender Studies,* Vol. 2, #2 (Sept. 2016), pp. 33–42. Gives useful context on the life and times of Admiral Keumalahayati, Cut Nyak Meutiz, and Cut Nyak Dhien and their military opposition to Dutch colonialism.

Note: More background on this period can be found in Steven Drakely, *The History of Indonesia* (Westport: Greenwood Press, 2005) see especially chapter 2, "Indonesia During the Colonial Period," pp. 23–50.

Orna Sasson-Levy, "Gender Performance in a Changing Military: Women Soldiers in 'Masculine' Roles," *Israel Studies Forum*, Vol. 17, #1 (2001), pp. 7–22. The author concludes that "Ironically then, women's achievements in the Israeli army might work to legitimize the military's gender regime, which is based on the subjugation of women" (p. 19).

Orna Sasson-Levy and Sarit Amram-Katz, "Gender Integration in Israeli Officer Training: Degendering and Regendering the Military," *Signs*, Vol. 33, #1 (Autumn 2007), pp. 105–133. Even the process of integration of women into the Israeli armed forces seems to reinforce gender inequality in terms of self-image in terms of evaluating "boy" and "girl" units.

Shelley Saywell, *Women in War* (Baltimore: Penguin Books, 1986). Wide-ranging account of women who have fought and led in battle. A lot of interesting vignettes here, many of which are fleshed out more fully elsewhere.

Claude E. Schaeffer, "The Kutenai Female Berdache: Courier, Guide, Prophetess, and Warrior," *Ethnohistory*, Vol. 12, #3 (1965), pp. 193–236. Long, in-depth, well-researched article on the Kutenai berdache, who took the derisive term as her own, Qanqon. The author describes her various careers of guide, courier, prophetess, and warrior. Quite a career.

Peter Schalk, "Resistance and Martyrdom in the Process of State Formation of Tamillam," in Joyce Pettigrew (ed.), *Martyrdom and Political Resistance* (Amsterdam: VU Press, 1997), pp. 61–83. Useful insights into female fighters among the Liberation Tigers of Tamil Ealam (LTTE). According to the author, women made up a significant number (3,000) of the rebels despite there being no women warriors in Tamil history.

Stacy Schiff, *Cleopatra: A Life* (New York: Little, Brown, 2010). A superb analysis of one of the most interesting and intriguing women in history, whose true strategic and tactical skill overwhelms her historical image as a courtesan. Schiff uses Cleopatra to give vivid and lasting insights into the world of Rome when it teetered between a republic and an empire and the forces for the latter won out.

Note: Interestingly, while classical-era writers such as Plutarch blame Cleopatra (and citing her "female and Egyptian" attributes) for Mark Anthony's disastrous defeat at Actium (Greece) in 31 BCE, modern military scholars give her more credit for the strategic decision to escape from that defeat together with the Ptolemaic treasury, with her naval squadron (held in reserve) leading the way. See David Califf, *Battle of Actium* (Philadelphia: Chelsea House, 2004) and especially Si Sheppard, *Actium 31 BC* (Oxford: Osprey Publishing, 2009).

James Schultz, *Running Eagle: The Warrior Girl* (Boston: Houghton Mifflin, 1917). (F) A charming novel making much of the Blackfeet woman in what is now Montana, a strong woman who counted coup and led in battle, ultimately becoming a leading warrior. Eventually she was killed by the Flatheads but not before she etched herself into Native American legend.

Simone and Andre Schwarz-Bart, *In Praise of Black Women I: Ancient African Queens* (Madison: University of Wisconsin Press, 2001). An amazingly lavishly—and lovingly—illustrated volume of many African warrior-queens, including Tiye, Queen of Egypt, the Queen of Sheba, Yennenga of the Mossi, Heleni of Ethiopia, and Beatrice Kimpa Vita, the Joan of Arc of Kongo.

Paul Sealey, *The Boudican Revolt Against Rome* (Buckinghamshire: Shire Publications, 1997). A good account of the sacking of Colchester, London, and Verulamium (outside present-day St. Albans) by "Boudican hordes" in 60 CE before those hordes were in turn crushed by Roman legions in the Midlands in 61 CE. Much archaeological evidence is promulgated herein.

Mary Lee Settle, *All the Brave Promises: Memories of Aircraft Woman 2 Class 214691* (Columbia: University of South Carolina Press, 1995). A charming and incisive look at the Women's Auxiliary Air Force (WAAFs) in action during World War II. This American woman signs up, endures much, and is almost killed by a V-1 bomb, but she serves the English well and truly.

Carole Seymour-Jones, *She Landed by Moonlight* (London: Hodder, 2013). Once-over-lightly account of Pearl Witherington of the SOE, who parachuted into wartime France and led a large unit of the Maquis for over a year, doing considerable damage to the German war effort.

Julia Denise Shayne, "Gendered Revolutionary Bridges: Women in Salvadoran Resistance Movement (1978–1992)," *Latin American Perspective,* Vol. 26, #3 (May 1999), pp. 85–102. Although there is very little on women in military action per se in this article, it does argue for their participation in the Revolution while showing what women can do in such situations, although they received very little credit for their efforts in building "gendered revolutionary bridges."

Julia Denise Shayne, Michael E. Allison, and Alberto Martín Alvarez, "Unity and Disunity in the FMLN," *Latin American Politics and Society*, Vol. 54, #4 (Winter 2012), pp. 89–118. If one studies revolutionary movements, one may be somewhat discouraged to share the conclusions of this article:

However, even with a cohesive FMLN, competing in a two-party race with the broadly popular Funes, and a deteriorating economic and security situation, the FMLN sill wone only 2.5% of the national vote. (p. 54)

Kathleen Sheldon, *African Women: Early History to the 21st Century* (Bloomington: Indiana University Press, 2017), see pp. 39–40 "Powerful Women."

Janann Sherman, "'They Either Need These Women or They Do Not': Margaret Chase Smith and the Fight for Regular Status for Women in the Military," *Journal of Military History,* #54 (January 1990), pp. 47–78. Two percent of the U.S. armed forces were women during World War II and they did not, according to Smith, receive the equality, benefits, and recognition they should have, so she fought for them. Amazingly ahead of her time, Senator Smith called for allowing women in combat in 1941. Strangely, Smith is rarely cited by feminists as a heroine.

Faegheh Shirazi, *Muslim Women in War and Crisis: Representation and Reality* (Austin: University of Texas Press, 2010). With focus on Iran, Iraq, Lebanon, and the Mahgreb (plus Aceh and Ambon), these essays look at a variety of women's roles. Especially interesting is the forcing of women to become suicide bombers in order to "save their honor."

Nicholas Shreeve, *Dark Legacy* (Crossbush Bindery: BOOKWRIGHT, 1996). Dark indeed, is the true history of the British in India, but for our purposes, notable for its chapter on Begum Samru (1752–1826), the Muslim woman who as a Nautch girl converted to Christianity and married a European mercenary Walter Reinhardt Sombre, inheriting his army (Europeans and Indians) and becoming the only Catholic ruler in India, as the Royal Highness of the Principality of Sardhana. A staunch supporter of the Mughal Emperor, she stood only 4½ feet tall, and her army occupied the left of the Maratha line at the battle of Assaye, which the British won under Arthur Wellesley, thus ending Maratha primacy in the Delhi region. She then ruled Sardhana for 30 more years under British overlordship. At one point her army exceeded 6,000 men.

Note: For a work focused more on the Begum herself, see Mahendra Narain Sharman, *The Life and Times of Begam Samru of Sardhana (A.D. 1750–1836)* (Sahibabad: Vibhu Prakashan, 1985). The broader context of the conquest of India is well covered in William Dalrymple, *The Anarchy: The Relentless Rise of the East India Company* (New York: Bloomsbury Publishing, 2019).

Anita Shreve, *Stella Bain* (New York: Little, Brown, 2013). (F) An American woman serving as an ambulance driver in France is wounded and suffers severe shell shock but eventually recovers. Along the way this novel gives a good sense of life at the front from a woman's perspective filling in what was traditionally a man's job during wartime in many cultures. Illuminating.

Adrian Shubert, "Women Warriors and National Heroes: Agustina de Aragón and Her Indian Sisters," *Journal of World History,* Vol. 23, #2 (Jun. 2011), pp. 279–313. Quite a cross-cultural comparison, this article looks at the warriorhood and life after death of Agustina de Argon, Jhalkaribai, and the Rani of Jhansi, Lakshmibai and concludes rightly that all are worthy of our attention, respect, and knowledge and that their subsequent handlings by history tell us much about the societies involved in those handlings. Shows how two heroes of the Indian Rebellion of 1857 have had two different afterlives in terms of their appeal.

Tsehai Berhane Silassie, "Women Guerrilla Fighters," *Northeast African Studies*, Vol. 1, #3 (Winter 1979–1980), pp. 73–83. Documents the activities of important female guerrilla fighters such as Wayzaro Shewaraged Gadle, Wayzaro Olamawarq Terunah, Wayzaro Shewanash Abreha, and Wayzaro Lakelash Bayan before and during the Italian occupation as well as its overthrow. Points out that in feudal Ethiopian society, their military leadership status depended on their existing landholdings (derived from their dead fathers or husbands). Often helpfully quotes the women fighting in their own words.

Note: For a modern overview account of the struggle for Ethiopia during the 1935–1941 period, see Jeff Pearce, *Prevail: The Inspiring Story of Ethiopia's Victory over Mussolini's Invasion, 1935–1941* (New York: Skyhorse Publications, 2014) and for Ethiopian efforts to pry themselves free of South African and British domination, see C. P. Potholm, *Liberation and Exploitation: The Struggle for Ethiopia* (Lanham: University Press of America, 1976).

Harleer Singh, *The Rani of Jhansi* (Cambridge: Cambridge University Press, 2014). Looking at the history and fable of gender in the 19th century, when Rani Lakshmi Bai, the Queen of Jhansi, fought the British during the insurrection of 1857 and in dying, became like Joan of Arc, a nationalist icon, a Rorschach test of gender attitudes, and an enduring legend. Lots of useful examination from the perspective of "Enslaving Masculinity."

Note: For some stunning illustrations of Lakshmi Bai, named for the Hindu goddess of wealth, see *National Geographic History* (Sept./Oct.) 2020, pp. 6–9.

Note: "Sepoys," the native levies trained by (usually) Europeans, fought on both sides of the Indian Mutiny of 1857. For an insightful overview of the sepoys and their military history, see John Lynn, "Soul of the Sepoy," *MHQ: The Quarterly Journal of Military History,* Vol. 17, #2 (Winter 2005), pp. 46–55. It is very clear that the English could never have conquered India without using large number of sepoys.

Note: See, for example, their use by Robert Clive in his victory at Plassey (1757) as described in Chuck Lyons, "Foundation of an Empire," *MHQ: The Quarterly Journal of Military History,* Vol. 20, #4 (Summer 2008), pp. 18–26. The mutiny of some sepoys in 1857 resulted in severe British reaction and the death of thousands of Indians, guilty and innocent: see Peter Harrington, "Portraits of the Mutiny," *MHQ: The Quarterly Journal of Military History*, Vol. 20, #3 (Spring 2008), pp. 90–93 for some of the images that sparked that repression.

Tiffany Sippial, *Celia Sanchez Manduley: A Life and Legacy of a Cuban Revolutionary* (Chapel Hill: The University of North Carolina Press, 2020). A major scholarly look at the first woman of the Cuban Revolution who fought in battle and organized logistics, resistance and policy. See especially chapter 4, "First Female Guerrilla: Life on the Front Lines of Revolution," pp. 77–104.

Note: An additional, even more laudatory wok on Sanchez is Nancy Stout, *One Day in December: Celia Sanchez and the Cuban Revolution* (New York: Monthly Review Press, 2013). Considerable detail of all facets of her life and the Cuban Revolution are presented here.

Rosemarie Skaine, *Women at War; Gender Issues of Americans in Combat* (Durham: McFarland and Company, 1999). Wide-ranging work dealing with how military service exposes the fault lines of contemporary society, feminism, and the demands of the military.

———, *Female Suicide Bombers* (Jefferson: McFarland and Company, 2006). Looks at female suicide bombers in Sri Lanka, Chechnya, and the Arab world and believes that "This is war, not suicide." Some interesting case studies.

Patricia Skinner, "'Halt! Be Men!': Sikelgaita of Salerno, Gender and the Norman Conquest of Southern Italy," *Gender & History*, Vol. 12, #3 (2000), pp. 622–641. Goes into considerable detail in fleshing out the dynastic, political, and military career of Sikelgaita of Salerno assisting in Robert Guiscard's two campaigns against the Byzantine empire (1081–1082 and 1084–1085) and shows how contemporary chronicles depict her as a very powerful figure in her own right, giving her the masculine title of "Duke" rather than "Duchess" at various points, highlighting her power, authority, and prestige.

Kenneth Slepyan, *Stalin's Guerrillas: Soviet Partisans in World War II* (Lawrence: University Press of Kansas, 2006). Insurgent and partisan in Soviet Union–occupied territory, some under the control of Moscow, others not. Useful insights into the day-to-day struggle against the Germans and their allies, and the tensions within and among partisan banks. See the excellent chapter on "The Crisis of Partisan Identity, 1943" with superb maps on p. 189 and p. 192. Partisans went from 100,000 to 181,000 during that year. A good section on women partisans can be found here.

Angela Smith, *British Women of the Eastern Front* (Manchester: Manchester University Press, 2016). Covers the gambit of British women in Serbia and Russia 1914–1920 and their trials and tribulations. While there are few references to British women as regular line fighters, there are references to a number of Serbian women, including Milunka Savic, Antonija Javornik, and Sofija Jovanovic, all of whom won many battle honors in both the Balkan Wars and World War I.

Catherine Smith, *Resistance and Localization of Trauma in Aceh, Indonesia* (Singapore: National University of Singapore Press, 2018). The author makes the point that Cut Nyak Dhien not only became a symbol of Acehnese resistance but that her life story created a dynamic that produced a "romanticized notion of women fighters as typifying the ideal Acehnese woman . . . women must be strong, brave, pious, and ready to fight alongside or in place of her husband" (p. 310).

Note: The long, long Dutch campaign to subdue Aceh lasted until 1905 with a vicious war starting in 1873. See Peter Hamburger, "Song of the Holy War," *MHQ: The Quarterly Journal of Military History*, Vol. 18, #4 (Summer 2006), pp. 32–41. The author traces the Aceh rebellion against the Indonesian state, both in terms of tactics and motivations, to the earlier resistance against the Dutch. Eventually the Indonesian government granted significant local autonomy to the region.

Helen Solterer, "Figures of Female Militancy in Medieval France," *Signs: Journal of Women in Culture and Society*, Vol. 16, #31 (1991), pp. 522–549. Argues that *Li Tournoiement as Dames* represents the "disturbing multivalence of the figure of the woman warrior" and thus "provides a scenario for realizing a female martial ambition" (p. 548).

Ron Soodalter, "Over Where? Cuban Fighters in Angola's Civil War: Castro Exports His Brand of Armed Revolution," *MHQ: The Quarterly Journal of Military History,* Vol. 28, #3 (Spring 2016), pp. 28–37. An engaging piece that manages to bring together the Yoruba-born leader of the 1843 slave uprising in Triumvirato, Cuba, "La Negra Carlota," Carlota Lucumi (another woman not mentioned but there in fact is Firmina) for whom the 1975 Cuban intervention in the Angola civil war and South African incursion was named: "Operation Carlota." The piece also shows Cuban women soldiers in action in Angola and is also a good introduction to the African and international forces at work as the struggle for Angola intensified. Over 500,000 people died in the Angola struggle.

William Shuman Sorsby, *The British Superintendency of the Mosquito Shore 1749–1787* (London: University College Doctoral Thesis, 1969). Sorsby gives a fascinating account of the interplay among the British, the Indigenous People, and the Spanish. Rafaela Herrera is mentioned in footnote 7 on p. 126.

Pat Southern, *Empress Zenobia: Palmyra's Rebel Queen* (London: Continuum, 2008). See especially the chapters "Septimia Zenobia Augusta" and "Aurelian and the Roman Recovery." Palmyrene expansion into Arabia, Egypt, and briefly into Asia Minor occurred while the Persians were back on their heels and the Romans were struggling with the invasions of the Goths. But that expansion was checked when Emperor Aurelian came calling in 272 CE. The Romans won the battles of Immae and Daphne and, according to this work, captured Zenobia as she fled on a camel. Provides lots of alternative sourcing for the sketchy record of Zenobia's time on earth and her departure from it.

Note: For additional background on Rome and its adversaries in the region see also David Nicolle, *Rome's Enemies (5) The Desert Frontier* (Oxford: Osprey Publishing, 1991).

Anne Speckhard and Khapta Akhmedova, *Female Suicide Bombers: Dying for Equality?* (Washington: Institute for National Security Studies, 2006). See especially the chapter, "Black Widows: The Chechen Female Suicide Terrorists," pp. 63–80. The authors note that 81% of suicide bombings have been carried out by women (there is a good table showing specific incidents) and believe that motivation is caused by a combination of the revenge imperatives, jihadist ideology of the 18th-century Wahhabist type and strong evidence of self-recruitment with nationalistic overtones.

Note: For a military overview of the Chechen war of 1994–1996, see Maciej Jonasz, "Chechnya 1994–1996," *Modern Warfare,* #51 (Jan.–Feb. 2021), pp. 44 54.

Amanda Spencer, "The Hidden Face of Terrorism: An Analysis of the Women in Islamic State," *Journal of Strategic Security*, Vol. 9, #3 (Fall 2016), pp. 74–98. Spencer argues that while only 1% of the women of ISIS function as frontline fighters and suicide bombers, 10% of them function as prison guards and patrol officers, including the Al-Khansaa Brigade which "operates as an all-female ultra-oppressive militia or police force" (p. 84).

Orin Starn and Miguel La Srna, *The Shining Path: Love Madness, and Revolution in the Andes* (New York: W. W. Norton, 2019). A very readable account of the bizarre Maoist rebellion in Peru that occurred from 1980 to 1991. Central to the process was the professor Abimael Guzman and his wife Augusta La Torre and Elena Iparraguirre. Seventy thousand Peruvians died.

Irene Stengs, "Dramatising Siamese Independence: Thai Post-Colonial Perspectives on Kingship," in Robert Aldrich and Cindy McCreery (eds.), *Monarchies and Decolonization in Asia* (Manchester: Manchester University Press, 2020), pp. 260–282. Provides considerable background and context for understanding the legendary Thai queen Suriyothai.

Matthew Stibbe, *Women in the Third Reich* (London: Arnold, 2003). See especially chapter 7, "From Total War to Defeat and Military Occupation" to examine the calumny that "The German soldier fought for six years and the German women for only five months" (p. 245).

Judith Stiehm (ed.), *It's Our Military Too!* Provides a set of interesting perspectives including "The Enemy Doesn't Care If You're Female," "Duty, Honor, Country: If You're Straight," and "Gender and Weapons."

———, *Women and Men's Wars* (New York: Pergamon Press, 1983). Arguing that "it is men who plan, prepare for, conduct, conclude, describe and define war," the editor provides a wide set of essays from women on pacifism, women in the military, and women in national liberation struggles.

Richard Stites, *The Women's Liberation Movement in Russia* (Princeton: Princeton University Press, 1978). See especially "Women against Women," pp. 278–316, for a complex examination of Russian women in the armed forces and combat during World War I and the Russian Civil War.

H. Henrietta Stockel, *Women of the Apache Nation: Voices of Truth* (Reno: University of Nevada Press, 1991). Based on extensive records and personal interviews with Apache descendants, this work highlights Apache women warriors including Lozen, Dahteste, and two seldom mentioned, both Mescalero Apaches, Siki Toclanni, and Goyen. Siki was at the battle of Tres Catillos with Chiricahua war chief Victorio. Captured, enslaved, and taken to Mexico City, she escaped after three years of captivity and made a successful journey back to her people after an arduous trek of 100 miles. Goyen, after her husband was killed by a Comanche raiding party, tracked the attackers for three days and eventually killed the chief before scalping him and returning triumphantly to present her trophy to her in-laws. See especially, "Apache Women Warriors," pp. 29–51.

Laurie Stoff, *They Fought for the Motherland: Russian's Women Soldiers in World War I and the Revolution* (Lawrence: University Press of Kansas, 2014). Although women fought in World War I in Russia under the Czar, the huge impetus for women in combat came under the Provisional Government from February to October 1917 when that government created separate all-female military units. See especially the chapter, "Russia's First All-Female Combat Unit." As many as 6,000 women were involved. The most famous was Maria Bochkareva, who was in the 1st Russian Women's Battalion of Death. Called "The Russian Joan of Arc," she fought for the Provisional Government and was wounded numerous times, eventually being captured by the Bolsheviks, and made it to the U.S. by way of Siberia, only to return later, begging the British and later Admiral Kolchak to let her fight. This time she was captured by the Bolsheviks (when Kolchak abandoned Tomsk) and shot on May 16, 1920. All told, 80,000 women fought for Russia in World War I and the Revolution. The Bolsheviks kept women in the army but broke up the sexually segregated units and integrated them into their male units. Note, the author also mentions Flora Sandes, the only British woman to have served officially in the military. She went to Serbia as a nurse and then joined the Serbian army, eventually rising to the rank of lieutenant.

———, *Russia's Women Soldiers of the Great War* (Lawrence: University of Kansas Press, 2018). Much material from her earlier work and most useful information on the Kerensky government's 16 women's combat units involving 5,000 women, including the 1st Petrograd Women's battalion, the 2nd Moscow Women's battalion of death and the 3rd Kuban Women's Shock Battalion. "In fact, women soldiers were often portrayed as more enthusiastic, better disciplined, more courageous, and more self-sacrificing than their male compatriots."

Elizabeth Stone (ed.), *Women and the Cuban Revolution* (New York: Path-finder Press, 1981). Fidel Castro speaks and makes the case for the participa-tion of women in war in his essay, "The Revolution within the Revolution" finding them "Doubly exploited, doubly humiliated" and hence highly moti-vated for change.

Mark Stoyle, "'Give Me a Soldier's Coat': Female Cross-Dressing during the English Civil War," *History: The Journal of the Historical Association*, Vol. 103, #358, pp. 11–34. A fleeting look at the women who, during the English Civil War (1642–1646), dressed up as men and, depending on your inter-pretation, actually fought with the Royal Army or simply threatened gender norms for the fun of it or, as prostitutes, were trying to capture the attention of some men. At least we know from the historical record that Charles I did not approve of any of it. Perhaps that is why he lost his throne and his head? Among other reasons perhaps.

Jozef Straszewicz, *The Life of the Countess Emily Plater* (New York: John Frow, 1842). Life and times of the legendary Emily Plater are presented as the 1830–1831 insurrection against Russian rule proceeds. Countess Plater becomes Captain Plater and is at the battles of Kowno, Schawle, and Scaw-lany before being taken sick, and eventually dying.

Amy Goodpaster Streve, *Flying for Her Country: The American and Soviet Women Military Pilots of World War II* (Washington: Potomac Books, 2009). A well-deserved paean to the women who flew during World War II. In that war, 400,000 women were in the military, including many in the Women Airforce Service Pilots (WASP), the Women's Flying Training Detachment (WFTD), Women Army Corps (WAC), and Women's Army Auxiliary Corps (WAAC). Particularly useful is the chapter on "Gender Issues."

Paul Strong, "Lotta Svard, Nacdhthexen and Blitzmadel: Women in Military Service on the Eastern Front," in Celia Lee and Paul Strong (eds.), *Women in War: From Home Front to Front Lines* (Barnsley: Pen and Sword, 2012), pp. 182–193. Illuminating a little-known set of Finnish and German women warrior involvement on the Eastern Front.

Jan Stronk, *Semiramis' Legacy: The History of Persia According to Diodorus of Sicily* (Edinburgh: Edinburgh University Press, 2017). Stronk brings to light one of the few detailed histories of Persia by examining the 1st-century account of Diodorus of Sicily. Unfortunately, there is little about our cherished Tomyris.

Pamaree Surakiat, "Thai-Burmese Warfare during the Sixteenth Century and the Growth of the First Toungoo Empire," *Journal of the Siam Society,* Vol. 93 (2005), pp. 69–100, puts this war and the actions of the Thai queen Suriyothai in the broader context of the rise of the Toungoo Empire and the Burmese expansion.

Jon Swan, "Never before a Case Like This," *MHQ: The Quarterly Journal of Military History*, Vol. 10, #4 (Summer 1998), pp. 98–101. As attested to by no less a student of the American Revolution than Paul Revere, Deborah Sampson enlisted in the Continental Army, fought in a number of battles (including Ticonderoga), and was wounded several times. Revere later helped her receive a long-overdue military pension.

David Sweetman, *Women Leaders in African History* (London: Heinemann, 1984). Breezy and sometimes lacking in definitive sources but a good introduction to this understudied subject. Some prominent African women leaders such as Amina of Hausaland and Nzinga of Angola stand out in both warfare and diplomacy. Written forty years ago, this work needs to be checked against more current sources but should stimulate further research.

T–Z

Blain Taylor, "The Saga of Captain Molly," *Strategy and Tactics*, #103 (March–April 2017), pp. 66–67. This short article focuses on another "Molly Pitcher," instead of the traditional one, Mary Ludwig Hays. "Captain Molly" Margaret Cochran Corbin (1751–1800), was a water carrier at the Battle of Monmouth in 1778 who, when her husband was wounded, took over the firing of his cannon. She too was wounded and captured by the British. When her wounds were discovered, she was paroled and became a Continental Army hero. She was given a uniform plus a soldier's half pay for life as a disability pension. She is buried at West Point.

Craig Taylor (ed. and trans.), *Joan of Arc: La Pucelle* (Manchester: Manchester University Press, 2006). A rich mosaic of 105 primary documents covering the life and times of the Maid. Heavy focus on her various trials and contemporary letters about her. Not much on her military activities per se, however. The author concludes that her impact on the eventual outcome of the Hundred Years War was due more to the breakup of the Burgundian-English alliance than to the activities of La Pucelle, although she is given credit for offering national hope after the English were stopped at the Loire and that they could eventually be ejected from French soil.

Steris Tepper, *The Gate to Women's Country* (New York: Doubleday, 1988). (F) This science fiction novel describes an ecotopia where women are in the process of breeding out the warrior strain in men. In the process, many ironic dimensions and developments emerge.

Tharaphi Than, "The Creation of the Burma Women's Army," pp. 70–92 and "Disbanding the Army and Communist women," pp. 93–110, in *Women in Modern Burma* (London: Routledge, 2014). Contrasting Burma's experience with that of the Philippines and Vietnam, the author argues that "the vision of the first Women's Army crumbled, partly because the army had to launch an earlier-than-expected attack on the Japanese but mainly because the concept was supported by only a few top leaders, while the rank and file thought it unimportant or unnecessary" (p. 89).

Note: For a well-written account of the Burma Campaign, see Frank McLynn, *The Burma Campaign: Disaster into Triumph 1942–1945* (New Haven: Yale University Press, 2011).

Dark Rain Thom and James Thom, *Warrior Woman* (New York: Ballantine, 2003 (F). Somewhat romanticized novel about the life and times of Nonhelema Hokolesqua (c. 1718–1786), the Shawnee woman known as "The Grenadier" for her height (6'6") and courage in battle. Wife of Chief Moluntha, she fought in the Battle of Bush Run (1763) between a British force and a mixed army of Shawnee, Mingo, Huron, and Delaware warriors during Pontiac's Rebellion. Later, Nonhelema initially favored neutrality in the American Revolution, but eventually sided with the Americans and was granted a pension by the Continental Congress after the war.

Vicky Thomas, *The Naga Queen: Ursula Graham Bower and Her Jungle Warriors, 1939–1945* (Stroud: The History Press, 2012). Carrying a STEN gun and a .38 caliber pistol, Ursula Bower became the senior woman of V Force in India, leading her Naga fighters against the Japanese. She appealed to General William Slim for equipment before the battle of Imphal when the Imphal Plain was "crawling with Japanese" and became a legend.

Tiffany A. Thomas-Woodward, "'Toward the Gates of Eternity': Celia Sanchez Manduley and the Creation of Cuba's New Woman," *Cuban Studies,* Vol. 34 (2003), pp. 154–180. By looking at the public and private acts of memory since the death of the Cuban revolutionary Celia Sanchez Manduley (1920–1980), the author skillfully turns those memories into the creation of a revolutionary prototype to be emulated by the faithful.

Note: For background reading on both Celia Sanchez and the entire Cuban revolutionary background, see Julia E. Sweig, *Inside the Cuban Revolution: Fidel Castro and the Urban Underground* (Cambridge, Massachusetts: Harvard University Press, 2004).

Alvin O. Thompson, *Flight to Freedom: African Runaways and Maroons in the Americas* (Jamaica: University of the West Indies Press, 2006). A wide-ranging look at a number of Maroon societies that mentions Grandy Nana of Jamaica in particular (describing her as wearing 9 or 10 knives) and also shows how various women "chafed under the burden of slavery and sought ways of escaping from it" (p. 76).

Virginia Thompson, "WAAF: Women's Auxiliary Australian Air Force," in Pennington (ed.), *op. cit.*, pp. 462–468. Tells the little-known story of the Australian women who from 1941 to 1947 were a branch of the Australian armed forces and involved 27,000. Machinists, signals traffic, intelligence, bomb armers, munitions experts, and many other positions were filled by them. They came under attack by the Japanese at various points and eventually paved the way for women to become regular members of the Australian air force after World War II.

John Thornton, "Elite Women in the Kingdom of Kongo: Historical Perspectives on Women's Political Power," *Journal of African History,* #47 (2006), pp. 437–60. While Kongo women never played as extensive political and military roles as their counterparts in Ndongo and Matamba, they were nevertheless deeply involved in the civil war surrounding the battle of Ulang (Mhwila) in 1665 and thereafter, says the author.

Helen Thorpe, *Soldier Girls* (New York: Scribner's, 2014). This account follows three young women who join the Indiana National Guard and serve in both Iraq and Afghanistan. Their deployments are of note, but so too are their reentries into American society. This reviewer was struck at how their reasons for entering the military paralleled so closely those of men.

Sharon Tiffany, *The Wild Woman* (Cambridge: Shenkman Publishing, 1985). Why cannot women be warriors without being considered "wild" is the central question of this work. It is a somewhat challenging book to read and understand, but a rewarding one. Let it provoke your thinking.

Pamela Toler, *Women Warriors: An Unexpected History* (Boston: Beacon Press, 2019). An unexpected present this: a breezy but well-done account of the many women who have fought throughout history, with lots of interesting tidbits gleaned from across time and space. A stimulating introduction to the growing field of "women in battle" studies.

————, "War List: Wonder Women," *MHQ: The Quarterly Journal of Military History,* Vol. 32, #2 (Winter 2020), pp. 28–30. A positive introduction to 10 women who fit the title, a rare article about women warriors in this journal.

Charles Townshend, *Easter 1916: The Irish Rebellion* (New York: Penguin Books, 2003). An easy-to-read yet incisive account, including the actions of Countess Constance Markievicz, who was an integral part of the uprising and almost paid for it with her life but was spared because she was a woman. Many pictures and accounts put her armed and at the center of the uprising, although whether or not she shot and killed a policeman is still held in question by some.

Note: Putting the subsequent Irish Civil War in context is Bill Kissane, *The Politics of the Irish Civil War* (London: Oxford University Press, 2005), while the Easter Rising finds its place in Irish rebellion history in Kevin Kenna, *All the Risings: Ireland 1014–1916* (Dublin: Currach Press, 2008). A wide-ranging look at the role of Michael Collins is an edited work by Gabriel Doherty and Dermot Keogh (eds.), *Michael Collins and the Making of the Irish State* (Boulder: Mercier Press, 1998).

Susan Travers, *Tomorrow to Be Brave* (New York: The Free Press, 2000). The amazing self-told story of this upper-class English woman raised in France. She joined the Red Cross in 1939 and in 1940 served with French expeditionary force sent to Finland as a nurse during the "Winter War." After the fall of France, she fled with the Free French to North Africa via Central Africa and the Horn and Syria. She became a driver during East African campaign. Trapped with 1 Free French Brigade at Bir Hacheim, Libya, she drove the commanding general and her lover in the breakout after the unit held off Rommel for 15 days. She eventually served in Italy and France and later in French Indochina as well after officially joining the Legion in 1945, resigning her commission in 1947 to raise a family. Received the Medaille Militaire and the Legion d'Honneur. In 2002 women were finally allowed to join the French Foreign Legion. Quite a story of quite an intrepid woman.

Note: Reading her candid account of war in the desert, one will be struck by the accuracy of her memory and how her observations about the war and life in the desert are corroborated by other writers. See, for example, Robert Citino, "Drive to Nowhere," *MHQ: The Quarterly Journal of Military History*, Vol. 22, #4 (Winter 1991), pp. 13–25.

Note: For further background on the French Foreign Legion, see Douglas Porch, "Legends of the Foreign Legion," *MHQ: The Quarterly Journal of Military History*, Vol. 3, #2 (Autumn 2008), pp. 20–29.

Sandra Gioia Treadway, "Anna Maria Lane: An Uncommon Soldier of the American Revolution," *Virginia Cavalcade,* Vol. 37, #3 (1988), pp. 134–143. She joined the Continental army with her husband and fought in several battles, including Germantown, serving under General Washington. Lane was wounded at Germantown, eventually receiving a pension from the Commonwealth of Virginia. Matter of fact. No big deal. Just went and was with her husband, did her job, and helped her country's revolution.

Jean Truax, "Anglo-Norma Women at War: Valiant Soldiers, Prudent Strategists or Charismatic Leaders?," in Donald Kagay and L. J. Villalon, *The Circle of War in the Middle Ages: Essays on Medieval Military and Naval History* (London: The Boydell Press, 1999), pp. 111–125. Presents a balanced view to counter both the underestimation and subsequent overcompensation assumptions of women at war in the Middle Ages, concluding: "The Anglo-Norman chroniclers clearly assumed not only that women were capable of making broad strategic decisions regarding the disposition of military forces, but also that their leadership in these matters would be accepted. A woman's presence with her troops was not only welcomed but provided them a powerful emotional rallying point" (p. 125).

Bonnie Tsui, *She Went to the Field: Women Warriors of the Civil War* (Guilford, CT: TwoDot, 2003). A highly readable account of some of the most famous (and some unknown) women who fought as men in the American Civil War: Jennie Hodgens, Sarah Wakeman, Loretta Velasquez, Sarah Edmonds, Anna Etheridge, and Francis Clayton.

Philip Tucker, *Cathy Williams: From Slave to Female Buffalo Soldier* (Mechanicsburg, PA: Stackpole Books, 2002). The truly amazing story of an African American woman, a slave born in Missouri who became a valued and celebrated member of the "Buffalo Soldiers," six Black units that fought Native Americans (in her case, Apaches) on the American plains following the Civil War. She was in the 38th U.S. Infantry.

———, *Martyred Lieutenant Sanite Belair: Haiti's Revolutionary Heroine: A New Look at the Fighting "Tigress" of the Struggle for Liberty* (New York: PublishNation, 2019). Despite its sometime purple prose and breezy style, this work gives the reader a sense of the life and times of both Sanite Belair and Marie-Jeanne Lamartiniere. Sanite in particular was a battle-hardened soldier who led men in battle and attained the rank of lieutenant before being captured and executed by a firing squad after refusing to be blindfolded.

Tucker also takes the interested reader through earlier literature that slighted the role of women in general and these two in particular.

Alan Tuelon, "Nanny—Maroon Chieftainess," *Caribbean Quarterly,* Vol. 19, #4 (December 1973), pp. 20–27. Gives a fascinating depiction of this brave woman warrior who defeated the British using guerrilla tactics and was granted her own town in the peace treaty that followed.

Stephen Turnbull, *Samurai Women 1184–1877* (Oxford: Osprey Publishing, 2010). A highly interesting set of revelations about the extent to which women warriors were an integral part of the samurai tradition up until 1877. Well-illustrated and often excitingly presented. Here are dozens of real and legendary warriors who fought as samurai and were present throughout much of the shogun period. Turnbull believes that "the exploits of female warriors is the greatest untold story in samurai history" (p. 4). And he goes on to prove it. The illustrations are superb as well. His earlier *The Samurai: A Military History* (New York: Macmillan Publishing Company, 1977) remains hugely comprehensive in illuminating the entire history and cultural aspects of the samurai during their long historical run as the dominant military caste in Japan.

Karen Gottschang Turner and Phan Thanh Hao, *Even the Women Must Fight: Memories of War from North Vietnam* (New York: John Wiley and Sons, 1998). The Vietnam wars against the French and the Americans and South Vietnamese through the eyes of the women who served in the North Vietnamese armed forces. Ironically, many women would end up suffering just as their male counterparts have throughout history. "The Return of the Warrior" is never truly easy whether the warrior is female or male.

Kathleen Turner, "The Rise of Female Suicide Bombers," *Counter Terrorist Trends and Analyses,* Vol. 8, #3 (Mar. 2016), pp. 15–19. Looking at female suicide bombers in Sri Lanka, Syria, Russia, and Chechnya, the author sees tactical (women are less likely to be watched closely) and strategic (women blowing up military and civilian targets get more attention and seem more devastating) reasons why they are on the rise.

———, "Soldiers and Symbols: North Vietnamese Women and the American War," DeGroot and Peniston-Bird *op. cit.*, pp.185–204. Poignant account of the hundreds of thousands of North Vietnamese women who fought in the Vietnam War from 1966. The author believes that 100,000 of them were involved in antiaircraft units and along the Ho Chi Minh trail in the "Long

Haired Army." Interestingly enough, these women did not feel the need to dress as men, and some found the Joan of Arc transvestite dimension troubling.

Meredeth Turshen, "Algerian Women in the Liberation Struggle and the Civil War: From Active Participants to Passive Victims," *Social Research*, Vol. 69, # 3 (Fall 2002). Looks at the changes in women's status from active resister during the Algerian Revolution and the subsequent efforts by radical Islamists to reduce their status to precolonial levels.

For a more comprehensive examination of the eight-year civil war she writes about, see O'Brien Browne, "Revolution Unleashed," *MHQ: The Quarterly Journal of Military History*, Vol. 23, #4 (Summer 2011), pp. 78–87 and Luis Martinez, *The Algerian Civil War 1990–1998* (New York: Columbia University Press, 1998). For additional context, the earlier decolonization struggle in Algeria is ably presented in Martin Evans, *Algeria: France's Undeclared War* (London: Oxford University Press, 2012).

Royall Tyler, "Tomoe: The Woman Warrior," in Chieko Irie Mulhern (ed.), *Heroic with Grace: Legendary Women of Japan* (London: M.E. Sharpe, 1991), pp. 129–161. Shrouded in mystery and legend, Tomoe emerges from this study a little clearer thanks to a 14th-century Noh play explicated by the author.

———— (trans.), "Death of Lord Kiso," excerpted from "The Tale of the Heike," *MHQ: The Quarterly Journal of Military History,* Vol. 25, #3 (Spring 2013), pp. 94–97. A powerful insight into the existence of a little-known female warrior class.

Note: For the full text of the tale of the Keike, see Royall Tyler (trans.), *The Tale of the Heike* (New York: Viking, 2012).

Stephanie Urdang, *Fighting Two Colonialisms: Women in Guinea-Bissau* (London: Monthly Review Press, 1979). Believes that women are "an explicit and integral part of the overall revolution" there but in addition to fighting the Portuguese colonialism they also need to struggle against traditional male-dominated social, economic, sexual, and political domination. The author also thinks attitudes would change faster if more women carried guns and were more deeply engaged in the cadre class.

Note: The war in Guinea-Bissau dragged on from 1963 until 1973. Its ebb and flow is introduced by Patrick Baker, "The Guinea-Bissau War of Independence (1963–1973)," *Modern War,* #53 (May–June 2021), pp. 18–27.

James Ure, *Seized by the Sun* (Chicago: Chicago Review Press, 2017). A short breezy account of Gertrude "Tommy" Tomkins, a WASP (Woman Airforce Service Pilot) whose love of flying cured her stuttering and gave her the freedom to fly a P-51 "Mustang." She disappeared ferrying one such craft. Quite illuminating as to the obstacles against women pilots. Somewhat amusing but irritating is the account of women successfully flying the largest plane of World War II, the B-29, in order to show male pilots how easy it was. When the top brass found out about this, they ordered it stopped as a "stunt." WASPs ferried almost 13,000 aircraft during the war and provided the military with over 60 million pilot hours.

U.S. Marine Corps, "Women in Combat? Insights Worth Repeating," *Marine Corps Gazette* (November 1997), p. 73. Are the demands of the Marine Corps different from those of other services? This article makes strong arguments against women in combat, at least for the type of warfare the Marines currently practice. Very challenging also are the cited words and views of Bowdoin Professor of Government Jean Yarbrough.

Mats Utas, "Victimcy, Girlfriending, Soldiering: Tactic Agency in a Young Woman's Social Navigation of the Liberian War Zone," *Anthropological Quarterly*, Vol. 78, #2 (Spring 2005), pp. 403–430. Although based on a single individual, Bintu, a Mandingo Muslim Liberian woman, Utas weaves a complicated typology that seeks to avoid the binary "victim" or "perpetrator" for women in war situations and argues that there is a range of realizable possibilities that are informed by social contexts and switching situations (i.e., one's male soldier protector is killed in battle) and thus social navigation is really a continuum.

Anthony Valerio, *Anita Garibaldi: A Biography* (Westport: Praeger, 2001). Romantic version of a romantic story that puts Anita at the heart of Garibaldi's efforts in Brazil and Italy, where she participated in the various battles such as Imbituba and Laguna and served in various capacities. The author claims she taught Garibaldi the guerrilla tactics of the gauchos. Anita, herself, lived to see the founding of the Roman Republic in 1849, but died of malaria soon thereafter.

S. Vanajakumari and P. Vimala, "Arc-Veera Mangai Velunachiyar in Antiquity India (1772–1780)," *Shanlax International Journal of Arts, Science, & Humanities,* Vol. 3, #4 (2016), pp. 23–76. A full and wide-ranging account of the Tamil queen by Vanajakumari and Vimala, pointing out that her resistance occurred 85 years before the more famous Jhansi Rani's struggle to the north.

Martin van Creveld, "Armed But Not Dangerous: Women in the Israeli Military," *War in History*, Vol. 7, #1 (January 2000), pp. 82–98. This long-time student of all things military gives the reader a brief history of the role of Jewish women in the military, estimating that 15% of the armed movements leading to independence were female. However, he argues that women drafted in the 1970s were the result of desperation on the part of the military and they have never been much of an asset except in support roles. He goes further, stating that unless the problem of women in the military is dealt with, "the IDF's days of greatness are definitely gone" (p. 98).

———, "The Great Illusion: Women in the Military," *Journal of International Studies*, Vol. 29, #2 (2000), pp. 429–442. Van Creveld is not a big fan of women in combat, nor even in the military, and he minces no words about his views. Using the example of the Israeli Defense Force and other combat formations, he makes a strong case against the use of women in war. Van Creveld is one of the military historians who commands a broad audience on this highly fraught subject, so his arguments need to be considered carefully. And he has observed women in action in a number of important contexts. At the same time, his knowledge of women warriors throughout history seems scant and disinterested indeed.

———, *Men, Women and War* (London: Cassell, 2001). The most holistic anti-women-in-war volume I have come across and it effectively marshals the many arguments against women in war. But, and this is strange and disturbing, he seems never to have read *any* of the books and articles cited here, undercutting many of his arguments. Strange, for, although he wants to save women from "The Maw of Mars," he does not allow them the right to choose their destiny. And he seems to know little about the cultures in which they have played a military role, which is quite surprising given his reputation.

———, "Warrior-Women of Dahomey," *Militärgeschichtliche Zeitschrift*, Vol. 39, #1 (2018), pp. 115–123. Van Creveld argues that the Amazons of Dahomey were not free, not agents of female empowerment, and did not have a very good life, although he makes little reference to their prowess in battle as attested to by the French Foreign Legionnaires who fought against them. At the same time, he is very correct in drawing the distinctions between the original, freer Amazons of the Scythian and Sarmatian peoples of the steppes, rightly indicating the warrior women of Dahomey paid a huge price: "To become warriors they had to surrender their womanhood, turn into men, and despise women, as they themselves said. To the extent that it is founded on fact, their fate was neither laughable nor enviable but simply tragic" (p. 123).

Note: There are many critiques of van Creveld and his works but one well worth noting here is Nina Liza Bode, *The Imaging of Violent Gender Performances,* Master's Thesis (University of Groningen, 2014). Using the case studies of Tanja Nijmeijer, Xarema Muzhakhoyeva, Wafa Idris, and Pauline Nyiramasuhuko, she cogently attacks his assertions that warfare is not for women because biologically they are incapable of the heinous actions that are central to war. By providing a refined and holistic image of the female participators of political violence she shows how they are as capable of any man in perpetrating mass slaughter. Refuting van Creveld's biological determinism, she puts women realistically in the space/time continuum of purposeful war acts including genocide. The case studies are worthwhile in and of themselves in showing as they do the wide range of motives and actions involved in these five women's stories.

Martha Vandrei, *Queen Boudica and Historical Culture in Britain: An Image of Truth* (London: Oxford University Press, 2018). This unusual work arises out of the author's desire to look at both the historical figure of Boudica and (perhaps more important) the way her story, image, and connotations have shifted over 400 years of British culture.

Brian Van Reet, *Spoils* (F) (Boston: Lee Boudreaux Books, 2017). Apparently not liking the idea of women in combat, the author gives her the giveaway name Cassandra, puts her in Iraq, where she is ignominiously captured, has her period, disgusts her Iraqi guards, attempts to convert to Islam, and kills an American soldier to prove her loyalty to her new faith before being killed herself. Goodness, what a strange work.

Gretchen van Slyke, "Women at War: Skirting the Issue in the French Revolution," *L'Esprit Créateur*, Vol. 37, #1 (Spring 1997), pp. 33–43. From 1800 until World War I, women in France were expressly forbidden to wear pants (while there was no comparable prohibition against men wearing skirts) unless they could petition for an exception (such as looking so much like a man that they would be mistaken for cross-dressing if they wore a skirt). This applied to women who wore pants when enlisting undercover in the armed forces.

Mac Vargo, *Women of the Resistance: Eight Who Defied the Third Reich* (London: McFarland and Company, 2012). Covers the likes of Vera Atkins,

Monica Wichfelt, Virginia Hall, Hannah Senesh, and Christine Granville. Truly intrepid women warriors showing great courage and amazing grit. Inspiring.

Note: Hannah Senesh's story is even more movingly told in Marie Syrkin, *Blessed Is the Match: The Story of Jewish Resistance* (Philadelphia: The Jewish Publication Society of America, 1947). Quoting her poem by the same name: "Blessed is the match that is consumed in kindling flame" (p. 24). There is also a fine chapter here on the inner workings of the Warsaw Ghetto Uprising, pp. 170ff.

Note: For an extensive accounting of the Jewish contribution to the overall defeat of Nazi Germany, see Martin Sugarman, *Fighting Back: British Jewry's Military Contribution in the Second World War* (London: Vallentine Mitchell, 2010). And Lucien Steinberg does a fine job in illuminating Jewish resistance all across Europe during the Nazi occupation, especially in his highlighting of revolts in the death camps of Sobibor, Treblinka, and Auschwitz in his *Not as a Lamb: The Jews Against Hitler* (Farnborough: Saxon House, 1970).

Agnes Carr Vaughan, *Zenobia of Palmyra* (Garden City: Doubleday, 1967). A classic study, albeit one with few non-European sources. Still the author is perhaps the best exigent on existing Roman accounts. She points out that Zenobia was a bit unlucky as Aurelian was soon to be assassinated, and she might well have survived his successor. This work is therefore well worth pursuing.

Marta Moreno Vega, Marinieves Alba, and Yvette Modestin (eds.), *Women Warriors of the Afro-Latina Diaspora* (Houston: Arte Press, 2006). A set of essays introducing a large number of Afro-Latina warriors (most broadly defined) covering a wide range of skill, talents, and influences.

Loreta Velasquez, *The Woman in Battle: A Narrative of the Exploits, Adventures, and Travels of Madame Loreta Janeta Velazquez, Otherwise Known as Lieutenant Harry T. Buford, Confederate States Army* (Madison: University of Wisconsin Press, 2004, reprint of 1872 edition). An amazing memoir despite some questionable assertions by the author. For example, did she really meet Abraham Lincoln when she was a spy? Could she really have shot U. S. Grant at Shiloh? But she did enlist to fight for the Confederacy, bringing her own horse and her own slave to various units and she saw action at First Bull Run, Ft. Donaldson, and Shiloh, joining various regiments as an officer and also serving as a spy, declaring "There was not a man in the Confederacy who was more willing to fight to the last than I was" (p. 78). Other women who fought for the Confederacy include Malinda Blalock, a veteran of three battles, and Mollie Bean.

J. F. Verbruggen, "Women in Medieval Armies," in Clifford J. Rogers, Kelly DeVries, and John France (eds.), *Journal of Medieval Military History: Volume IV* (Woodbridge: Boydell Press, 2006), pp. 617–634. This Belgian author gives us a different take on Joan of Arc, quoting the Duke of Bedford who claimed the French king gave his superstitious people "a troubled woman of low repute, who wore men's clothing and carried herself licentiously" (p. 132) and adds other women warriors of the period, namely Elenore Helwisa de Nevers and Isabella de Conches (1091–1092) of Aquitaine, "Bruges Matin" women of 1302, the Great Margot, the women of Toulouse (1217–1218), Ermingardis, Viscountess of Narbonne (1134), and others.

Christine B. Verzar, "Picturing Matilda of Canossa: Medieval Strategies of Representation," in Robert A. Maxwell (ed.), *Representing History 900–1300: Art Music, History* (University Park: The Pennsylvania State University Press, 2010), pp. 73–92. Well-illustrated, this chapter provides a look at the many dimensions to this extraordinary woman, one of only two ever to have a sepulchral monument for her in St. Peters. Features her centrality to the Investiture Crisis and shows her receiving the Book of Prayers and Meditations from Bishop Anselm of Canterbury on his way back from Rome.

Jeanmore Vickers, *Women and War* (London: Zed Publishers, 1993). Seemingly more interested in keeping women out of war than in doing well in war, the author does provide some accents on "Women in Action," "The Impact of War on Women," and "Moving Toward a Non-Violent World."

Barbara Victor, *Army of Roses: Inside the World of Palestinian Women Suicide Bombers* (New York: Robinson Publishing, 2004). Traces the lives of five women caught up in the Intifada and concludes that they are driven by "terrible despair" and are more victims than warriors.

Gilberto Villahermosa, "Angels of Death: Ludmilla Pavlichenko and the Red Army Female Snipers in World War II," *World at War*, #66 (Jun.–Jul. 2019), pp. 84–86. Ludmilla, credited with 309 kills, personified these women snipers who were found by the Soviets to be more patient, more creative, more careful, and more obedient than their male counterparts.

Natalya Vince, *Our Fighting Sisters: Nation, Memory and Gender in Algeria 1954 to 2012* (Manchester: Manchester University Press, 2015). Looks at the many roles women played in the Algerian struggle for independence, including providing logistical, nursing, spying, and psychological support as well as direct participation as members of the Maquis and bombers such as Zhor Zerari, Djamila Bouhired, and Zohra Drif.

————, "Colonial and Post-Colonial Identities: Women Veterans of the 'Battle of Algiers,'" *French History and Civilization,* Vol. 2 (2009), pp. 153–158. Traces the trajectory of these women explaining how they became *Mujahidats* (women resisters), what they did during the war, and what happened to them after it.

Lyuba Vinogradova, *Avenging Angels* (London: Maclehose Press, 2017). Dozens of individual interviews with Soviet women snipers are put in the context of campaigns in the Kerch Peninsula, the Leningrad Front, Operation Bagration, and Czechoslovakia. Soviet female snipers served as individuals, "couples," and even companies of 60 or more.

————, *Defending the Motherland* (London: Maclehose Press, 2015). A breezy, sprightly account of Soviet female aviators, including those who flew the U-2s and Yak-1s in the battles from Moscow to Stalingrad to the Caucuses and beyond. Filled with memorable portraits of individual women and useful pictures of many. Chapters include "Girls—Pilot a Plane" and "Stop Flirting There's a War On." Particularly poignant is the case of two women navigators who salvage a silk parachute and make it into undergarments only to be informed upon and sentenced to ten years at hard labor for destroying state property. Luckily, their commander voided the sentence and restored them to active duty.

Jocelyn Viterna, *Women in War* (London: Oxford University Press, 2013). Based on 230 interviews with El Salvadorian women, the author looks at "Gender, Violence and the Micro-Processes of Mobilization" to conclude it is not easy being a female in a wartime situation. This work is very interested in the gender truths that the 12 years of war threw up as women were mobilized for combat and concludes that for many women, gender norms were widespread even under the tutelage of the Farabundo Martí National Liberation Front (FMLN) in which numerous women served in combat from 1980 to 1992. Over 75,000 people lost their lives.

William Vollmann, *The Ice-Shirt* (New York: Viking, 1990). (F) A curious blend of the sagas and travelogue to real places and dreamscapes along the Viking trail to Greenland and Vineland. See especially, "Freydis Eiriksdottir or How the Frost Came to Vineland the Good," pp. 129–340. As the pregnant Freydis confronts the Skraelings, she shouts "Oh, you would like me to take my shirt off, would you? I'll show you, you savage thralls, you Hell meat." "Sharpening" her sword on her breasts, she attacks, and the Skraelings flee, but the Vikings decide the future is not on their side and subsequently sail back to Greenland.

Marguerite Waller and Jennifer Rycenga (eds.), *Frontline Feminism: Women, War and Resistance* (New York: Garland Publishing, 2000). A wide-ranging collection covering ethnic and gender violence, militarism and sexuality, and feminist resistance to war, as well as soldier and state considerations and the exploration of women in and by war.

Wiebke Walther, *Women in Islam* (London: George Prior, 1981). Puts the military actions of such Muslim women as Umm Umara and Hind Bint 'Utbah into a set of much-needed religious, social, and economic broader contexts.

Note: For a useful overview of the battle of Yarmuk (636) in the context of the Byzantine Empire, Muslim Caliphate, and Sassanian Empire, see David Nicolle, *Yarmuk AD 636: The Muslim Conquest of Syria* (Oxford: Osprey Publishing, 1994). Another critical battle, one that began the *Tottenritt* of the Byzantine Empire, was Manzikert (1071), is well covered in David Nicolle, *Manzikert 1071: The Breaking of Byzantium* (Oxford: Osprey Publishing, 2012).

Note: Good sources for the rise of the Islamic armies and their evolution from infantry ground pounders and light skirmishers to the magnificent and very successful Arab light horse cavalry include Brian Carey, Joshua All-free, and John Cairns, *Road to Manzikert: Byzantine and Islamic Warfare 527–1071* (Barnsley: Pen and Sword, 2012), Anthony Pagden, *Worlds at War* (New York: Random House, 2008), Tom Holland, *In the Shadow of the Sword: The Birth of Islam and the Rise of the Global Arab Empire* (New York: Doubleday, 2012), and especially, Robert Hoyland, *In God's Path: The Arab Conquests and the Creation of an Islamic Empire* (London: Oxford University Press, 2013).

Note: Many studies of Islam underplay the importance of the early military victories of Muhammad. Unlike Jesus, who operated with the coming Kingdom of God in mind and established no earthly state, Muhammad and the early Islamic movement depended on initial military success to save the religious polity that he had formed in order to avoid having the concomitant religion stillborn. See Richard Gabriel, "The Warrior Prophet," *MHQ:*

The Quarterly Journal of Military History, Vol. 19, #4 (Summer 2007), pp. 70–78.

William Ware, *Zenobia, Queen of Palmyra* (Boston: Estes and Lauriat, 1838). (F) A historical romance celebrating the life and times of Zenobia, Queen of Palmyra, and her eventual defeat in the Third Century CE at the hands of the Emperor Aurelian, who laid siege to Palmyra and eventually captured her. Very praiseful of her: "Julius Caesar himself, Piso, never displayed a better genius than this woman."

Clare Johnson Washington, "Women and Resistance in the African Diaspora, with Special Focus on the Caribbean, Africa, and USA," *McNair Scholars Online Journal,* Vol. 2, #1 (Jan. 2006), pp. 352–377. Points out that while passive resistance was the most widespread tactic in slave actions, there were a number of women who took to violence in their search for better conditions as well as freedom. Interesting are her short portraits of Queen Mary Thomas of St. Croix and Granny Nanny of Jamaica.

————, *Women and Resistance in the African Diaspora, with Special Focus on the Caribbean (Trinidad and Tobago) and U.S.A.* (Portland State University: Master of Science Thesis, 2010). A wide-ranging coverage of many women who fought in many different ways for emancipation and women's rights. Useful vignettes and photographs abound.

Jack Weatherford, *The Secret History of the Mongol Queens* (New York: Broadway Books, 2010). Surprising assertions about the strategic and military roles played by the daughters of Genghis Kahn and the bold assertion "Without Genghis Khan's daughters, there would have been no Mongol Empire." Interesting account of Manduhai Khatun the Wise (c. 1449–1510) who reunited the Mongols after the empire had fallen into warring factions. The author suggests that since the Mongols were illiterate, the Muslim, Christian and Chinese chroniclers edited out the activities of these powerful women.
    Note: For an introduction to Mongol warfare, see Stephen Turnbull, *The Mongols* (Oxford: Osprey Publishing, 1995) and Erik Hildinger, *Warriors of the Steppe: A Military History of Central Asia, 500 B.C. to 1700 A.D.* (New York: Sarpedon, 1997). An outstanding look at Genghis Khan is provided by Frank McLynn in *Genghis Khan: His Conquests, His Empire, His Legacy* (New York: Da Capo Press, 2015) while Jack Weatherford makes a series of important counterintuitive points in his *Genghis Khan and the Making of the Modern World* (New York: Crown Publishers, 2004), while the classic overview of the Mongol impact on Central Asia and beyond remains René

Grousett, *The Empire of the Steppes: A History of Central Asia* (Rutgers: Rutgers University Press, 1970). Peter Jackson provides an in-depth examination of the interaction between the Mongols and the people of Islam in his *The Mongols and the Islamic World: From Conquest to Conversion* (New Haven: Yale University Press, 2017).

Graham Webster, *Boudica: The British Revolt Against Rome AD 60* (Lanham, MD: Rowman & Littlefield, 1978). Puts the revolt of the Iceni on a par with the Jewish Revolt of 70 CE as being sparked by both religion and terror. Admits that the bravery of Boudica and the Iceni was undercut by their lack of discipline and their continuing reliance on outmoded chariot warfare and poor weapons. Good map on p. 92 shows the Roman forts of the era—there were quite a few. Not much about Boudica or her military prowess per se, but the work is heavily grounded in archaeological finds of coins, pottery, and other artifacts.

Elizabeth Wein, *A Thousand Sisters: The Heroic Airwomen of the Soviet Union in World War II* (New York: Balzer and Bray, 2019). An in-depth, year-by-year examination of the roles played by women in the Soviet air force. Fully one third of Soviet pilots in 1941 were women, and their astonishing feats during the war now seem somewhat overridden by their under-utilization after the war.

Batya Weinbawn, *Islands of Women and Amazons: Representation and Reality* (Austin: University of Texas Press, 1999). Sees Amazonian legends everywhere from Homeric tales though the medieval period, also China, India, Native American cultures, and Pacific Islanders as well as popular culture up through and including "leisure primitivism."

Judith Weingarten, *The Chronicle of Zenobia: The Rebel Queen* (Cambridge: Vanguard Press, 2006). (F) From Tadmor-Palmyra in what is now Syria, Zenobia led a rebellion against the Romans from 269 to 272 CE. When her husband the ruler died, she took over and led her armies to victory, eventually taking over Arabia and Egypt until she, like Boudica, was defeated by the Romans who decided that allowing a rebellion to succeed was not an option. This long, somewhat fanciful novel gives the reader something of a flavor for her life and times.

Ruth Weiss, *The Women of Zimbabwe* (London: Kesho Publications, 1986). This early account by a journalist underscores the variety of roles and extent of the contributions of women to the successful Zimbabwe revolution. Accounts of Teurai Ropa Nhongo "Spill Blood," Siyathemba Mlilo, and Tainie Mundondo illuminate that story.

Margaret Collins Weitz, "Soldiers in the Shadows: Women of the French Resistance," DeGroot and Peniston-Bird, *op. cit.*, pp. 135–153. A much-needed look at the hows and whys of women getting less credit for their participation in the French Resistance. Uses two case studies, Seanne Bohec and Sonia Eloy, to show the similarity of motivation and the differing orientations. Makes the seldom-illuminated point that Charles de Gaulle refused to have anything to do with any Resistance group that received training or support from the British. Also illuminates the women who fought in the Greek resistance, Helen Ahrweiler, Elemi Fourtouni, Maria Karra, and Levendokaterini of Crete.

   Note: For concise background on the various elements of the Greek resistance to the Germans and the subsequent groups fighting in the Greek Civil War (1943–1949), see Edward Lengel, "Postwar Agony in Greece," *MHQ: The Quarterly Journal of Military History*, Vol. 28 # 4 (Summer 2016), pp. 53–59.

Julie Wheelwright, *Amazons and Military Maids* (London: Pandora, 1989). This work grew out of the author's earlier master's thesis at the University of Sussex and covers quite a wide range of subjects, including many of the usual suspects, including Flora Sandes, Maria Bochkareva, Christian Davies, Deborah Sampson, and Loreta Velasquez. Many, many pictures of Flora. For a further exploration of the theme of female empowerment when wearing men's clothing in the military and beyond, see her chapter, "Becoming One of the Boys," pp. 50–59.

Lyn Webster Wilde, *On the Trail of Women Warriors: The Amazons in Myth and History* (New York; St. Martin's Press, 1999). Amid some flights of fancy (their "bright, burning vital power"), the author does pin down the grave of the earliest woman warrior, found in Georgia dating from 1200 BCE and explores the shores of the Black Sea for Scythian and Hittite women warriors.

Bel Irvin Wiley, *The Life of Johnny Reb: The Common Soldiers of the Confederacy* (Baton Rouge: Louisiana State University Press, 1978). An updated version of the 1943 edition, which was way ahead of its time in its accent on "common folk" and "little people." "Women in the Ranks," pp. 334–335 shows, however, that previously, historians often did not look too hard for signs of real women in real combat.

————, *The Life of Billy Yank: The Common Soldiers of the Union* (New York: Bobbs-Merrill, 1951). While the author declares "Not all who wore blue were men," he really does not make much of an effort to find out who or what they were. He also seems genuinely perplexed about the whole concept, relying mostly on somewhat lurid press accounts of the time. Seems happy that he did not unearth any examples from the Confederacy.

June Willenz, *Women Veterans: America Forgotten Heroines* (New York: Continuum, 1983). Profiles women in the service during World War II and looks at what happened to them afterward.

Kenneth P. Williams, "The Tennessee River Campaign and Anna Ella Carroll," *Indiana Magazine of History*, Vol. 46, #3 (1950), pp. 221–248. An amusing little diversion of a woman who claimed she gave the strategy for the Union's success in the western theater, an assertion which turns out not to have much merit but one has to give her high marks for hectoring President Lincoln and General Halleck so steadily.

Amrit Wilson, *The Challenge Road: Women and the Eritrean Revolution* (Trenton: The Red Sea Press, 1991). "Remember the women who have been martyred fighting" begins this work, which contains a number of life stories of women in the struggle; see especially the chapter "Fighters," pp. 87–110.

Catherine M. Wilson, *When Women Were Warriors* (Boulder, Colorado: Shield Maiden Press, 2008). (F) This self-published trilogy creates an interesting world (a mystical ancient proto-Celtic one) where women, such as the protagonist Tamras, are true warriors, where lesbian love is honored, and men are on the fringes of important matters.

Peter Wilson, *The Thirty Years War: Europe's Tragedy* (Cambridge: Belknap Press, 2009). Extremely detailed account of the entire Thirty Years' War and its devastation, including 20% of the total population of Germany dying. Lost in this sauce are a few examples of women in action (as opposed to camp followers and their children as "armies" usually involved almost as many civilians following in their wake). For example, the Swedes were repelled in battle by women at Biberach in 1632 (p. 924).

Note: See also Paul Lockhart, "Attack on the White Mountain," *MHQ: The Quarterly Journal of Military History,* Vol. 28, #2 (Winter 2016), pp. 58–63. The author provides an excellent introduction to the Thirty Years' War, the most destructive European war until World War II. Weaves an intriguing tale of "how a two hour battle led to 30 years of war, redrawing the map of Europe" (p. 59).

Note: For two other useful works to help gain appreciation for some of the weapons and tactics that enabled women dressed as men to participate, see Keith Roberts, *Pike and Shot Tactics 1560–1660* (Oxford: Osprey Publications, 2010) and Robert Brzezinski and Richard Hook, *The Army of Gustavus Adolphus* (Oxford: Osprey Publications, 1993).

Rex Winsbury, *Zenobia of Palmyra: History, Myth and the Neo-Classical Imagination* (London: Duckworth, 2010). The 3rd-century CE warrior queen of Syria was defeated by Emperor Aurelius, originally from Serbia and a superb warrior in his own right ("The Achilles of his Era"?). See especially the chapter "Arms and the Woman: Zenobia Goes to War." Zenobia played in the broad seam between the Persian and Roman Empires, both under duress when she staged her rebellion. Gibbon, Chaucer, and a host of others made much of Zenobia—and much of that was very romanticized. In reality, Zenobia was a tough woman in a world where toughness mattered, but she and Palmyra obviously had certain limits when taking on the most powerful military actor in the Mediterranean world.

James E. Wise and Scott Baron, *Women: Iraq, Afghanistan, and Other Conflicts* (Annapolis: Naval Institute Press, 2006). A very good collection of first-person female accounts of their service at war. Examples from the U.S. Coast Guard, Marines, Army, and Army Paratroops. A very poignant appendix listing all the women wounded in these wars is included. The work clearly suggests that there is now a very blurred distinction between "combat" and "non-combat" with many women in transportation, supply, and other areas already in "combat" due to IEDs and ambushes and urban violence against "safe areas."

Note: 7,400 U.S. women served in Vietnam, mostly as nurses compared with (as of February 2008), 195,600 women who have served in Afghanistan and Iraq, with 25,000 in war zones at the height of those wars. Over 100 American women had been killed in Afghanistan and Iraq as of 2017.

C. J. Worthington (ed.), *The Woman in Battle: A Narrative of the Exploits, Adventures and Travels of Madam Loretta Janeta Velazquez, Otherwise known as Lieutenant Harry T. Buford* (Hartford: T. Belknap, 1876). A woman warrior of the Confederacy tells her story of fighting, spying, and operating beyond gender norms. Absorbing from beginning to end.

Diana Wright, "Female Combatants and Japan's Meiji Restoration: The Case of Aizu," *War in History*, Vol. 8, #4 (November 2001), pp. 396–417. Documents in considerable detail the female warriors who fought in the "Woman's Army" or Joshigun. Many received in-depth combat training and fought to the death.

James Yates, "Artemisia of Caria: The West's Only Fighting Female Admiral," *Strategy and Tactics*, #266 (Jan.–Feb. 2011), pp. 35–36. Short, breezy introduction, one paying close attention to her first fleet action off Euboea (opposite Thermopylae). Pindar said this battle in particular "laid the shining foundation of freedom," as it greatly weakened the Persian fleet.

Bill Yenne, *The White Rose of Stalingrad* (Oxford: Osprey Publishing, 2013). Despite the misnomer—she was actually the "White Lilly of the Donbas"—Lidiya "Lilya" Litvyak was the highest-scoring women air ace of all time, with a total of 18 credited kills. She disappeared during her last dogfight, and her remains were never found. Lilya flew her Yak-1 as a free hunter in the famous 586 Regiment.

Jane Yolen, *Sea Queens: Women Pirates Around the World* (Watertown: Charlesbridge, 2008). Who knew "Some of the greatest pirates ever known were women?" The author gives us Alfhild, Grania O'Malley, Anne Bonney, Mary Read, Rachel Wall, Mary Anne Talbot, and Ching Isao from across the globe, including Holland, England, America, and China.

Alfred F. Young, *Masquerade: The Life and Times of Deborah Sampson, Continental Soldier* (New York: Alfred A. Knopf, 2004). This stalwart woman jointed the Fourth Massachusetts Regiment of crack light infantry as "Robert Shurtleff" and served 17 months from May 1782 to October 1783, being wounded at the Battle of Tarrytown. This work meticulously records her entire life and points out that in August 1782, the Continental Army consisted of over 12,000 men.

Helen Praeger Young, *Choosing Revolution: Chinese Women Soldiers on the Long March* (Champaign: University of Illinois Press, 2001). A very valuable historical document, showing clearly why women joined the Revolution and why these chose to go on the Long March. Very detailed and quite poignant as women describe their sufferings and tribulations before, during, and after the Long March as well as their triumphs. Quite detailed and probably will remain the definite account of the Long March women in their own words.

Note: Helen Praeger Young, "Women at Work: Chinese Soldiers on the Long March, 1934–1935," DeGroot and Peniston-Bird, *op. cit.*, pp. 82–118 also relies on survivor recollections. She uses interviews with 23 survivors of the Long March to represent activities of the 2,000 women who accompanied the various army groups. Although primarily doing logistic, propaganda, education, and recruitment and taking care of the wounded, some women were known to have been in battles. Interesting to note the many disagreements between and among the various army groups, especially the 1st Front Army and the 4th Front Army.

Note: As a result of the Long March and the Communists, ability to avoid many pitched battles with the Japanese during World War II, they eventually emerged much stronger at the end of the war than they were when it began. For a major turning point in their struggle with the Nationalist Government of Chiang Kai-shek, see Harold Tanner, *The Battle for Manchuria and the Fate of China: Siping, 1946* (Bloomington: Indiana University Press, 2013) and Michael Lynch, *The Chinese Civil War 1945–1949* (London: Osprey Publishing, 2010. Jung Chang and John Halliday provide striking and seldom seen evidence of Mao's failures, military mistakes and totally callous behavior on the Long March. Due to all three, his army went from 80,000 down to 10,000. See their *Mao: The Unknown Story* (New York: Alfred Knopf, 2005), especially chapters 12–14, pp.130–170. A somewhat more positive interpretation of Mao's role on the Long March can be found in Philip Short, *Mao: The Man Who Made China* (London: T.B. Tauris, 2017), see especially "In Search of the Grey Dragon: The Long March North," pp. 304–337.

Note: For a stimulating look at the process by which contemporary Chinese relate to the Long March, the struggle against the Japanese during World War II, and the Chinese civil war, see Rana Mitter, *China's Good War: How World War II is Shaping a New Nationalism* (Cambridge: Harvard University Press, 2020).

Marina Yurlova, *Cossack Girl* (Somerville: Heliography, 1934). Sprightly written account of the Kuban Cossack Marina Yurlova, who followed her father into World War I, finally got her own sword and horse, was wounded several times, and was awarded several St. George Crosses. Eventually escaped the Bolsheviks by fleeing east with the Czech Legion.

———, *Russian Farewell* (London: Michael Joseph, 1936). The further adventures of our heroine as she makes her way to Vladivostok, Japan, and eventually England after meeting the Prince of Wales. Brief meeting à la *Dr. Zhivago* with her Czech Captain A (last seen in Omsk!) before departure from her beloved Russia.

David Zabecki, "Artemisia at Salamis," *MHQ: The Quarterly Journal of Military History* (Summer 2014), pp. 38–43. The best short account of the Battle of Salamis and the role of the first recorded female admiral in it. The very fact she was trusted with a portion of the entire fleet suggests great competence, and her insights prior to the battle proved to be prophetic. The author places great emphasis (rightly) on the approval of Xerxes of her before, during, and after the battle. Artemisia argued against fighting the battle on the ground that the Persians had already achieved their goal by burning Athens and believed that the Greek allies would not stick with them for the winter season. Xerxes also witnessed her brave action in the middle of the battle and subsequently afforded her full battle honors and sent his sons home with her on her ship while he accompanied his army back by land.

This astute investigation of the subject gives the reader a sense to see both the originality of Artemisia *and* the high quality of her advice to Xerxes. Given her small contribution (five ships out of 1,207 in the Persian fleet) and the fact that she is a woman, it is of note that Herodotus and Xerxes makes so much of her intelligence and advice. Most exegetes when focusing on Artemisia point out the importance of her insistence that Xerxes not commit his fleet to the Battle of Salamis. But, and this is very important to note, her subsequent advice for Xerxes to return to Persia and leave his general Mardonius behind with chosen land forces presages the actual events and while sounding cynical to our modern ears nevertheless was extraordinarily apt. In the world of that time, Mardonius *and* the army were simply "slaves" of the king and his to do with whatever he wanted. Of course it was a disaster for Mardonius, but the King of Kings was safely back in Persia when things turned sour. Leaving them in Greece, he simply goes home to the rest of his empire relatively unscathed before the fateful Battle of Platea, where the Persian army is destroyed by the Greeks.

———, "The First Female Ace," *Military History,* Vol. 37, #2 (Jul. 2020), p. 18. Celebrating the accomplishments of Sr. Lt. Lydia Litvyak, the Russian woman who shot down 18 German planes during 1942–1943, including Leutnant Hans Fuss, a German 71-kill ace himself. Litvyak was eventually shot down and killed at age 22.

Yasmine Zahran, *Zenobia: Between Reality and Legend* (London: Stacey International, 2010). This work portrays Zenobia as a Hellenized Arab, one who ruled toward the end of Palmyra (which ran from the 3rd Century BCE to the 3rd century CE) and led her conquering armies in Arabia, Egypt (which at the time produced one-third of Rome's grain) and Mesopotamia. The author argues that existing Arab sources have her committing suicide rather than enduring the shame of being paraded at Aurelian's Roman victory parade. Another version has her dying en route to Rome.

Rafiq Zakaria, *Razia, Queen of India* (London: Oxford University Press, 1966). Calling her "a monumental figure," the author paints a loving, even lavish, portrait of her. Illustrated and presented with a variety of poems and other sources, the work has her dying in action and concludes with the epithet "weep not for her!"

Joshua Zimmerman, *The Polish Underground and the Jews, 1939–1945* (Cambridge: Cambridge University Press, 2015). Makes the case that the Polish Underground had a wide range of relations with the Jews of Poland, ranging from providing help to acts of roundup and murder. Interesting examination of the little-known Women's Mine Laying Patrol of the Home Guard, the patrol led by Dr. Zofia Franio.

Werner Zips, *Black Rebels: African-Caribbean Freedom Fighters in Jamaica* (Princeton: Markus Wiener, 1999). Focusing on the Maroon communities in Jamaica (with various references to resistance movements in Surinam and Brazil) as representing part of a pattern, the author helpfully explains the appeal of the Maroon life quoting the Jamaican saying "Bush, Bush no Have no Whip," to explain the powerful pull of these communities and the stark duality of the choice. Good material on Nanny Town and a continuum of resistance. Unfortunately, no index.

Stanley Zucker, "German Women and the Revolution of 1848: Kathinka Zitz-Halein and the Humania Association," *Central European History,* Vol. 13, #3 (1980), pp. 237–254. This article puts women at the heart of the various revolutions especially during the planning and run-up to the events.

Index

Index

Gogun, Alexander, 118
Gokcen, Sabiha, 31
Goldman, Nancy Loring, 118, 139
Goldstein, J. S., 118–19
Goldstein, R. James, 119
Goldsworthy, Adrian, 10, 117, 119
Gonzalez, Robert, 48n9, 119
Gordon, Bob, 120
Gordon, D. A., 162–63
Gordon, Mary, 120
Gore-Booth, Eva, 108–9
Gotterman, William, 120
Gottlieb, Julie, 120
de Gouges, Olympe, 99, 142
Gowrinathan, Nimmi, 120
Goyen, 204–5
Gozen, Hangaku, 18
Gozen, Tomoe, 18, 213
Graden, Dale Torston, 120
Graff, David, 120–21, 181
Graham-Bertolini, Alison, 121
"Gráinne Mhaol, Pirate Queen of
    Connacht" (Murray, T.), 171
Grammaticus, Saxo, 121
Granit-Hacohen, Anat, 121
Granville, Christine, 169, 215
Grayzel, Susan R., 121–22
"The Great Illusion" (van Creveld),
    214
Green, Miranda, 122
Greer, Michèle, 86
Grigg, Nanny, 33, 193
Groen, Janny, 122
Gronke, Monika, 122
Ground Zero (Francke), 114
"Growing Trends of Female 'Jihadism'
    in Bangladesh" (Moshina), 168
Gruffydd, Gwenllian ferch, 140
Gudrid of Iceland, 64
Guerrillas and Generals (Lewis), 153
guerrilla tactics: Aragon in, 21, 198;
    Ethiopia and women, 52n45; Nanny
    with, 19, 33, 183–84, 186, 210, 216,
    228; women with, 30, 74, 84, 141,
    157–58, 189, 198, 200

*Gunpower, Masculinity, and Warfare in
    German Text, 1400–1700* (Brugh),
    79
Guns and Guerilla Girls (Lyons),
    157–58
Gunson, Niel, 51n33, 123
Gupta, Alisha Haridasani, 123
Gupta, Archana Garodia, 123
Gusterson, Hugh, 48n9, 119
Gutmann, Stephanie, 123

"'Habits Appropriate to Her Sex'"
    (Cardoza), 84
Hacker, Barton C., 123–24
Hagemann, Karen, 84, 113
Hallam, Andrew, 126
Hallam, Nicola, 126
"'Halt! Be Men!'" (Skinner), 199–200
Hancock, E., 126
Han E (Han Guanbao), 32–33
Hanley, Catherine, 124
Hannoum, Abdelmajid, 52n48, 126
Hao, Phan Thanh, 211
Harrington, Peter, 126, 189
Harrison, Kathryn, 126–27
Hasanov, Zaur, 125–26
Hasselaar, Kenau, 20, 178
Hatshepsut (queen), 8, 85, 95, 133, 160,
    191
Hatshepsut (Roehrig), 190–91
Hausaland (Koslow), 146
Hauser, Ewa, 127
Havens, Thomas R. H., 127
Haverty, Anne, 127–28
Hay, David, 128
de la Hay, Nicolaa, 27, 165
Hays, Mary Ludwig (Pitcher, Molly),
    74, 175, 206
Heath, Jennifer, 128
"Hebrew Gender and Zionist Ideology"
    (Feldman), 112
Hebrew Women Join the Forces
    (Granit-Hacohen), 121
Hegar, Mary Jennings, 128
Hegseth, Peter, 128

ONE WORD MORE

Keep looking for women warriors.

There are still many to be discovered, rediscovered, or highlighted.

It's your job now.